JAMES PLUMPTRE'S
BRITAIN

JAMES PLUMPTRE'S
BRITAIN
The Journals of a Tourist in the 1790s

EDITED *by* IAN OUSBY

with a Preface by
JOHN JULIUS NORWICH

HUTCHINSON
LONDON SYDNEY AUCKLAND JOHANNESBURG

First published in Great Britain in 1992 by
Hutchinson

Random Century Group Ltd
20 Vauxhall Bridge Road, London SW1V 2SA

Random Century Australia (Pty) Ltd
20 Alfred Street, Milsons Point, Sydney, NSW 2061, Australia

Random Century New Zealand Ltd
PO Box 40-086, Glenfield, Auckland 10, New Zealand

Random Century South Africa (Pty) Ltd
PO Box 337, Bergvlei, 2012, South Africa

A catalogue record for this book is available from the British Library

ISBN 0-09 175430 5

Typeset by SX Composing Ltd, Rayleigh, Essex
Printed in Great Britain by Butler and Tanner Ltd, Frome, Somerset

CONTENTS

ACKNOWLEDGEMENTS

My greatest debt is to the Syndics of Cambridge University Library for their permission to publish these journals. I owe special thanks to the staff of the Library's Manuscripts Room, Maps Room and Rare Books Room for their patience, particularly when I seemed bent on testing the truth of Dr Johnson's remark that a man will sometimes turn over a whole library to make a single book. At Clare College I have been helped by the Archivist, Suzanne Johnston, and the Fellows' Librarian, Roger Schofield; at Queens' College by the Archivist, Iain Wright.

The staff of the following organisations have also been generous in their assistance: Local Studies Department, Birmingham Reference Library; Cambridge County Record Office, and its Huntingdon Branch; Catholic Record Society; Cleveland County Archives; English Folk Dance and Song Society; Essex Record Office; Eton College Archives; Hartlepool Central Library; Norfolk Record Office; Public Record Office; St John's College Library, Cambridge; School of Scottish Studies; Squire Law Library, University of Cambridge; Trinity College Library, Cambridge; Trinity College Archives, Oxford; University Botanic Garden, Cambridge; University of Cambridge Archives.

I am also grateful to J.H. Baker; Aidan Bellenger; Christopher Birkinshaw; Geoffrey Day; Pat Harper; Rev. Peter Ievins; Clive King; Robin Kirkpatrick; D.A. MacDonald; Hazel Mills; Michael Grosvenor Myer; Oliver Padel; Roy Palmer; J.G.A. Pocock; Michael Sharratt; Patricia Sigl; Dorothy Stroud; Rev. J.H. Thomson; David Yorke; and particularly to John Mayhew, without whose help I should still be blundering around the various public archives into which my search for information about Plumptre and his family led me, and my editor, Euan Cameron. Annette Kelley probably does not realise how valuable her support and encouragement have been.

PREFACE

The last decade of the eighteenth century in England was unlike any that had gone before. The French Revolution had cast long shadows across the Channel—shadows that grew more menacing still after the execution of the King in 1793. To all but the most hidebound reactionaries, it was clear that the old order was changing, the old values were no longer to be accepted without question. New ideas were in the air: political ideas about liberty, philosophical ideas about reason, aesthetic ideas about nature.

To the Reverend James Plumptre, the first of those categories would have been of little interest. Fitting comfortably as he did into the educated English upper middle class, he was perfectly content with his station in life and would have bitterly opposed any interference with the status quo. The second would have shocked him deeply. Unlike many of his companions of the cloth, he took his religion very seriously indeed, and never hesitated to voice his displeasure at what he considered misplaced levity or irreverence. He was, however, no puritan; and the third category of ideas had awakened in his heart an immediate and enthusiastic response, providing him with his principal motivation for undertaking the journeys that he describes in the following pages.

Twenty years earlier, Plumptre would have been happy—in company with the vast majority of those of his compatriots who thought about such things at all—to accept Edmund Burke's division of the wonders of nature into two groups only, the 'Beautiful' and the 'Sublime'. Since then, however, a Hampshire parson named William Gilpin had suggested a more important distinction: that of whether or not the natural phenomenon composed into a picture. Beautiful or sublime it might or might not be: the question was, could it be seen and presented as a work of art? And so the cult of the Picturesque was born, its disciples spreading far and wide with their prospect tubes and their Claude glasses, the better to reduce the Lake District or the High Peak to the well-bred dimensions of a gilt frame on a dining-room wall.

Gilpin himself makes a brief personal appearance towards the end of this book, and we may regret with Plumptre that he did not also make the acquaintance, when he visited their estates in 1799, of the two wealthy landowners who, more than anyone else, put his ideas into practice: Uvedale Price of Foxley in Herefordshire and Richard Payne Knight of Downton, near Ludlow. We can console ourselves, however, with the reflection that we have probably not missed much—for Plumptre is a master when it comes to leaving things unsaid. How infuriatingly little he tells us, for example, about the celebrated Ladies of Llangollen, from whom he accepted an invitation to breakfast!

But there: he does not pretend to be a portraitist of the famous.

Plumptre's real subject is the small incidents and the ordinary people (whose dialogue he captures so marvellously) he encounters in the course of his travels. The overriding interest of these journals lies not in the brilliance of his writing but in the fascinating picture they convey of what it was like to travel in England and Scotland almost exactly two hundred years ago. Even in England, conditions were grim enough; Plumptre is at his best when he describes his difficulties with the local landlords—and, in particular, landladies—of the inns at which he is unfortunate enough to have to stay. As for Scotland, he frankly gives up in disgust; having read his account of the horrors of Glen Falloch, we can understand why. True, the innkeepers may not have been entirely to blame: by his own account Plumptre frequently comes through to us as insufferably arrogant and overbearing and more often than not, one suspects, he got no more than he deserved. Yet the impression is inescapable that—leaving aside the quality of the services they provided—the people of these islands in the age before the railways were ruder, worse-tempered and infinitely more unhelpful than they are today. And the weather wasn't very much better either.

Whether or not this is a matter for rejoicing depends, I suppose, on our capacity for *Schadenfreude*; but in other respects Plumptre wins hands down. He knew nothing of modern-day tourism, of the coach parks and the camping sites, the hamburger stands and the soft drink stalls, the litter and the clutter that now disfigure all too many of the places that he gazed at in astonishment, seeing in them only further proof of the glory of God's creation. Not for a moment would I suggest that I would rather have lived in his age than in my own; but I can't help feeling that the sight of Windermere as he beheld it, or the joy of walking through country where the motor car (and the filling station) was unknown, would have been well worth the occasional 'gaunt gnat'—one of his more memorable images—or even a sheetless bed or two.

JOHN JULIUS NORWICH

GENERAL INTRODUCTION

This selection is drawn from the travel journals kept by James Plumptre during his tours round England, Scotland and Wales between 1790 and 1800. None has been published before, apart from three brief extracts[1] which were privately printed a few years ago. The manuscripts are among the papers he carefully preserved until his death in 1832, strongly hinting in his will that his executors might wish to edit and publish them 'together with such a memoir of myself as may be useful or interesting to the World at large'.[2] They ignored the suggestion and Plumptre's papers apparently lay in his vicarage at Great Gransden until 1914, when the widow of a later incumbent who had written a history of the parish[3] presented them to Cambridge University Library.

It is not hard to guess why Plumptre's executors baulked at the task of becoming his editors. His many sermons, essays, plays and editions of other men's work had never brought him more than minor, local fame during his lifetime. After he died, his reputation shrank to the doubtful immortality of a short, inaccurate entry in *The Dictionary of National Biography*, that Valhalla of the obscure, and the occasional passing reference in scholarly books. Besides, the vast jackdaw miscellany of his papers—all the flotsam and jetsam hoarded by a man who could never resist scribbling a note and never bring himself to throw it away—baffled even his own otherwise tidy habits and can still dismay even the most patient researcher.

Easily the most substantial items in the collection, his travel journals record all the eight tours he made from the age of nineteen, when he was a Cambridge undergraduate, to the age of twenty-nine, when he had become a clergyman and don. He began with a brisk ride from Norwich to Stratford and the Midlands. The taste for walking that he developed on later tours enlarged rather than restricted the scope of his journeying. From Cambridge or, later, his parish at nearby Hinxton he set off to north Wales (1792); the Peak District (1793); Scotland, the Lake District and the Peak District (1796); the West Riding of Yorkshire, the Lakes and north Wales (1797); and the north-east coast, Scotland, the Lakes and north Wales (1799). Of these tours, the last was by far the most ambitious, taking four and a half months and covering 2236 miles—1774¼ of them on foot, as he noted with triumphant exactitude. By contrast, 1800 saw only a five-week round of London, the southern counties and the Isle of Wight, and then, as a curious tailpiece to his walking career, a trip to the source of the river Cam.

The nature of the written record varies as much as the journeys themselves. Its roughest form is what Plumptre called his 'memorandums': hasty notes jotted down, on the spot or at the end of the day, in leather-bound pocket notebooks with brass clasps. Those for 1796 hardly get beyond the bare record of dates and places, and so have been excluded from this edition, but his memorandums for the 1797 and first 1800 tours are full enough to deserve selection. After the 1790, 1792, 1793 and second 1800 tours he wrote up short journals presumably meant for circulation among friends and family. It is probably no accident that on all but the first of these occasions he had a companion, whom he may well have had in mind as his first reader. Fittingly, the 1799 tour received the most elaborate treatment. From the detailed memorandums taken on the road—two notebooks survive and there was presumably a third—he prepared a three-volume 'narrative' which has all the hallmarks of being intended for publication.

Plumptre apparently offered the 1799 narrative to a London bookseller, Joseph Mawman, who declined it on the grounds that it 'would be interesting to private friends but not to the public'[4]—almost, but not quite, as dusty a rejection as his fictional near-contemporary Dr Syntax is shown receiving in one of Rowlandson's illustrations. Yet the passage of time can lend even the ordinary, fugitive or trivial details noted by travellers a significance, as well as a charm, they might not have held for contemporaries. All Plumptre's journals have ripened in this fashion during the two hundred years since they were written. He made his journeys during the critical decade when the enthusiastic, pioneering expeditions of earlier travellers were being organised into itineraries and circuits that the modern tourist can easily recognise, and indeed often still follows. He took with him the large curiosity of the eighteenth-century traveller, recording his impressions of a provincial theatre performance, an interview with a local celebrity or a chance encounter on the road in the same detail as a visit to a country house, a castle or an abbey; he was fascinated by coalmines, new manufacturing processes and agricultural improvements as well as by waterfalls, lakes and mountains. His descriptions bear the stamp of a man whose first and last love was the theatre: a sharp eye for the detail that brings a character to life, a marvellous ear for dialogue and a love of crafting the episodes of the journey into comic scenes, even when it requires casting himself as the butt of the joke.

His relish for drama, in both the specific and the wider sense of the phrase, sounds the most consistently personal note in journals otherwise lacking the unmistakable, individual voice that announces the great diarist or the great traveller. Though he could be odd in all sorts of unexpected ways, the nervous tension of a Pepys or the vehement originality of a Cobbett had no place in his milder nature. Indeed, he was at heart a conventional man. If he quotes a great deal from poets, antiquarians and moralists, that is not just because he liked to air his reading but because he delighted in agreeing with other people, particularly people who had written books. In his social life, quarrels and disputes made him deeply uneasy;

with a pen in his hand, he often sought to blur differences of opinion that separated him from those who had already written on the same subject. His strongest ambition was to be at one with the most enlightened, most respectable sentiments of his day.

This is what historians usually mean when they call someone 'representative of the age' or describe them as speaking with 'the voice of the age'. The phrases may be bland but the state they seek to describe is not, for the spirit of a particular time is never a smooth and uniform entity, however much retrospective description tries to make it seem so. The spirit of the 1790s lay precisely in the divisions and uncertainties provoked by the emergence of Romanticism, the growth of the Evangelical movement, the example of the French Revolution abroad and the threat of answering discontent at home. When he set out on his first tour at the age of nineteen in 1790, Plumptre was also exploring this conflicting variety—or, if not its full range, then at least the part of it congenial to a gentleman of his background and generation. When he finished his last tour a decade later he had come home not just in the literal sense but also in the sense of having found, to his own satisfaction, a point of rest among the shifting currents of his time.

A note at the end of this introduction explains how the selection published here has been drawn from his journals and how the problems posed by their sometimes rough and ready text have been dealt with. Short introductions to each journal give the necessary details of his routes, travelling companions and so forth. It remains here to supply a version of that memoir which Plumptre hoped he might one day receive, putting his travels in the context of his life and his life in the context of his age.

James Plumptre was born on 2 October 1771, the third son and tenth child of Dr Robert Plumptre and his wife Anne (or Ann), at the President's Lodge in Queens' College, Cambridge, thus beginning life at the main power base of a family comfortably entrenched in the university and well connected elsewhere. The family's history typified the workings of what even a sympathetic historian calls 'unreformed Cambridge' and of the Church of England during its most worldly phase. Its position by the 1770s had already prompted the poet Gray, who kept his eye on the Plumptres' rise to power from a neighbouring college, to translate Dr Plumptre's motto, *Non magna loquimur, sed vivimus*, as 'We don't say much, but we hold good livings'.[5]

Before his election to the Presidency of Queens', Dr Robert Plumptre had served as a Fellow of the college and then, in 1755, acquired the livings of nearby Wimpole and Whaddon, together with a Prebend's stall in Norwich cathedral the following year—a little clutch of clerical preferments which had all previously been kept warm for him by his older brother and all came the Plumptres' way by the favour of Lord Chancellor Hardwicke, owner of Wimpole Hall. Dr Plumptre did not surrender them on his return to Queens' in 1760. Indeed, he later added to his quiver the Knightbridge Professorship of Moral Theology or Casuistical Divinity, for the sensible reason that 'though small in value, yet it has the recommendations of having nothing to do for it, [and] of interfering with no other preferment'.[6] This was more than could be said of the Vice-Chancellorship, which he twice assumed with the reluctance of a man who disliked administrative duties.

In all these capacities he carried out his obligation to his patron family by defending the Whig interest in Cambridge; other interventions in university affairs identify him as a liberal and reformer in his own right. At Queens' he used his influence to make sure that the Combination Room never ran short in its supply of Plumptres. During his presidency both his elder sons, Joseph and Robert, and a nephew were elected to fellowships, as well as three of his wife's relatives. Her family, the Newcomes, further extended the network, for they ran the Hackney public school that Dr Robert Plumptre had attended. Later generations of Plumptres would get their first education at Hackney alongside later generations of Newcomes.

The Hackney school, Cambridge, a college fellowship, preferment to a parish with an income that made it possible to settle down and marry, and perhaps a deanery or a master's lodge waiting to cheer the latter end of life: this was the pattern James Plumptre was naturally expected to follow. More than that, it was the male Plumptres' inheritance. Dr Plumptre could provide his eldest daughter with a dowry and leave respectable annuities for his widow and five surviving unmarried daughters, yet he had not led the sort of professional life that accumulated any great personal fortune or holdings in land to bestow on his three sons. Joseph and Robert got small sums of money and James, as the youngest and least advanced in life, the unexpired leasehold of a very small property in Hampshire.[7] Their real legacy had already been given to them: in the family name, the university and clerical connections that went with it, the social status and the earning power it put easily within their grasp.

So it was more or less inevitable that the main stages of Plumptre's career should conform to the family type. He spent his schooldays at Hackney with several Newcome cousins as fellow pupils and his uncle Henry as his master. He entered Queens' College soon after his father's death in October 1788; the exact date of his arrival is not clear, but the university registered his matriculation at Easter 1789. In December 1790 he changed to Clare College, an unexpected step in a career otherwise so easily predictable and hence one that will need to be examined in more detail later. For the rest of the decade his progress held no surprises. He took his degree in 1792, spent two years preparing for 'the profession to which the wisdom and kindness of my parents had intended me'[8] and was ordained on Palm Sunday 1794 by James Yorke, Bishop of Ely, a younger son of the Hardwickes and an old family friend who had already given his oldest brother Joseph Plumptre his first living. The previous month Plumptre had been elected to a fellowship at Clare College.

A brief spell standing in for the ailing Vicar of Gamlingay was followed by his first real experience of pastoral duties when, in 1797, he went to the little Essex village of Hinxton. Within easy reach of his rooms in Clare and temptingly close to the coach road that led to London, the parish nevertheless became the centre of his life for the next several years. He formed a close partnership with the local squire Edward Green, another newcomer as well as a man of his own age and enthusiasm. Together, they formed a Friendly Society, introduced Jenner's new smallpox vaccine,[9] organised gardening competitions and sought to combat the lure of the Methodist meeting house in nearby Duxford. The manuscript 'Account of the Parish of Hinxton', which Plumptre started in 1802, testifies to the pride he took in his work, though also to its difficulties: out of a population of about 270, his best efforts still harvested only about 20 regular communicants.

Plumptre was in effect curate in charge of Hinxton. He himself always stuck to his formal title of Sequestrator, a reminder of his lifelong regard for ecclesiastical niceties but also of the relative insecurity of his appointment. It came to an abrupt end soon after Edward Green died unexpectedly in 1805. The personal loss was 'the most sudden shock I ever experienced';[10] the professional loss cast its shadow over the next few years. Plumptre fell back on his fellowship and waited for a satisfactory living to come vacant. He unsuccessfully proposed a course of university lectures on English poetry, took care of his brother Joseph's parish at Stamford in the months following his sister-in-law's death, pursued his literary interests, did pastoral work at Cambridge jail, preached sermons wherever he could find a friendly pulpit and took good care to publish them. In all, the Fellow of a small college with few good livings in its gift and fewer still close to Cambridge, he waited nearly seven years.

He had turned forty by the time he at last became Vicar of Great Gransden in May 1812. The appointment promised to meet ideally the needs of a man who sought a comfortable living that would not completely sever him from the city and university where he had spent most of his life. Great Gransden lies in a pleasant stretch of the Chilterns just over the Huntingdonshire border about twelve miles east of Cambridge, and it had been well endowed by Barnabas Oley, a Fellow and benefactor of Clare in the seventeenth century. Yet what Plumptre found there was certainly very different from the picturesque, well-groomed little village that greets the modern visitor, and probably below his expectations. Neglected by an absentee vicar for the previous seventeen years, the parish was suffering its way through the agricultural depression that accompanied the end of the Napoleonic Wars. Even Oley's handsome brick-built vicarage next to the church was 'in a ruinous state':[11] its repair forced Plumptre into debt and delayed his final removal from Clare until the spring of 1813.

By the beginning of the next year he was sufficiently established to turn his attention to the only remaining want in his life. His last sermon to the university had attacked, in forceful language by his own mild standards of debate, the injunction forbidding most college fellows to marry, hinting darkly at the encouragement it gave to 'disgraceful' conduct by some members of the university and the frustration it caused others. Yet when he stressed that his grounds were not personal but doctrinal—the Protestant suspicion of celibacy and the Evangelical belief that fornication was the 'national sin'[12] of the Regency—he was probably speaking the exact truth. The New Year's resolution in his diary for 1814, 'I will look out for an Help meet for me', confirms that he was unattached and hardly pulses with romantic ardour. A brief flurry of tea engagements with a Miss Morris in June may represent his most determined effort in this direction, though at the end of the year he was still forced to report of his resolution: 'Unsuccessful'. By 4 April the next spring, however, he could record in the same businesslike way: 'Called on Mrs Robinson made a proposal of marriage: accepted'.

Plumptre's courtship of Elizabeth Robinson took place in Cambridge. He married her on 6 June 1815 at the old church of All Saints opposite Trinity College, when he was nearly forty-four and she nearly forty-five. These bare facts, and the additional detail that she had been born in Edgware, are almost all we know of her.[13] Plumptre's silence about her family and life before their marriage is not in itself suggestive, since the care with which he noted details of his male ancestors, school friends and colleagues in Cambridge and the Church is everywhere matched by a corresponding lack of interest in documenting his female connections. The 'Mrs' by which he first styled her was presumably just the honorary title adopted at a certain age by unmarried women, including several of his own sisters, for there is no hint of a previous husband or children by a previous marriage. Nor did she bring a fortune to her marriage bed: the £90 Plumptre received directly from her and the promissory note for £250 from the Charles Finche (or Finch) who acted as a witness to the wedding were apparently her only dowry.

Plumptre's diaries for the Great Gransden years hint that his marriage, like his parish, brought its trials and disappointments. She suffers from rheumatism, nettle rash and the blister; he summons the local doctor, administers leeches, prays at her bedside morning and evening, and is himself confined to the sofa for days on end by the return of an old complaint, apparently of the bowels. 'Wife too ill to go to church' becomes a familiar refrain, particularly during the long winter months, soon joined by 'Wife out of tune', 'Wife still out of tune', 'Wife quite out of tune'.[14] The tensions begin in August 1819 when, after being 'very unsettled' for several days, she confides 'an important secret'.[15] They continue for the next few years in quarrels over domestic affairs, like the management of their servants: 'Wife very unpleasant on the subject of W^m,[16] and 'Words with wife about Betsy's being dressed in a silk dress: insisted upon her taking it off'.[17] In the spring of 1822 Elizabeth Plumptre spends part of an insomniac night 'in her room for 3 hours reading, and particularly her Journal', is 'very insulting after dinner'[18] and refuses to admit the doctor whom Plumptre has taken into his confidence. The entry for 30 March records a crisis: 'Wife very much out indeed: talked of going away: was obliged to ring for W^m'. Plumptre, who had for several years made a point of marking 6 June by a private reading from the prayer book, observed the custom in 1822 with gloomy anxiety: 'Our Wedding Day. I read the Marriage service over—and prayed'.

And there this cryptic record ends. A number of his Great Gransden diaries are missing, and the surviving ones shed no further light on what his wife's important secret might have been, or where the balance lay between her nervous irritability and his view of a husband's domestic authority. The couple resumed their social round of drinking tea with the parishioners, receiving visits from Plumptre's sisters and his brother Robert, going to market in Huntingdon and St Ives, and taking occasional trips to Cambridge and London. The purchase of a pony chaise caused much brief excitement until it was abandoned when the pony insisted on going downhill too fast, and their life became increasingly confined to the parish.

Plumptre continued to read widely in plays and devotional works and to publish books with the same stubborn, conscientious energy he brought to his pastoral duties. He formed Friendly Societies and won a dispute over his right to appoint his parish clerk—small, fragile triumphs in a village where the agricultural depression touched even the Vicar's purse. Unable to find a tenant for his glebe farm, he was forced to make himself expert in the market price of pigs and remedies for crop disease ('sow Soot on . . . wheat taken by the wire worm').[19] The man he hired to run the farm merely brought problems of a different sort: 'Brand at the Public House in morning; serious conversation with him in the evening'.[20] The cycle of Brand's alternating drunkenness and repentance ran its course for several years, typifying all the daily chores that filled the last stage of Plumptre's life: admonishing a parishioner's errant wife, trying to stop the miller from grinding on a Sunday, taking medicine to a young boy with the ague, rebuking the children in the next village who stole his turnips, and breaking up a disorderly scene in the local pub, where the beery voices of the regulars insisted that they 'did not care a pin' for him and 'would come there for all any parson or bishop'.[21]

He died on 23 January 1832, a few months after his sixtieth birthday, leaving a will punctiliously dutiful in its concern to make his small resources provide for his widow but mainly preoccupied with gestures of affection for old friends from Cambridge and with the fate of his library and private papers. The executors managed to pay a lump sum of £800 to Elizabeth, who remained in Great Gransden until her death four years later. Plumptre was buried in the chancel of the parish church, where a wall tablet still marks his memory, but his grave was later moved to join his wife's beside the outside wall. The creeping fingers of ivy have obliterated their headstones.

On the face of it, then, Plumptre's career followed a course mapped out by family history without achieving the distinction that rewarded many of his relatives, particularly of an older generation. His father finished life as President of Queens' and his cousin (and brother-in-law) John died in the Deanery at Gloucester, while Plumptre himself merely ended up in glum rustic isolation at Great Gransden: a youngest son born just too late to get his feet properly under the family table and forced to make do with leftovers from the festive heyday of its power in university and Church. Yet this portrait glosses over his travel journals and, indeed, much of his activity during the 1790s; and it pays scant attention to the books he published throughout his life. All these show a man who began by being ill at ease with at least part of his family inheritance and finally embraced values far removed from the worldly, genial Whiggery of the past.

Plumptre, after all, began the 1790s in the aftermath of his father's death with his decision to move from Queens' to Clare College. In a life until then so circumscribed by family tradition, even this small defection a quarter of a mile downriver is significant. Though he nowhere bothered to record the exact date when he took up residence at Queens', his diaries in old age were still noting 17 December, the anniversary of his departure. Like the poet Gray's decision to move across the road from Peterhouse to Pembroke, it marked an era. Queens' was home ground, while at Clare he was 'unrecommended and without either friends or interest'.[22] Or perhaps the point was that after his father's death Queens' no longer felt like home ground, for its new President, Isaac Milner, was markedly hostile to the spirit in which Dr Robert Plumptre had governed the college and at once set about establishing a very different regime. Regarding several of the fellows he had inherited as 'Jacobins and infidels',[23] he went outside the college to appoint new tutors over their heads. His tactless energy soon swept away the Whig and latitudinarian atmosphere of Dr Plumptre's day and made Queens' a bastion of the Tory and Evangelical party.

The fact that James Plumptre eventually came to have more in common with Milner's views than with his own father's would not have made the change at Queens' any less distressing to a recently bereaved young man of nineteen. Even in later life he never warmed to Milner and appears to have scanned his writings with a jealous eye for any hint of disrespect to Dr Plumptre's memory. Soon after his arrival at Clare, he testified with some bitterness to the 'austerity' with which his tutors had treated him at his former college. He made the criticism in 'A Letter to a Friend on his going to reside in the University,' an unpublished essay full of elder-brotherly advice to an imaginary freshman: set aside time for study, be cautious in the choice of friends, don't get into debt, 'shun Newmarket' and so forth. Yet among these platitudes a revealing passage depicts the start of his own undergraduate career as an awful warning.[24] Liberated from school and deprived of 'the best and wisest of Parents', he behaved with 'every boyish and giddy passion unrestrained' and became a 'libertine' in his excesses. His tutors' harsh and unsympathetic reaction so intensified the 'state of warfare' that reformation demanded a fresh start at a new college, where he was lucky enough to find a kindly and sensible tutor in John Dudley.

There is no need to take at face value the violent language Plumptre used to condemn his own youthful misconduct. He already had enough of the Evangelical in him to know that preachers are more convincing if they confess they have once been lost sheep and to enjoy exaggerating even mild truancy into near-fatal encounter with sin. Yet the austerity of Queens' under Milner had inflamed into temporary rebellion a discontent with his studies that dated back to his days at Hackney—'slavery', he called them in this essay and, elsewhere, 'a rugged and gloomy pilgrimage'.[25] For all his old-boy loyalty to school and university, Plumptre never 'took much, I may almost say any, delight in the usual routine of a classical education'.[26]

His real interest had been awakened at the age of eleven by his first visit to a London theatre and a school production of *King Lear*: 'My love for the Drama was fixed from that time'.[27] However uncongenial its formal curriculum, the Hackney school had at least a saving grace in a tradition of amateur theatricals that made him, in his own artlessly grand phrase, 'both an actor and an author'[28] by the time he entered Cambridge. 'The Olio', a pantomime he had written at school, was laid permanently aside but during his short spell at Queens' he still found the time to polish up his farce, 'Plot upon Plot', for undergraduate performance, to adapt Shakespeare's *Henry VI* plays (retitled 'The Wars of York and Lancaster') and *Richard III* in the hope of interesting a London management, and to plan a comedy. While this burst of enthusiastic activity hardly qualifies as libertine excess, it comes as no surprise to hear the more sober tones of the middle-aged clergyman admit that it 'interfered too much with what ought to have been the object of my studies'.[29]

Plumptre applied himself more earnestly to his studies under the friendly guidance of John Dudley at Clare, and his career progressed steadily from graduation to a fellowship, ordination and his assumption of pastoral duties at Hinxton in the course of the 1790s. Yet this new earnestness still left room for the theatre, and the same decade saw his early enthusiasm grow into real literary ambition. *Osway*, the leaden tragedy he published in 1795, and the two stiffly pedantic essays on *Hamlet* which followed shortly afterwards suggest an attempt to incorporate the solemn fruits of his academic studies; so perhaps did the tragedy about Mary, Queen of Scots, he planned but apparently never wrote. Yet his real métier lay elsewhere. The characteristic plays of the 1790s shows the same light-hearted love of eccentric character and farcical episode that distinguishes his travel journals. Both are identifiably the work of the sociable, fun-loving man who liked to entertain the company in the evenings by singing one of Mr Dibdin's comic songs or imitating the famous actors and actresses of the day.

Written for an undergraduate audience in 1793, 'The Senior Wrangler' was too stuffed full of Cambridge in-jokes to have deserved a wider audience or achieved publication, but two other comedies did. *The Coventry Act*, apparently the play he had meditated at Queens', was privately staged in 1792 at the Norwich home where his family had settled after Dr Robert Plumptre's death. As well as Plumptre and his sisters Anne and Annabella, the cast included Amelia Alderson, the future Amelia Opie, whose own play 'Adelaide'[30] he also staged there. The next year his comedy was revived for a professional performance at Norwich's Theatre Royal, establishing a friendly connection with the theatre company that lasted throughout his life, and became his first published work. *The Lakers*, though it failed to find the London home he had aimed at, was published in 1798. Like its predecessor, it enlivens a slight romantic plot with songs and comment on contemporary manners; its genial satire of enthusiasm for the Picturesque and Lake District tourism links it closely to the travel journals of the 1790s.

Otherwise, Plumptre's life looked anything but single-minded or unified. He sat down to begin *The Lakers* in the same year he went to Hinxton, a young man equally enthusiastic at the prospect of immersing himself in the duties of his parish and of making a reputation (and a few hundred guineas) on the London stage. After both the Covent Garden and Haymarket theatres had turned the play down, its publication marked, for a while, the end of his involvement with the stage. The preface he added describing in ingenuous detail his failure to interest the London managers sounded for the first time a note of disappointment that would be heard more loudly when he returned, in a rather different spirit, to the drama in later decades. One of Plumptre's many small oddities was his persuasion that the best way to introduce a book was a blow-by-blow account of his difficulties finding a publisher for it.

It would not do to exaggerate the extent of his literary ambition and its disappointment. Family background, an essentially conventional character and a growing sense of vocation at Hinxton all assured that he never seriously debated earning his living by the pen. Besides, there were particularly strong reasons for keeping his distance from the professional theatre: never a respectable walk of life, it was increasingly denounced by moralists of his generation as epitomising the fashionable, public immorality that set the tone for society as it moved towards the Regency. Plumptre was praising his old school when he remarked that the theatrical tradition of Hackney had never bred a professional actor, just as Hannah More was citing irrefutable evidence of Garrick's solitary virtue in a tarnished milieu when she recorded that she had never met another actor at his dinner table.

More than a passing amusement yet, even at the height of his youthful enthusiasm, unthinkable as a career, the theatre represented a side to Plumptre's nature that he never managed either to suppress or to fulfil. In this regard, one could argue, Cambridge and all the male inheritance of the Plumptres thwarted him—or at least placed him on the horns of a dilemma—in a way that Norwich and their female inheritance did not thwart his sisters Anne and Bell. Anne Plumptre,[31] in particular, carved out precisely the sort of minor literary niche for herself that her brother never quite achieved. Born in 1760, she was eleven years older than him and thus in her early thirties when they joined in amateur theatricals at Norwich. After she moved to London with Bell and their mother in 1794, she published novels, travel books and translations from the French and German. Her versions of August von Kotzebue's sentimental dramas, though overshadowed by the success of rival work by Sheridan and Elizabeth Inchbald, represent a particularly intense burst of activity at the end of the decade. She took from Norwich the 'intellectual Jacobinism'[32] for which the city was known at a time when Milner's Toryism was winning the day in Cambridge. After the Treaty of Amiens established a brief peace with revolutionary France in 1802, she went with Amelia and John Opie on the journey that led, finally, to her best book, *Narrative of a Three Years' Residence in France* (1810), notable for its spirited defence of Napoleon.

Literally and metaphorically, this is a longer, bolder journey than any her brother undertook. There was always more of Cambridge than Norwich in his disposition. Watching the literary world from the sidelines, he attacked Kotzebue's popularity as proof of the declining morals of the time. Growing up in the age of revolution, he remained steadfast in his loyalty to Church and King: the young traveller deplored the Jacobinical pamphlets he saw on sale in Kelso market, while the older clergyman described in gloating detail to his congregation the supposed deathbed terrors of the arch-infidels Voltaire and Tom Paine.[33] In particular, he regarded the feminism of Mary Wollstonecraft with acute dislike and looked with stern disapproval even on milder bluestockings. The satirical portrait of the wild-flower enthusiast Beccabunga Veronica in *The Lakers* was meant, he explained in an extraordinary passage, to show that 'the study of Botany [is] not altogether a proper amusement for the more polished sex; and the false taste of a licentious age, which is gaining ground, and corrupting the soft and elegant manners of the otherwise loveliest part of the creation, requires every discouragement which can be given'.[34]

Yet the complications of his own nature guaranteed that these differences did not estrange him from Anne. The private papers and diaries that note details of all the Plumptre menfolk leading lives, and apparently holding views, very much like his own never speak of them with more than polite cordiality; for all the various visits he paid his brothers, there is no hint of common interests, let alone enthusiasms, that drew them together. Of Anne, fellow lover of plays and travel, he always writes with evident warmth. The books he published in later life take a certain pride in mentioning her achievements, however much they might run counter to his own settled views. And the obituary he wrote on Anne's death in 1818 defends her career and opinions as evidence that Dr Robert Plumptre had 'brought up his children to think for themselves'.

For all his caution and innate conservatism, Plumptre was not content to remain sheltered within the college and the parsonage. Smaller and safer in their compass than Anne's trip to France, his travels round Britain in the 1790s are none the less also adventures. His journals certainly breathe an atmosphere of youthful excitement and discovery. In fact, he has a pleasant knack of looking eagerly at more or less anything the journey brings his way; his travel journals indulge the same voraciously miscellaneous appetite that swelled all his private papers to such bulk. Arriving at Malham, he notes the name of the pub and its landlord but cannot resist adding, 'his ears stick up'. When he walks out of Kidderminster after several frustrating hours spent waiting for a coach that failed to turn up, his eye is still fresh enough to take in the spectacle of 'a mob collected round a house to see a virago with a soldiers helmet in her hand scolding her servant'. Yet in all this miscellany, one theme recurs again and again, reminding the reader that Plumptre belonged to the same generation as two other travellers of the 1790s: Wordsworth, his senior by just a year, and Turner,[35] his junior by only four years. What he most hoped to find in his travels was a particular experience of nature that typified the mood and the values of his age.

Of course, the breakdown of neo-classicism had by then been underway for long enough to assure that by no means all Plumptre says about taste or landscape is peculiar to him or to his generation. There is nothing surprising in his relative indifference to the great Baroque and Palladian houses of a previous age, where he can usually think of nothing better to do than copy down the inaccurate catalogue of paintings and statues that the housekeeper rattled off as she showed him round: one reason why this selection usually omits such passages is precisely because they are tediously familiar from so many previous travellers' accounts. By the same token, his condemnation of formal effects like the parterres and cascades at Chatsworth merely reiterates a taste that had come to dominate English landscape gardening since the fashion for the Picturesque had first begun to assert itself several decades earlier. Even his love of untouched countryside—Wales and the Lake District are obviously his favourite regions—can often be expressed by quoting a classic as well established as Thomson's *The Seasons*

12

or dipping into more recent authorities like William Gilpin, Uvedale Price or Richard Payne Knight. Gilpin, of course, was already the most influential traveller of the late eighteenth century whilst Price and Knight, advocates of a wilder Picturesque, led the new fashion—though not all their disciples showed Plumptre's dedication in actually seeking out these men and their estates.

With its emphasis on the rules of taste, Picturesque appreciation could easily remain confined to mere connoisseurly appraisal of nature: travellers quizzed carefully chosen scenes through their Claude glasses, approving one here and criticising one there, like spectators making their way through the Royal Academy Exhibition. While going in for his full share of this genteel exercise, Plumptre also knew its limitations. His satire of Miss Veronica in *The Lakers* wittily managed to show how easily the fashion for the Picturesque could degenerate into affected jargon and hollow exclamation. Like many of the Picturesque authorities themselves, he yearned to find in landscape a source of real and unaffected feeling. That is what he is striving for when he pauses on the summit of Skiddaw to remember the divine author of the scene or when he includes these sentences in an otherwise unremarkable description of Hartlepool:

> A promontory stretched far into the sea in the distance, while the declining sun, retiring among the dark blue clouds, cast its gold and purple glow over the whole. The clouds soon gathered into a bank-like mass, the sun sinking behind it, tipped its edge with burnished gold, and cast its radiant glory upwards in an extensive circle over the brightened atmosphere.[36]

Its cadences are rather too conscientiously studied, yet the passage hints at the delicacy of feeling we find in Turner's watercolour studies by the seashore. It certainly conveys the special value people of Plumptre's generation attached to delicacy of feeling and the special role they assigned to nature as teaching it. Elsewhere we find the same spirit repeatedly announced in his attitude not to landscape but to animals, a subject that, perhaps more precisely than any other, traced the changing values of the eighteenth century and the emerging sensibility of Romanticism. The young man who sets out on his travels in 1790 still has in him enough of the exuberant brutality of an earlier period to enjoy 'a most pleasant little course' after a hare. Yet even here the victim is called a 'poor' hare: just the sort of epithet bestowed on it by Thomson and Cowper in their attacks on hunting and cruelty to animals. Their lesson has been more fully digested, indeed is being loudly proclaimed, by the time he comes to mourn the death of the dog that accompanied for most of his 1799 tour. And among the equipment for his last tour in 1800 he notes, ruefully, the old shooting bag 'still stained with the blood of some poor harmless feathered animal, which, in times now past, I had deprived of life out of wantonness; but I was not displeased to reflect upon the change, when it was the companion of the pencil instead of the Gun'.[37]

It is no coincidence that Plumptre the hunter went on horseback whilst Plumptre the sketcher sensitive to the sufferings of animals went on foot. 'Pedestrianism', to use his own heavily Augustan term for a very un-Augustan activity, had more than cheapness and convenience to recommend it, however much these considerations helped make it fashionable with young men of his generation, like Wordsworth and Coleridge, who otherwise lacked the means to make any sort of tour, Grand or domestic. Seeing the country on foot typified the spirit in which they sought out nature, making it not just a spectacle admired from the window of a carriage or a passing scene briefly soliciting an outburst of feeling but a way of life, simple, pure and wholesome, in which they could immerse themselves. The dress they wore, the food they ate, the places they lodged all proclaimed the walker's rejection of despised luxury and ostentation. In this spirit we find Plumptre relishing boiled eggs, bread and cheese beside a spring in Wales, or sitting down to a 'delicious repast' of barley cake, butter and milk with cream in it at a statesman's house in the Lake District. Usually he puts up at very modest inns, where he might find a used chamber-pot beneath his bed or be asked to share his room with a drunken maltster; in the Lake District he is eager to stay in the homes of the country people.

Only in Scotland does he find these humble arrangements too uncomfortably spartan to tolerate. Elsewhere they satisfy the same desire not just to see but to join in the life of ordinary people that makes him jump at the chance of carrying a letter for a Lake District statesman or hitching a lift with a couple of servants driving their master's carriage. With his Scotch plaid and his knapsack containing a small, deteriorating supply of linen, Plumptre likes at moments to fancy that he has left luxury and ostentation so far behind as almost to shed his class identity. In fact, he does manage to get himself mistaken variously for a bagman (commercial traveller), a surveyor for the local inclosure, a grocer from Liverpool and, because of his cropped hair without powder, a 'Democrat'.[38]

That is going too far: it embarrasses and annoys him in the same way that being shown into the servants' pew in church does. The contradiction between his yearning for the simple, natural life and his reluctance to surrender his social rank affords much unconscious comedy in his journals, while also pinpointing a quite serious dilemma. 'Were an Hermitage built in these grounds', he exclaimed at Hackfall in 1799, 'I could well hermitize here—at least for the summer half year'.[39] This states the yearning for nature and simplicity in the most familiar, conventional language of eighteenth-century feeling, as the fashion for dotting hermitages about Picturesque gardens demonstrates. They were meant more for elegant amusement than real use, as places to hold a tea- or dinner-party not as places to live, even for the summer half-year. Plumptre knew this perfectly well, of course, and elsewhere got impatient with this sort of genteel play-acting. The Earl of Dysart's *cottage orné* on the Isle of Wight looked just artificial and silly: 'A Cottage is the residence of an English Peasant, and when it becomes *Orné* it is Frenchified and has lost its character: it is like ... a good english dish, spoiled by French Cookery'.[40]

The 'fairy Palace of the Vale'[41] where the Ladies of Llangollen lived their life of retirement came closer to being the genuine article, which is presumably why Plumptre was drawn to it three times in all. Yet the number of his visits, let alone the list of fashionable fellow visitors he met there, suggests how much the Ladies led their retired life in the glare of polite curiosity. He found an example with more direct bearing on his own aspirations when he stumbled on four French emigré priests in their tiny cottage by the Durham coast and shared with them a simple meal of home-grown food served with hand-made utensils. Despite the language barrier and the more formidable barrier of their Catholicism, the encounter plainly moved him and left him thoughtful. He was pursuing, we may say, a vein of thought he would take up again the next year in the first of his journals for 1800, when he paid a visit to his cousin Frank Newcome, a young man of his own age who had abandoned the law and quarrelled with his family to become the curate of a remote parish, lodging with a local cottager's family.

'Is he right in his mode of life?' Plumptre asked his journal when he came away. However strong his distaste for family quarrels or his doubt about his cousin's temperament, Plumptre already knew that this mode of life was right for himself. In the wide register of the age's sensibility, admiration for nature and simplicity could variously prompt Lord Dysart to build his *cottage orné*, make Wordsworth decide to settle at Dove Cottage and, not so long afterwards, turn Shelley into the radical Hermit of Marlow. In Plumptre's case it led back to what, with something less than complete irony, he had already called his 'Hinxton cot'.

To confirm the debt his brand of pastoral idyll owed to the Evangelical movement in general and to Hannah More in particular hardly needs Plumptre's own later acknowledgement of the momentous influence the Cheap Repository Tracts had over him from the moment he first encountered them in 1797,[42] or his references to distributing these tracts on his last tour. Indeed, he had shown all the makings of an Evangelical ever since he had interpreted his reformation of 1790 in the fervid language of religious conversion. His straightforward piety coupled with political conservatism, his contempt for luxury coupled with fear of democratic levelling, his genuine admiration for the poor coupled with incorrigible obtuseness about the real ground of their discontent: all marked him as a natural recruit. Even his renunciation of blood sports, like the growing avoidance of alcohol and gambling that his travel journals also record, agreed with leading goals in the Evangelical campaign to reform contemporary manners.

And in resolving to seek contentment as a clergyman whose life set an example to the humblest of his parishioners he was, in a sense, resolving to step into the village world of the Repository Tracts themselves, where such clergymen and their parishioners make frequent, idealised appearances in the blunt type and smudged woodcuts.

If Plumptre's travel journals record the spiritual history that turned the stage-struck enthusiast of 1790 into the earnest young clergyman of 1800, the transformation itself explains why he should then have stopped travelling. Indeed, it explains why, in striking contrast to the ambitious journey of 1799 that took him to Scotland, the Lake District and Wales, his last tour should describe a narrow circle round his native region. For Plumptre had in effect decided to cultivate his own garden—more or less literally so, given the horticultural bias of the second 1800 tour. The faith that sustained him at Hinxton and then Great Gransden did not require a large and curious experience of the world, merely the sense of vocation necessary to devote himself to the duties of his own parish. In later life, he took the occasional trip to the seaside, as to London; he made a brief pilgrimage to scenes connected with his favourite poet, Cowper; and, though he seems to have meditated a book on pedestrianism, did not get beyond a few preliminary notes before he let the project fall. Really, he had made his final judgement on his travels in 1811, when he wrote on the flyleaf of his 1799 Journal: 'I am ashamed to think how much I have travelled and to how little advantage to myself and others'.

So Plumptre gave up travel in much the same spirit in which he had renounced blood sports, gambling and strong drink. It was harder to give up the theatre, however strongly the Evangelical revival of the old Puritan attack on the immorality and unlawfulness of the stage seemed to demand it. Yet had not Hannah More herself repented of her previous career as a playwright? He attempted to follow suit in 1801, selling his large library of plays and buying religious books instead; but, he recorded engagingly, he soon found himself getting interested in 'convivial Songs'.[43] He was always much less successful than Hannah More and William Wilberforce in repressing a natural sense of fun.

When he published his *Collection of Songs* in 1805, he pruned and revised their texts to deprive them of any offence, a policy he also followed in his various editions of fables and in *The English Drama Purified*, the collection of non-Shakespearean classics of the English stage he published in 1812. It belonged to the same era as Dr Bowdler's *Family Shakespeare*, when delicacy of feeling shrank into prudery, and piety hardened into a witch-hunt against 'heathenism', and like Dr Bowdler's work sought to ensure 'that nothing should remain which can occasion a blush on the cheek of modesty, or grieve the heart of piety;—in short, that nothing should appear inconsistent with the faith, the conversation, and the practice of a Christian'.[44]

If public memory had run in a different channel we might now speak of 'plumptreeing' texts rather than 'bowdlerising' them. Yet comparison between the two censors does not adequately convey the real spirit of Plumptre's work. While Bowdler wished to preserve Shakespeare the classic poet for reading aloud in genteel parlours, Plumptre was attempting the altogether trickier task of keeping the contemporary stage alive yet acceptable to the Evangelical definition of morality. That is the continual burden of the steady stream of books and pamphlets about the theatre that began with *Four Discourses on Subjects Relating to the Amusement of the Stage* in 1809 and ended with *A Letter on the Subject of a Dramatic Institution* in 1820. With stubborn good will, they try to mediate between two apparently antagonistic extremes: reminding playwrights of their obligation to avoid vice, and reminding Evangelicals that plays could act as a power for good. The curious mixture of clergymen and fellow Evangelicals (like Dr Bowdler himself) with actors and theatre managers on the list of subscribers to *The English Drama Purified* suggests the sort of reconciliation he proposed. So too does *Mrs. Jordan and the Methodist*, one of the *Original Dramas* he published in 1816, by dramatising a chance encounter between a notorious actress and a serious-minded preacher which, to their surprise, reveals a common bond of good-heartedness and charity.

As a play, *Mrs. Jordan and the Methodist* is no better than any of the other works in a volume which shows how fatal the touch of Hannah More could be to the literary imagination. Yet, in its way, it expresses a last kindly thought from a man who never thrived on antagonism and always observed a sort of dogged honesty in trying to accommodate the different sides of his own nature. To see these sides in creative, unreconciled tension we need to turn back to the travel journals where, for example, we can find this encounter with one of the bad poor of Wimpole, who has failed to win a prize in the local gardening competition:

> She said "they had the prizes whose gardens were not so good". I however doubted it, but gave her a Cottage Cook which I said was better than giving her a guinea & which she in her turn did not assent to.

If Plumptre the clergyman here looks the very embodiment of the priggish Evangelical running up against what Dickens would call a tough subject, then that is precisely because, with barely conscious artistry, Plumptre the writer has made us see the encounter as a dramatic scene—and himself as a character in it—with just such comic possibilities.

A NOTE ON THE TEXT

Plumptre's travel writings amount to more than 350,000 words in all. My selection reduces them to rather less than one-third of that length.

This still permits the short journals of his tours of the Midlands (1790), north Wales (1792), the Peak District (1793) and the Cam (1800) to be presented almost entire. The ellipses (. . .) that signal omissions appear only rarely, marking those points where Plumptre was tempted into an unduly lengthy quotation or an antiquarian catalogue of a country house or a cathedral—the twin curses of eighteenth-century travel writing.

The omission of these elements from the 1799 Narrative does much to reduce its original bulk of about 250,000 words, for the hope of publication encouraged Plumptre in his habit of quotation and his love of antiquarian detail to a much greater extent. Moreover, concern for the privacy of the friends and relatives whom he visited along the way often blunted his account of these occasions—quite sharp in his original memorandums book for the tour or the less formal context of his other travel journals—into politely generalised compliment. Above all, his policy of sticking to a detailed day-by-day narrative forced him to fill out the paragraph or the page even on a day when nothing much happened and to offer a conscientious report of even those places that did not really interest him. Instead, my selection breaks the narrative up into a series of headlined extracts. (Where my headline does not simply indicate the place or person described in the extract, it has been borrowed from Plumptre's text or the summary notes he put at the beginning of each day's narrative.) The result still follows the main lines of his journey and observes the rough proportions of space devoted to the several different regions he visited, while highlighting those occasions when Plumptre was most engaged by what he saw.

I have adopted the same approach to quarry the rough, lengthy 1797 Journal and the 1800 Memorandums for passages which stand by themselves. The 1796 Memorandums have been omitted entirely, as too bare and too cryptic to need preserving.

Plumptre appended notes to all but his hastiest travel writings, sometimes at a much later date, registering a query, adding a fact or citing a quotation he judged relevant. Only one of them has seemed worth printing entire (1799 Narrative, 'Descent into a coalpit', 24 May), though I quote or summarise others in my own footnotes.

In trying to preserve the flavour of what Plumptre wrote, I have followed his spelling in its obedience to eighteenth-century convention ('shew', 'surprize', 'croud'), its inconsistencies ('kitchen'/'kitchin', 'average'/'avarage') and its personal oddities ('partere', 'butress'). I have also kept his use of capital letters, ampersands, underlining (as italics), double underlining (as underlined italics) and superscript letters for abbreviations. (The limitations of modern typesetting force me to put 'S^t.' and 'M^r.', whereas Plumptre, when he remembered the full stop, usually put it underneath rather than after the superscript letter.) I have not spelled out the shorthand abbreviations he used in his most hurried moments, notably in the 1797 Journal: not just 'y^e', and 'y^t', the customary eighteenth-century abbreviations for 'the' and 'that', but also '⊥^{r}' for 'perpendicular', '⊙^{r}' for 'circular' and the delightful '~~tine' for 'serpentine'.

His often haphazard spelling of people's names has been left untouched; identifying footnotes silently supply the necessary correction. Place names are a bigger problem, for Plumptre wrote before their spelling was standardised by the Ordnance Survey and he was often just attempting a phonetic transcription of what he heard the locals say. Thus, for example, he rendered Hoylake as 'Hoilick', Thaxted as 'Thackstead' and Yazor as 'Ayzer'. Rather than tampering with what he wrote, or festooning it with *sic*s and corrective footnotes, I supply in Appendix 1 a glossary listing those cases where his spelling differs from the approved modern form.

Odd words and phrases are marked with a *sic*. Those points where his handwriting is illegible, or where he left a gap but forgot to fill in the missing detail (usually a figure), are also noted. I make no attempt to record all his many deletions, which are usually quite trifling. When they are interesting, or clarify the sense of a passage left unclear in the revised version, they appear between angle brackets (< and >).

Some intervention has none the less been unavoidable. I have silently corrected obvious slips of the pen that led Plumptre to spell a word wrongly; write the wrong word ('too' for 'two', 'of' for 'on', 'pen and Inn' for 'pen and Ink'); repeat a word; forget a comma in the middle of a list; and fail to open or close brackets or inverted commas. Though in general content to follow his punctuation, I have sometimes needed to introduce a full stop or a capital letter (or both) to mark the division between sentences. In particular, the 1797 Journal and the 1800 Memorandums—as the least formal of Plumptre's travel writings—string long chains of phrases, clauses and apparently complete sentences together with dashes or no punctuation at all; I do not think my silent revision has altogether destroyed their breathless rush.

JOURNAL [1790]

[*Editor's note*. A pocket-size notebook with worn leather covers and pages of blotting paper bound between ordinary writing paper holds the earliest and shortest of Plumptre's travel journals to survive, describing the first leg of a six weeks' tour made in 1790 when he was an undergraduate of nineteen. On 17 September he set off from Norwich, the family home since his father's death two years before, to ride round Norfolk and through the Midlands to Warwick, Stratford and Worcester. His account breaks off among the Malvern Hills: if a second notebook concluding the tour ever existed, it has disappeared. However, the sketch of his itinerary in the surviving volume shows that he made his way back across the Vale of Evesham and the Cotswolds to Oxford, along the Thames valley to London and north via Cambridge and Ipswich to Norwich. He arrived home on 4 November, methodically noting that he had travelled 498 miles and spent £17 7s 7d.

The following month Plumptre moved from Queens' to Clare College. His autumn journal belongs to the turbulent period following his father's death when enthusiasm for the stage distracted him from his studies. As a tourist, he brings a conscientious eye to the antiquities of Warwick and Worcester, and responds with some warmth to the scenery round Bewdley and Stourport, but he is above all a theatrical pilgrim. He inspects playhouses, notes the companies touring East Anglia and the Midlands, collects playbills, identifies himself as a 'player' during a chance encounter on the road and pays homage to Shakespeare at Stratford, a town still lacking a theatre but firmly established on the tourist map since Garrick's Jubilee celebrations some twenty years before. In short, he does everything a stage-struck young man could hope to do on his holidays except actually seeing a play performed.

Their common interest in theatre explains Plumptre's visit to Lumley St George Skeffington (1771–1850) of Skeffington Hall, an old schoolfellow from Hackney but also a dandy remote from the country parsonages where Plumptre normally found his friends. Skeffington himself managed only a few 'Skeletons of Plays' (as Byron called them) before exhausting the family fortune and sinking into the chronic bankruptcy of his last years. In the meantime, however, he had helped Plumptre's theatrical ambitions by encouraging him to write *The Coventry Act*, the 'new farce' of which this journal speaks. Though their plan to stage it at Skeffington Hall was abandoned for a private performance in the humbler surroundings of the Plumptres' home in 1792, Skeffington still lent his fashionable name to the play by contributing a prologue for its professional production at Norwich's Theatre Royal and its publication in 1793. Plumptre acknowledged the favour with a dedication to Skeffington's mother, which spoke proudly of his 'friendly intimacy' with her son.]

I left Norwich on Friday the 17th. of September 1790 at about ½ past two, and had a very pleasant ride to Dereham, where I drank Tea, and from thence had a most charming ride by moonlight to Swaffham. Dereham is a neat Town about 16 miles from Norwich. There is no regular theatre there, but occasionally strolling companies come there, when a temporary one is built for them. Swaffham is also a neat town. It is 12 miles from Dereham.

This Town neither can not boast of a Theatre, but has also at times a temporary one, built for any companies that come there. There is a very good assembly room, which is often let to People who come there with—Lectures on Heads—Brushes—Attic entertainments—Dramatic olios—&c &c.[1] Here I took up my abode for the night at the Crown Inn, where I was well treated and had a most comfortable bed in a neat clean Room. I amused myself till bed time with reading the story of the Merchant Abudah from the first volume of the tales of the Genii,[2] which I hired from a circulating-Library for one penny. The next morning, after eating my breakfast and paying my bill, I proceeded on my journey to Lynn; and arrived there at eleven, making 3 hours of the 14 miles; Tho' to say the truth the day was very hot and, as I had plenty of time before me, I thought it needless to melt down my fat without a cause. Lynn is a large, but not a very pleasant Town. It is very dirty, and the narrow streets are ill-paved. Here I waited with Mr Oswyn (who came from Wisbeach that day to take my Sister back) till four oclock for my Sister, who came in the coach from Norwich. As soon as she arrived we got our dinner, which by the by was a very bad, the House (The Dukes Head) and the People belonging to it being very dirty. After dinner we walk'd down to the river side, and from thence to the Theatre. The Theatre is not a very large, but it is neat and has pretty good accomodations both before and behind the curtain. The Scenes which are pretty good ones belong, together with the House, to the corporation. They have always Plays there during the time of the Mart which is in February. It has at different times been occupied by different companies, but for the Two last years by the Norwich Company. The Man who shew'd the House said he was sure I was a north-country man by my brogue, and when I told him that I was born and brought up at Cambridge, said he knew better.

NB he is the first person that ever told me I had the brogue.

At Six oclock my Sister and Mr Oswyn set out in Mr O's chaise and I accompanied on the outside on my horse. We got to Wisbeach about ½ past nine. The ride was not unpleasant, but I caught a bad cold, from the fogs and dews of the fens. Sunday the 19th. I rested.

Wisbeach is not a very large town, but it is neat. My brothers house[3] where I sojourn'd is a very good one. The River Neine runs thro the Town, and by being not far from the sea, makes it a place of considerable merchandize.

The Theatre is small, and has only Pitt and Gallery. It belongs to a gentleman of the Town, who has granted a lease of it to Miller and Robertson, who come there every summer for about six weeks or two months with their dramatic corps. Besides this Scraggs company[4] were there last winter for three months. They fitted up a house adjoining the Methodist meeting house in deadmans lane for a theatre; as Miller (who has a lease of the regular one) would not be so blind to his own interest as to let them have his. I left Wisbeach on the 21ˢᵗ. along with my Brother. The day was most unpleasantly windy, and being full in our faces, we were much incommoded by the dust. We got to Peterborough about three oclock, and dined with Mʳ Strong,[5] a friend of my Brothers. The Country from Wisbeach to Peterborough is very disagreeable indeed, being in the middle of the fens. After dinner, my brother went with me to see the Cathedral. The outside is most magnificent indeed, but the inside has been lately fitted up in a modern way, which by no means tallies with the antique grandeur of it. In this Cathedral were buried Catherine of Aragon wife to Henry the eighth and the unfortunate Mary Queen of Scots: But her body has since been removed to Westminster Abbey, and the monument is pull'd down and removed into the garden belonging to the Sacrilegious Dean. From the top of the Cathedral there is a large and extensive view. You see Whittlesey Mere some little way off and have a distant view of Crowland Abbey. The Town is not a very good one. I had no time to see the Theatre. I slept at the Angel Inn. Hitherto I had got my portmantua on by some conveyance or another, but not finding one from here to Wansford I was thrown into the utmost distress, and at last prevail'd upon myself to take it behind me. So leaving my brother at Peterbro, I set forwards with my portmantua behind me on the 22ⁿᵈ and got on very well till within about a quarter of a mile of Wansford. When my new straps broke and down came my portmantua. What a dilemma! however I took it up in my arms and got it safe to the Haycock Inn where my allpropitious fate had provided a carrier who was just going to set off for Uppingham. I gave it the carrier and after waiting there about half an hour pursued my journey. The Country from Wansford to Uppingham is beautiful indeed, being hilly and varied delightfully with wood and lawn; and made a fine contrast to my fenny ride the day before. I got to Uppingham about ½ past 12. Here I took a refresher of bread and cheese and ale. And then took a walk about the Town. It is small and dirty, the Houses both great and small are built of stone as are most others in this part of the Country. After waiting here about an hour I set forward and arrived at Skeffington[6] about 3. There is no Theatre at Uppingham, but there is occasionally a temporary one built for any strollers that come. The last company that was there was Hownslow's. The Road from Uppingham to Skeffington is hard and stony and very much up and down hill, and what is very extraordinary and at the same time a great nuisance on a turnpike road, there are a great number of gates. The country is beautifull. At Skeffington, I received that friendly welcome from the family, which I expected, and which I should wish to receive wherever I go. Skeffington is situated on the turnpike road and is exactly half way between Uppingham and Leicester. The House is five hundred years old, but is at the same time both large and convenient. There is a most charming collection of paintings, done by the first masters; and is reckon'd the second in the county, the Duke of Rutlands being the first. The furniture is old and pertakes of the grandeur of former days. In the Hall (which I take to be about 32 by 22) are two of the largest china bowls I ever saw. In other parts of the House also are pieces of old and valuable china, and also several Roman and other antique urns and vases. The Drawing room, which is over the Hall and exactly the same size, is wainscoted and floor'd with one oak tree which was cut off the Estate. Two of the Paintings which particularly attracted my notice, were an original of Henry the Eighth by Hans Holbein, and another of Queen Elizabeth (taken when she was sent prisoner to Woodstock) by Zukero.[7] The Hall is most admirably calculated for a private Theatre and is I believe to be made use of for that purpose next year. The grounds about the House are not very extensive, but are laid out to the best advantage. In the Paddock before the House are some [blank space] sheep.[8] These are remarkable for their large horns. The Rams having four. And being curiously marked black and white. S^r W^{ms}. Estate is very extensive, and in the most beautiful and fertile country imaginable. The family hours were breakfast at nine. Dine at four. Drink tea at seven. Sup at nine and retire to soft slumbers soon after eleven. Between breakfast and dinner it was our constant practice to ride when the day would permit. The following is a journal of what I saw in my rides.

Thursday the 23^d. the Day was so rainy that we could not stir out.

Friday the 24th. walk'd round the grounds. Then rode to Tilton a village about 2 miles off to see a curious monument of a Knight Templar in the church. From thence to a Hill called Robin Tiptoes Hill, to see a most beautiful and extensive view. Why or wherefore this Hill came by the name I could not learn. Coming down the Hill the dogs (a spaniel and a greyhound) put up a Hare and we had a most pleasant little course, in which the poor Hare became a victim to the superior speed and strength of the Dogs. We rode home from Hence and had Company to dinner.

On Saturday 25th. Rode to Burrow Hill formerly a Roman Station to see one of the finest views that it is possible for the imagination to form. You see over an immense tract of country which is varied with Hill and dale, wood and lawn. Several noblemens Houses present themselves to view round about, and the Derbyshire Hills in the distance, terminate the prospect in a most romantic and luxuriant manner. We rode Home a different way from that we came. After dinner the clergyman of a neighbouring parish came in and set with us the rest of the Evening.

Sunday the 26th. I went to church. The church is old, and by no means neat. On one side of the chancel is a place seperated from the other part of the church in which are several handsome monuments of the Skeffington Family.

Monday the 27th. Rode to Norton to see a new church.[9] This church is built in a very handsome manner of stone in the style of a Cathedral. It is an obscure place, where it is situated as no turnpike road runs near it, and there are no Gentlemens Houses of any note within four or five miles. It was built by Mr Green and cost [*blank space*] pound.

Tuesday the 28th. We dined with Mr Green at Rolleston. After dinner I sung my song of Queen Mab,[10] for the first time in public, and received great commendations for it. And was complimented on my close adherence to the text of Shakspear. We walk'd home by moonlight, and a delightfull walk it was, in such an Evening "as the gentle Jessica stole from the Wealthy Jew".

Wednesday 29th. I had meant to leave Skeffington, but was prevail'd on to put off the evil moment till the morrow, which I consented to without much pressing. We rode out thro' a most picturesque part of the country and my friend and I laid the plot of a new farce to be performed at Skeffington next year. After dinner I gave my imitation of Mrs Mattocks[11] in the Epilogue to the Widow of Malabar and received great applause for it.

Thursday the 30th. I left Skeffington, about ½ past eleven, with great regret; and indeed how could I feel otherwise at leaving a house, where I had received such civility, and spent my time so agreeably. I got to Leicester about one where I learnt that the races (it being race time) were just going to begin. I went accordingly to the course and saw two heats ... After the race I went back to the Inn, and found it was too late, to stay and see any of the Curiosities. Namely the bed that Richard the third[12] slept in the night before he was kill'd and several others, which I *purposely* went round by Leicester to see. (As I could have gone a near road from Skeffington to Harbro'.) So I eat a piece of Cold Beef, and made a fruitless attempt to get some playbills, and then set off for Harbro about 4 oclock. At Kibworth, a place about six miles on this side Harbro, I espied a playbill on an Inn window shutter and stop'd to enquire about it. There was no play till the next night, when Richard the third and the Agreeable Surprize[13] were to be perform'd. As it was impossible therefore for me to stay till the next night, on many accounts, I got two bills and rode off as fast as I could, being under some apprehensions lest I should be benighted. I had got on about two miles farther, when I met a woman, who enquir'd how far it was to Leicester. Upon my telling her it was about eleven miles she appear'd sorrowfull and said "She was a poor Soldiers wife who was quarter'd at Leicester, and that she must get on there before she could stop as she had no money in her pocket. That she had travel'd a long way that day, and was quite fatigued". I told her I was sorry for her, and if a shilling would be of any use to her (giving her one) that there it was, and I would advise her to stop and sleep at Kibworth. And that if ever she heard a player abused, to stand up for him and say, "I met with one once, who upon my asking charity of him, gave me a shilling out of his stock, although he had not sufficient to take him to the end of his journey". We parted and I got on to Harbro' about ½ past six. When I got to the Inn, I wrote a note to my friend Wartnaby,[14] and sent it by a Boy, who brought me back word that he was gone to Leicester to stay the week. Here was a great disappointment to me, as I had reckon'd much upon spending the evening with him. To console myself I went to the printers (who printed for the company at Kibworth who had been at Harbro' just before) and got some old bills for which I gave him a shilling and the Dog had the impudence to *weigh* it. I eat and slept at the Inn and the next morning got to Northampton to Breakfast. Northampton is an excessive neat and clean Town. There is a fine market place, which is the fashionable Mall for the Ladies to walk on. There is also a large and handsome church, to which charles the second was a great benefactor. His statue is placed over the portico. There is no regular play-house there. A company (Pero's) generally come there every year and have latterly erected a Theatre for the time; formerly they used to fit up the riding school. I left Northampton about eleven and reach'd Daventry about one. It was statute day there, but there was nothing worth seeing. I found my friend Andrew[15] in good health and spirits. I dined with him, and drank some of his good port afterwards. After tea I found my stomach much indisposed, so I went to bed (at the Wheatsheaf) and the next morn-ing woke perfectly recover'd. I breakfasted with him, and about ½ past nine set forwards on my journey. Daventry is a small Town, and I fancy pretty clean. I cannot speak to a certainty as I saw it at a disadvantageous time. The first day being statute, the next fair day. The fair was for Beasts (cows, oxen, and sheep) and cheese. They have occasionally players there, when they fit up the assembly room. The last company that was there was Marriots. From Daventry on the 2nd of October I went to Southam and from thence to Warwick. As soon as I got to the Inn I inquired if I could see the Castle and they told me not without I wrote a note to his Lordship. I therefore immediately penn'd a note in the punctilios to his Lordship to this effect.

Mr James Plumptre (of Queens College Cambridge) presents his com-pliments to the Earl of Warwick and would esteem it a Favour if he would permit him to see the Castle.

Warwick Arms Octr 2nd. 1790.

I received back in answer from his Lordship that I was welcome to see the Castle as soon as I pleased.

I immediately set out, and as I approach'd the Castle was struck with the awful magnificence of such a pile of building. It formed a perfect *scene*. The inside is of a more modern structure, having been lately fitted up; But does not fall short in point of magnificence. The Hall is the largest I ever saw, and would do most admirably for a private Theatre. The other Rooms are also large and magnificent. There are not many pictures in the House but what there are, are good. In the Dressing Room to Queen Annes bed-chamber is an original of Anne Bullen[16] by [*blank space*]. There is a neat chapel to the Castle and a little beyond that is an armoury, in which is the armour of the Earls ancestors. I wanted to have ascended the lofty battlements, but was told by the good Lady[17] who shew'd me the apartments that my Lord did not suffer it. The grounds about the Castle are rich and luxuriant in the extreme, and the River Avon running close by the Castle makes it altogether appear like an enchanted spot. I next went to see the playhouse but could not gain admittance. The outside is not of a very promissing appearance, and is situated in an inconvenient and dirty part of the Town. It is built of stone. The last company that was there was Beynon's. I enquired after playbills but could not get any. The Town of Warwick as far as I saw of it, is not a very good one, nor by any means clean. The high street is a pretty good one, but the others seem very indifferent. I left Warwick about ½ past four and got to Stratford upon Avon about six. It was too late that Evening to see any of the curiosities of the place, so, after I had been to the printers and got as many Playbills as I could, I contented myself with spending my Evening at the Inn (The White Lyon).[18] This is a very large and good Inn. And they gave me a good supper and a clean and comfortable bed. The next morning I was up with the Lark to quaff the inspiring waters of the softflowing Avon. And then went and saw the Town Hall. It is a large Room and well fitted up. At one end is an awinspiring likeness of our Immortal bard, done from an original in the possession of M[r] Jarvis, at the other a painting of Garrick at the bust of Shakspear, by Gainsborough. The Picture of Shakspear together with a statue of him in a nich on the outside were presented by Garrick at the time of the Jubilee. That of Garrick the corporation were at the expence of. The next place I saw was the church. In the chancel lie interred the remains of our immortal bard with a marble slab on which are these lines written by himself before his death.

Good friend, for Jesus' sake forbear
To dig the dust inclosed here.
Blest be the man that spares these stones,
And curst be he that moves my bones.

The cause of these lines, seems to have been a dread of having his bones mix'd with others in a large charnel Room on one side the chancel; which he always express'd a disgust at. There is also a monument with a three-quarters statue of him writing and these lines written under it.

Judicio Pylium, Genio Socratem, Arte Maronem,
Tera tegit, Populus moeret, olympus habet.[19]

The monument was of plain stone, but is now painted over, and in my opinion much the worse for it.[20] A short time before the Jubilee a company of Players (Wards) were in Stratford and Advertised a Play, the receipts of

THE THEATRE
at
WORCESTER.

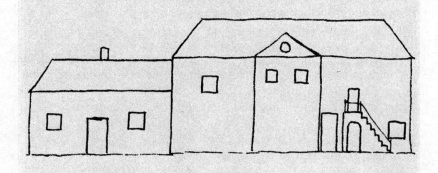

The THEATRE.
at
WISBEACH.

Sketches from the 1790 Journal

which were to be appropriated towards cleaning Shakspears monument. This Plan was approv'd by the inhabitants, who thought it a proper mark of respect to his memory, and everybody almost was there, a large sum of money was obtain'd, and with it they paid the expence of Painting it. The Third and last Place, was the House where he was born.[21] This is an old and shabby house and is inhabited by an old woman. The front Room was the shop where Shakspears Father and Mother follow'd the Trade of wool-combers. In the inner Room, on one side the fireplace, is a chair fix'd into the wall, where our bard used to sit. Here I sat myself down, and found an enthusiastic ardor spread itself all over my frame which prompted me to take out a knife to cut off a sacred relic. Upon this the old woman, who had watch'd me narrowly, said she would not have any cut off, as M[r] Garrick had charged her never to part with the least bit of it. So I departed without it.

I went to Sharp's,[22] the man who had Shakspears mulberry tree, and bought several relics of the original. When I had done all these things I return'd to the Inn, and when I had eat my breakfast set off, and pursued my journey through Alcester, Bromsgrove and Droitwich; and arrived at my Brothers at Worcester[23] about ½ past Six, nothing material having happend by the Way. Stratford upon Avon is a largish Town and is neat and clean. They have no Playhouse there; but have often a Temporary one built for any Company that comes there. Beynons was the last that was there, in about September 1789. They used formerly to lend the Town Hall on such occasions, but since it has been new built (which was at the time of the Jubilee in Sept[r] 1769) they have always been forced to build one for themselves or hire a barn.

Worcester is a large and populous city. The streets are some of them wide and well-paved, others very narrow and dirty. There are a great number of very large and handsome shops in the city, particularly china shops, for which article Worcester is very famous; a large manufactory being carried on there.

The Theatre is a neat brick building, and is situated in *Angel* Street, a proper place for such an Edifice. The inside is commodious and well fitted up. There are good dressing Rooms and also a Green Room. There are Boxes, Pitt and Gallery and when full, it holds between seventy and eighty pounds.[24] It was built about ten years ago by Whitley, who had the management of the company, but is now the joint property of several proprietors. Miller's company is the one that performs here, their season is for about 3 or 4 months in the Winters, and at the race time which is generally in August. The performers are, I am informed, in general very good. I obtain'd a few playbills from the man who shew'd me the House.

On Tuesday October the 12th. I rode with my Brother to Stone, a living of his about 13 miles from Worcester. We dined with a gentleman in the neighbourhood, and after dinner a letter came to him with a playbill enclosed. This was a bill of a Company at Bewdley, a Town about 5 miles off. It was for the next night, when "All the world's a stage"[25] and "The Agreeable Surprize" were to be perform'd. The parts of Diggory and Lingo by a girl only 14 years old. This set me all on fire, and the next morning I proposed to my Brother our going, but he, not being so dramatic as myself, set his face entirely against it, and I was obliged to relinquish the idea. We rode that morning (the 13th.) thro Kidderminster and Bewdley to Stourport and from thence home again. This ride is reckon'd the grand Lion[26] of Worcestershire and is indeed a most delightful one. The ride from Bewdley to Stourport is along the banks of the Severn, and some parts of it are romantic to a degree. This view I almost think I prefer to those in Leicestershire, on account of the river; water being so great an addition, and the Leicestershire views are deficient in this point. On the morning of the 14th. I walk'd over to Kidderminster and got some Playbills from the man who printed them for the Company at Bewdley: and soon after 12 o'clock my Brother and I set out on our journey Homewards. My Brothers House at Stone is small, but very neat and convenient, and contains a great deal of Room considering the size. There is a neat Garden, or rather shrubbery before the House, and a good Kitchen Garden behind. The country round is very pleasant, and being a sandy soil you may walk out at all times except while it is actually raining without being incommoded by dust.

The Cathedral at Worcester makes a most venerable appearance, and impresses awe on the mind of every beholder. It is built of the stone of the country, which not being of a very durable nature, is in many places mouldering away very fast, yet not so much as to endanger the building, but adds much to the look of it in point of antiquity . . .

The Malvern hills are to the West of Worcester about 8 miles. I rode there on the 19th and was much pleased with it. The Malvern Wells are two miles from the Town of Malvern. These Waters are good in all scorbutic disorders,[27] the Baths are neat and convenient, there is a good house for the accommodation of those who come for the benefit of the Waters; Where all live in one family after the manner of Buxton and other public watering places. There is a terrace up one of the Hills nearest this House which winds up by a gradual ascent, till it reaches the Top. From thence is a most extensive view all over Worcestershire, Glostershire, and Herefordshire.

A JOURNAL:
OF A TOUR THROUGH PART OF
NORTH WALES,
IN THE YEAR 1792

[*Editor's note*. Plumptre's second tour took him to north Wales in the summer after he received his BA. A few years earlier the wobbly start to his undergraduate career had endangered the prospect of his taking a degree at all, but the change from Queens' to Clare College in the winter of 1790 steadied him, largely by bringing him under the influence of a more sympathetic tutor in John Dudley (1762–1856), still young enough to be a friend as well as a representative of college authority. Plumptre never missed the chance of paying tribute to Dudley, from the dedication of *Osway* (1795)—a play, significantly, about friendship—to the final, unqualified statement in his will that he owed his old tutor 'my degree, my fellowship and by consequence my living'.

In a sense, the 1792 Journal itself is another tribute for, though he cuts only a shadowy figure in its pages, Dudley was Plumptre's companion on the tour and it seems likely that Plumptre wrote so careful a record for his eyes and in hope of his approval. If this is the case, then the older man was a pleasantly unexacting moral guardian who required less than various Evangelical mentors would later demand of Plumptre. The latter's interest in the jail at Flint and praise for the House of Industry at Shrewsbury strike a note of social concern absent from his 1790 Journal, where such institutions would have caught his eye only if they could be adapted as playhouses. Yet they still take up much less space than the compelling description of the interlude (or popular play) he is lucky enough to see at Llangollen.

Of course, Plumptre and Dudley did not go to Wales to look at plays or ponder social problems. They went for the same reason that drew travellers like William Gilpin, Sir Richard Colt Hoare, Wordsworth and Coleridge: to admire its wild natural scenery of valley and mountain, lake and waterfall. Return visits in 1797 and 1799 would extend his knowledge of the country, just as reading the Picturesque writers would make him progressively fluent in the fashionable rules for appraising it, but in 1792 he brought a fresh enthusiasm and, when that left him speechless, a copy of James Thomson's *The Seasons* to pillage for quotation. Still popular nearly fifty years after the publication of its final text in 1746, Thomson's rich Virgilian pastoral offered more than useful passages to pin on particular mountains or waterfalls. It celebrated a natural simplicity that Plumptre went to Wales to experience for himself, if only briefly and as a tourist. He finds it in an open-air meal made even more tasty by denouncing the luxury and extravagance of the rich, in the freedom of walking rather than taking inconvenient and expensive chaises, and (like so many contemporaries) in the example of the Ladies of Llangollen. The fleeting glimpse of them here is merely a prelude to longer accounts in 1797 and 1799, yet their life of friendship and rural retirement embodies sentiments already cultivated with youthful eagerness by Plumptre, walking through Wales with the friend to whom he owes most in the world.]

Part 1

The following is the Journal of a Tour, through part of North Wales, taken by myself and another Gentleman, in the long vacation of 1792. We were limited in our time of absence from College, and the principal object of our excursion was sea-bathing: for which purpose we fixed upon Park-Gate, as being near to Wales, and from whence we might, with the greater ease, take a Tour to see a country, of which we had heard much, and had a great desire to travel through: but, as we had not time to see all we wished, we resolved to make the most of that of which we were masters, and see that part which was most worthy our attention, and at as little expence as possible. As Park-Gate, therefore, was our head quarters I shall give a short description of that Place, and then proceed to our Welch Tour.

Park Gate,

is merely one row of Houses by the sea side, and is only resorted to as a bathing place; for which purpose the accommodations are tolerably convenient, and that is as much as can be said in favour of it. The shore is bad, being stony; and, in many places, there are large beds of muscles and pieces of rock covered with barnacles, which are dangerous; so that it is hardly possible to bathe there, except at high tide, unless you take a boat and go out with one who is acquainted with the shore. Board and Lodging is not unreasonable, 17^s..6^d a week being the usual charge. The Assembly House is the best and most genteel rendevous there: we scarce ever set down to dinner a number less than twenty. They have Card Assembly's once a week, but have neither dances, a Coffee House, nor Circulating Library, places much wanted for the company to resort to in their leisure moments. Nesson, which is about a mile off, is the Post town, Park Gate being only a Hamlet to it. The scene here is often enlivened by the Dublin Packets going to and returning from Ireland, which often exhibit scenes the most curious and entertaining; but, excepting at those times, the spot is uncommonly dull; for, unless you have a pleasant party of your own, you have little society; the company who resort to this place being chiefly Chester people, who keep much to themselves, and associate little with strangers. To one fond of Sailing, there are fine opportunities of enjoying that most healthy and pleasant diversion; the boats are good, and the terms reasonable, and the owners themselves civil. The country about Park Gate itself is not pleasant; but the Welch Hills on the other side of the River Dee give a wonderful richness to the Prospect. On the opposite shore to Park Gate stand the Towns of Holywell and Flint, with the noble ruins of Flint Castle; these are crowned by the welch Hills which extend as far as the sight each way. The country on the welch side is finely cultivated, and bears more the appearance of a Garden beautifully laid out, than any thing of the kind I ever saw before. On my first approach to Park Gate, I think I saw this country in the height of perfection. The morning was gay and chearful; but, on a sudden, the clouds lowered over the cheshire side, a barren and disagreeable country, and a violent storm of thunder and lightening raged over it, while the sun shone full and splendid upon the beautiful and fertile Hills of Wales, which were seperated from us by the Dee at high tide.

Nearer to the sea, about ten miles from Park Gate, stands Hoilick, now only a few Houses; but, by the spirited exertions of Sir J. Stanley, who is building a commodious Hotel for the reception of visitors, is likely to become a favourite bathing place, as the situation is more pleasant, and the shore far preferable for that purpose than Park Gate. We saw this spot in one of our morning Walks.

The Equipment and Journey.

On Friday, the 27th. of July, having staid a week at Park Gate we set off on our Tour through Wales. But, before I give a detail of that, and what we saw on it, it may be necessary to give some account of our plan and equipment. Our first intention was to hire an one-horse chaise from chester, and our next to hire horses; but, as the expence of either would have been considerable, and anything of the kind frequently an incumbrance, and horses

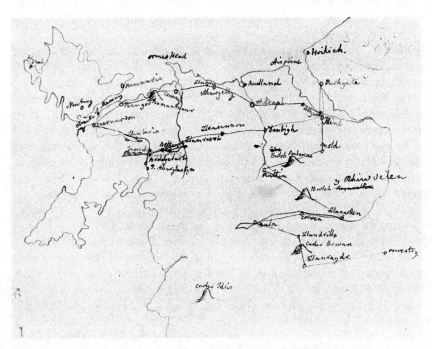

Plumptre's sketch map of the route for his 1792 Welsh tour

perhaps, as is often the case with hacks, unable to perform the journey with us, we resolved to set out on foot. Our next care was to contrive a conveyance for the little luggage we wanted on our journey, and here we soon accommodated ourselves. We had a Knapsack made large enough to hold two shirts, two pair of stockings, neckcloths, pocket Handkerchiefs, shoes, &c; and, as the pack was light, and we carried it by turns, it was no inconvenience to us. We also took a book, a small bottle covered with wicker and a small tin drinking can; we had a general plan of our Tour sketched out, and a map of North Wales: and, thus accoutred, we set off gay as Larks, resolved not to let any thing be a difficulty to us.

The morning was fine; and, at six o'clock, we took a boat for Holywell. We had a pleasant sail, and landed at the Greenford banks, from whence we walked two miles over the sands to Holywell. And here, curiosity bad us to see the famous well of S^t. Winefred.

S^t. Winefred's Well,

is a spring of the purest water which boils with vast impetuosity out the stony bottom of the well, which is covered with a fine arch of gothic architecture, supported by pillars. The first rise of this well is by some accounted a miracle. The following is the account of it delivered to us by the person who shews the well:

"In the year seven Hundred lived Winefred, a virgin of extraordinary sanctity, who made a vow of chastity during life, and dedicated herself to the service of God".

"An Heathen Prince named Cradoc, having often attempted her chastity in vain; met her some time after upon the top of the Hill near Holywell church, and struck off her head, which rolling down the hill, was taken up by the priest of Holywell, who did, by divine assistance, replace the head on Winefred's shoulders, who was thereupon restored to life, and lived fifteen years afterwards".

"At the very instant Winefred was restored to life, this spring arose in that very place; no doubt in order to perpetuate the Memory of so great an action; and Winefred being made a saint, the holy Priest of Holywell named the spring S^t. Winefred's Well. The waters seem to be of a singular Nature, and not to be excelled; for from the original rise of the spring to this day, the water, by bathing therein, performs wonderful cures; it heals those troubled with the leprosy and many other diseases; restores the lame to the use of their limbs, as well as sight to the blind; and strengthens such as are recovered of the small-pox. The Physicians are of opinion the water is of that excellent nature as not to be equalled in the Universe; which has caused so great a resort to the place, that, from a few Houses, Holywell is increased to a great market Town, and is rendered sufficiently convenient to accommodate a great number of visitors; and the bathing rendered as agreeable as at any other Wells or Baths".

"It has been proved by experiment, that this spring rises more than one hundred Tons of water every minute. This experiment was tried for a wager, on Tuesday the 12th of July, 1731, Mr Price the Rector of Holywell, Mr Williams, Mr Wynn, D^r. Taylor and several other Gentlemen of Holywell, as also several strangers, being present; when, upon the water being let out from the well and bason, which hold together Two hundred and forty Tons of water, it filled again in less than two minutes".

"The bason is more than four feet deep, yet so transparent is the water, that the minutest particle may be seen at the bottom of it".

"The water, as it flows from the Well, turns a number of mills, used for various manufactories, and then runs into the River Dee".

The Man of whom we hired our boat at Park-Gate, told us that the following Sunday was a great day at Holywell, called S^t. Sunday; and that the Roman Catholics came from far and near to do honour to St Winefred and bathe in the well on that day. But why on that day in particular he could not tell us, nor can I imagine any reason, as it was neither the anniversary of her first or second death, one being the 22nd of June, the other the 3^d. of Novr. according to Pennant.[1]

Having seen the Well, we went on to the Town, eat our breakfast at an Inn, took our Dinner in our knapsack, and proceeded on our Journey towards S^t. Asaph. And, now, a scene presented itself to us, different to anything we had before witnessed. We were upon the high road from Chester to Holyhead, and our way lay over hills and mountains. Sometimes barren hills presented themselves to our view; and, at other times, fertile valleys: the sea too on our right was often a pleasing object. On each side of the road were mines of lead and calamine, and the miners at work in them: the women we met were dressed in men's hats and long blue cloaks, the usual dress of the country, and were knitting as they walked along.

We had travelled about 7 miles from Holywell, when a high and steep hill presented itself, which we did not climb without some labor; but, when we got to the top, one of the finest prospects it is possible to paint, opened upon us at once:

The Vale of Clwyd,

extending above 20 miles. I never in my life beheld so rich and varied a prospect: groves and lawns, cornfields and pastures, Villages, Towns and Castles alternately attracted our attention. To the East it extended, till it was lost in itself, the eye not being able to carry us to the end; but the town and castle of Denbigh formed a most pleasing and noble point of sight. The Town and Cathedral of S^t. Asaph stood below us upon a rising mound in the bottom of the Vale, about 3 miles off. To the West stood the ruins of Rudland Castle; and beyond that, the sea and Ormes Head mountains delightfully varied with light and deep shade, and forming with the waters at their base some of the most charming bays imaginable terminated the view; whilst to the South, the Hills which terminated the other side of the Vale, were toped by a long chain of mountains, and beyond those, almost lost in the clouds, the high mountain of Snowdon. There was one of the summits of this mountain which presented a craggy and nearly $\perp^r$ side to us, I suppose 300 feet high, which seem'd detach'd from the rest and nodded terror upon every object around it: it struck us with wonder at that distance, and afterwards, upon a closer view, with dread and horror. We were lost in the contemplation of this wonderful and pleasing scene for some minutes, and then descended in continued admiration. The city and cathedral of

S^t. Asaph

are little worth attention, the former is shabby in its appearance with no good Houses except the Palace, which was then undergoing great alteration and improvement. This Cathedral as it is called, but in fact it deserves no better name than a parish church, being inferior to many in England, merited our notice only for it's neatness within and without. The situation is wonderfully fine. There is a neat and elegant bridge over the Elwy soon after you leave the Town, and this river then joins the Clwyd. We proceeded towards Abergeley.

Our Dinner.

About two miles short of Abergeley, a dell by the side of the road, In which was a pure spring covered by lofty Trees, afforded us a shade, under which we eat our Dinner. A large stone over which we spread a clean Handkerchief, served us for a Table; and two others by the side of it, for seats. Our Repast consisted of eggs, boiled hard for the conveniency of carriage, and bread and cheese. Our bottle we had filled with brandy, so that we mixed our brandy and water at the spring as we wanted it; this made us a drink at once refreshing and safe, even when heated with walking: Here I may say we truly enjoyed ourselves.

Ye Rich and Proud! who move in the higher sphere of life, I never envied you less, than in that moment. How many of you, even then, were feasting in your splendid Halls and grand Saloons, the choicest dainties of your own and foreign countries spread upon your tables, which your sated appetites scarcely enjoyed; the jolly glass, sparkling with merriment and wit, passing it's baleful rounds; whilst, crouded at your boards, the summer-flies of prosperity, light, airy, pert and insincere, sat tasting the sweets that lay before them, ready to flit away at any whisper of mishap borne on the fickle gale.—Our situation was more humble, more sincere. Our's was the simple meal, which hunger made delicious. Our's the slaking draught, which health had sanctioned us to take: and our society

from all the stormy passions free
That restless Man involve; we heard, and only heard,
At distance safe, the human tempest roar,
Wrapt close in conscious peace.[2]

When we emerged from our dell, we ascended a high hill immediately
above it to see the country. We had but just eaten our dinners, and were
little used to climing; it was hard work for us, and the view scarcely repaid
us for our labour; but it served to prepare us for the far greater fatigues we
were afterwards to undergo in climing the vast mountains. We wished
when we got to

Abergeley.

to have taken a chaise on to Conway that Evening; but, though it is a
public bathing place, and much resorted to, there is not one kept in the
Town; and as it was too early to stop for the Evening, we walked on
leisurely 2 miles and a half farther till we got to

Llandulas,

vulgarly called Black-and-blue which is nearly the english to the word, *du*
or *dee* signifying *black*, *las blue*; this is a small village about a quarter of a
mile from the sea and here we took up our quarters for the night. We were
told at Abergeley, that we should get accommodations there, and a good
old woman at the turnpike told us in welch English the *Nobles* resorted to
this place; and we, in consequence of this report, formed a comfortable
idea of the accommodations we were to meet with, and were much surprized when we were directed to a mean looking House for our Inn. But I
believe it was more that we had raised our expectations too high, and the
appearance of the Inn that caused our surprize, than any real disappointment with regard to our ideas of welch travelling. For we got a good supper, comfortable Lodging, and were very civilly treated. Almost close to
Llandulas are vast lime rocks, at which we saw the men at work: these supply Liverpool. They told us the Holyhead mail passed by at eight in the
morning; we got up to bathe at seven; and, whilst we were dressing, it
passed by, so we bore our disappointment with all proper Philosophy, and
after breakfast again set out on foot.

This morning was as fine as the former, and the road pleasant, sometimes
mountainous, and sometimes through vallies; till we got upon Penman
Ross, and next to Conway Ferry. It was unfortunately low water, so that
we did not see the Castle to the greatest advantage; but it nevertheless
formed a rich object in the fine view before us. We ferried over; and, upon
refusing to give the men more than their demand, they grumbled at us. I
am happy in taking the opportunity of saying, that this was the only incivility we met with in Wales. From the accounts I had received, I had

formed but an ill opinion of the lower class of people in these parts; but, saving this instance, we found them universally civil and obliging, and always thankful for any trifle we gave them. At

Conway

we dined, and after dinner walked out to see the Town and castle.

I saw few places in the course of our Tour, which gave me more pleasure, and satisfied my curiosity so much as this: it gave me a perfect idea of the ancient mode of fortifying Towns. The Castle, which is now a neat and elegant ruin, stands upon a rock, and has a fine command of the river and surrounding country. The old walls, which entirely enclose the Town, are yet remaining, and the towers and battlements sufficiently perfect to shew their forms and use. The Town is small but neat. The Church is but indifferent; there are some fine Yew Trees in the church yard. When we had satisfied our curiosity we set forward on our Journey. Just out of the Town we passed a hay field, and saw the hay carried in sledges, which are much used in these hilly parts. About five miles from Conway we got to the vast and hideous mountain of

Penmanmaur.

The road along the side of this mountain is cut out from the rock, just broad enough for two carriages to pass. On the one side is a steep precipice, the bottom of which the sea dashes against; there is only a slight parapet as a defence from this tremendous fall. On the other side is the wild and ragged mountain, threatning to crush the affrighted traveller to atoms every step he takes. Nor is his apprehension groundless: for frequently

> with mighty crush,
> Into the flashing deep, from the rude rocks
> Of Penmanmaur heap'd hideous to the sky,
> Tumble the smitten cliffs;[3]

sometimes blocking up the road, and sometimes breaking down the fence in its fall, and carrying it with it to the waters. When we arrived at the foot of the mountain, we turned to the left, and began to ascend. We were fifty minutes in gaining the summit. The whole way was steep and laborious, and sometimes danger attended our progress, the loose stones rolling away from under us, as fast as we took our feet from off them. These stones are the remains of British fortifications, which are now scatter'd over the side of the mountain, but the top of the mountain exhibits more than loose stones, the vestiges of walls and towers being easily discernible. But, when we reached the top our labour was well repaid; the Evening was fine and clear, and we commanded an extensive view over the Isle of Anglesea to Ireland; and over some parts of North Wales; but here our view was confined by the adjacent mountains; we could plainly see also the Isle of Man; and great part of Lancashire, and Cheshire. The air here was extremely rarefied and cold: but we tied our silk Handkerchiefs round our necks, and buttoned up our coats; and we had fortunately some wine in our bottle, which we had brought from Conway; this was extremely grateful to us, as we were somewhat fatigued with the difficult ascent. When we left Conway, our wine was red port; but was, when we drunk it, without even a S^t. Winefred's miracle, become *mountain*. There is a spring of fine water at the top of this mountain; a thing I believe not very usual, as the water generally descends, and forms springs in its way, and scarce ever rises to the top of the mountain. The height of Penmanmaur, as measured by Mr Caswell from the sands is 1545 feet.[4] We descended and got to a small village at the foot of the mountain, the other end of the road, from that which we ascended. Finding ourselves fatigued, we stoped at a public-House to get some refreshment. Tea and bread-and-butter was our repast; and, so much refreshed were we with it, that we resolved to get on to Bangor that night; whereas, when we first stopped here, we thought we should only be able to get on to Llanaber, 2 miles farther. It was here we saw a most beautiful Kitten; I called to her, and she looked up in my face as much as to say *Dim Saxenag*[5] and the good woman of the house told me I must address her by the appellation of *Tittoo*: the idea of a Cat's not understanding English diverted me much. It was near eight o'clock when we left this place; but the Evening was calm and serene, and the moon shone gloriously, and we had a pleasant walk to Bangor, which we reached at about ten.

Bangor,

Like all the Towns in North Wales, is small, neat and clean. The cathedral is shabby and is the only church in the Town. Being Sunday, we attended divine service once in welch, which was performed in the body of the cathedral as the parish church; and afterwards the English cathedral service, in the choir. The situation of Bangor is pleasant, being upon the banks of the Menay. We intended going over into the Isle of Anglesea after church to see Beaumaris; but the weather was too rainy to permit us. In the afternoon it cleared up, and was very fine, but we could not for want of time then go over to Angelsea; so we took a chaise, determined to make Sunday a day of rest, and got to Carnarvon between seven and eight: our ride was very pleasant, along the banks of the Menay, with a fine view into the Isle of Angelsea.

Carnarvon.

Having ordered supper and beds, we walked to the Castle. The situation of which is very fine, commanding the straits of Menay and River S^t. Helens;[6] but I think inferior to that of Conway. The Castle is grand and awful, there is a sullen majesty about it, not to be surpassed; but it wants the neatness and elegance of Conway. Up one of the Towers, called the Eagle Tower, there is still a staircase remaining; we went up to the top; from whence we had a fine view, nearly the same as what we saw in our way from Bangor, only to far greater advantage. In this Tower is the apartment, now in ruins, in which Edward the second was born. There is much of the old Walls still remaining, but they are not so perfect and compact as Conway. The Town is pretty and clean. We bathed the next morning before breakfast, the water here I think was clearer and finer than any salt water I ever met with. During our breakfast the Harper of the Inn played to us. The tone of the Harp is I think wonderfully sweet, and the welch music so delightfully pathetic, and well adapted to it, that I do not wonder at the influence the welch bards had over the people, when they had such inspiration in their power. After breakfast we set off

To Llanberris.

The road was tollerably good and plain for about five miles, when we got to a village by the side of a Lake.

Here we hoped to have got a boat up the Lake to Llanberris; but, unfortunately, one had set off to go up to the Copper works, about half an hour before; and there was not another to be had. We met here an intelligent and civil Peasant; he advised us to keep a path by the side of the Lake up to Llanberris; but, if we did not like that way, he said, by striking up to the right, towards the top of the mountains, we should find the high road thither. We kept the lower path some time, but found it so extremely wet and boggy, that we resolved to find the high road, and, for that purpose, ascended the mountains. When we got to the top, we found an English footpath: from the situation it appeared to be the road and yet was, as we thought, too insignificant and rugged to be an high road. We, therefore, went still higher up to the top, but could see no other either there or down the other side, we then returned to the path we had rejected and followed it some way, till we saw at a distance in a field, Haymakers at work; we made up to them but no one could speak English; we pointed to the path and pronounced, *pareen am a forth a Llanberris*? (which is the way to Llanberris?) he answered *yea a* (yes).[7] We went a little farther, and met with more here, upon our speaking, we were answered in our own language; and never did sounds strike more pleasing upon my ear! We had lost our way; we were among strangers, who could not understand us; we were cold; wet; and hungry; and our own language brought a thousand agreeable sensations at once crouding in upon my mind. We conversed; he pointed us the path and gave us directions for the rest of our way: and we got down to Nant Beris. This is a wild and Romantic Vale, bounded by the mountains of Snowdon. There are two fine lakes in it joined by a river. On a rock, by the side of one of them, stands the ruins of Castell Dolbadern, consisting of a round tower, and some fragments of walls. From hence our road lay by the side of these lakes to Llanberris. The road was steep and craggy and often cut in the form of stairs from the rock. At the end of the farthest Lake we crossed a rude bridge over the stream, which filled the Lake, and soon, indeed before we were aware of it, found ourselves at

Llanberris.

Llan signifies a church; and, as we could not see one, or anything like a Town or Village, we enquired of a man we met, which was Llanberris? He told us this was. Where was the Public House? We were close by it.—We were now in the most wild and romantic part of wales, the church was so low that it was almost hid by the yew & birch trees which surrounded it, the Town, as they called it, was a few stone huts, and the public House no better than the others. All of them are but one story high, for it seems that the winds in winter up the vale are so strong, that an house of any height would be in danger from them. Our Host told us that they frequently are so powerful as to blow the water from the lake up to the village, which is more than a quarter of a mile off; that it not only blew the waters up, but formed a thick mist in the air, so as to obscure the prospect. We entered the House; and, rude and rugged as it was, were happy to find ourselves at our Journey's end, and in company with one of our own country. For, upon asking our Host, if he was an Englishman, he said he was a york-shire-man, though Honest. He had

A venerable aspect:
Age sat with decent grace upon his visage,
And worthily became his silver locks;
He bore the marks of many years well spent.[8]

The Hotel at Llanberris

Sketch from the 1792 Welsh tour

41

He had much consequence in his appearance, for he was a farmer, and had labourers under him. And, though in this superior situation, he told us he often dined upon bread and butter; his men had a mess of ale and bread then boiling for them. <Ye English Farmers and labourers, who live in plenty and affluence, yet bear your good fortunes with discontent, hear this and blush, if all shame has not forsaken you.> We asked our Host if he had any meat? he said, no. Had he any eggs? yes; and Bacon? He made no reply, but, with an arch look of satisfaction, went into an Inner room and pulled a large piece of Bacon from out a box of meal, at which his countenance extended into a broad grin. The Room he shewed us into was both parlour and bedchamber; it had a slate floor, but it was summer; and though the bed was not what we should have had at home, yet the sheets were clean and a white coverlid spread over all. And though eggs and bacon was the best fare we could get;

> our stomachs
> Made what's homely, savoury: and weariness
> Can snore upon the flint, when resty sloth
> Finds the down pillow hard.[9]

Our Host took care to inform us, that he had had Great Folks lodge with him. Sir Joseph Banks and Sir George Shuckborough[10] had occupied this apartment. With the latter he had been up Snowdon the year before to boil water, to measure the height of it, and determined it to be [blank space]. Pennant makes it 1189 yards and 1 foot above the level of the sea.

After dinner we walked out to see the situation and country round. Llanberris is most strikingly romantic: it is in a Vale surrounded by barren and lofty mountains, about a quarter of a mile or more from the Lake, as I before mentioned; a rapid stream runs close to the village, and there are some trees, a rare sight in this part, mixed with the huts, which compose the village. In the church yard are some fine old yew trees. The meadows here are chiefly fenced round with stone walls, composed of the loose stones which fall from the mountains, and are placed together here by the labourers, serving a double purpose, to clear the ground from the incumbrance, and also to fence it. Here the labourers, as well as those we saw on our way hither, were making hay, up to their ankles in water. The grounds being all boggy from the quantity of water which descends from the mountains. When it is made, they carry it on their backs to the stacks, as the rugged country will not permit them to use either carts or sledges and indeed the contracted limits of the fields seems to render such vehicles scarcely necessary. The Vale began now to grow narrower, and we soon found ourselves in a wild and dreary dale. The sky too began to darken, and the clouds resting upon the tops of the mountains, formed an amphitheatre: torrents of water falling on all sides from the mountains formed innumerable cascades, and joining at the bottom rushed in a roaring torrent over it's rocky bed, till it found a more quiet receiver in the Lake below.

> Amazing scene! Behold! the glooms disclose,
> I see the rivers in their infant beds!
> Deep, deep I hear them, lab'ring to get free!
> I see the leaning strata, artful rang'd;
> The gaping fissures to receive the rains,
> The melting snows, and ever-dripping fogs.[11]

Excuse me, gentle Reader, if I grow enthusiastic; but such scenes must be inspiring to the most inanimate observer. Forgive me, therefore, if the recollection of them warms me afresh, and makes me burst forth in poetic rapture. We ascended one of the mountains and the top presented us with still wilder and higher rocks than we could see from the bottom. Here we had a second and nearer sight, and by its nearness more awful (being over our heads) of that high and perpendicular cragg seen from above S[t]. Asaph. Below us was a deep and gloomy glynn, with a large and frowning lake at the bottom, but all was still and silent as death. We descended, and measured our paces back to our lowly, but hospitable cottage. Our Host had treated with a guide to conduct us to the highest peak of Snowdon the next morning. We were to be up by two, to reach the summit by sunrise, to have the view before the mists from the lakes and mountains exhaled into vapours to intercept our sight. Our good Hostess made us some milk porridge with their excellent oatmeal for our suppers, and we early retired to bed. But the next morning brought rain and disappointment; it was too wet to attempt ascending. So we took our natural rest, had our breakfast, shook hands with our host, and again set forward, the weather being somewhat clearer.

To Beddgelert.

Our road, according to our Host's directions, was up the dale we went the preceeding evening, and over the mountain to the Lake side, from whence we were to find a broad and beaten way to Beddgelert. We pursued our road up the dale, but when we got to the foot of the mountain, I proposed going a short way farther before we ascended, as the ascent was less steep and not so high. We got to the top of the mountain with some difficulty; our way was over a pete bog, and we were almost constantly enveloped in clouds and mists. When we were at the top, we looked down, but could see no lake; all we could see was a thick mist, and black and white clouds flapping together beneath us. We continued to proceed and, at a distance, the bottom of the valley presented itself, but no Lake was to be seen. We were doubtful whether we should pursue our course or not, when we heard a shepherd's boy at a distance. We hailed him, and by signs, and the little welch we were masters of, made him understand our wants. He accompanied us down the mountain, but the way was slippery and dangerous: I twice fell, but got no farther damage than getting wet. We gave him a few halfpence, and he pointed us the path we were to pursue. We walked on and were obliged three times to ford a river up to our knees, which ran through the vale: Presently we got to a large and fine Lake about a mile long. This I fancy was the Lake our Host meant when he gave us our directions, and he misunderstood us, when we told him of the one we had seen; for, as we afterwards learned, had we gone down to that, we must have crossed another mountain, higher than the one we went over, before we could have got to the Vale we were now in. After we had passed this Lake, the Vale grew narrower and our path lay up the side of one of the mountains, and near some huts. At the door of one of these sat one of the most lovely girls I ever beheld. There was a healthy bloom in her countenance, accompanied with a native modesty not to be equalled; she was neatness herself; and a black ribband, bound round her hair, gave an elegance to her appearance, resembling some of the finest statues of Antiquity. <Thou beauteous work of nature's perfect hand, your image yet lives within my heart! There it remains in colours, glowing as the life, which, not even distance, can efface.> We went to another cottage, a few paces farther, but met with no better success here; there were only two Tailors, and those of even less value than English Taylors, for they could not inform us what we wished to know even in a *ninth* proportion. So good by, ye things "of shreds and patches".[12]

Another Lake soon opened upon us, and presented us with a most beautiful and picturesque view; we followed its waters till they again run only in a smaller stream, when we crossed a curious and fantastic bridge, and passing by Dinas Emrys soon arrived at

Beddgelert
or as it is called
Bethkelert.

This is a most pleasant village, in a beautiful tract of wet Meadows at the junction of three vales, near the conflux of the Glas Lyn and Colwyn.

It takes its name, as we were informed by a guide we took on our second tour, from the following legend.

A Farmer had a favourite Dog of the name of Gelert. He went out one day into his fields to work, and left his child in a cradle, and his faithful dog in the room with it. When he returned, he found the cradle overturned, the child bloody, and the Dog lying by it. In the first transports of his rage, he killed the dog; and, after, when it was too late, discovered the fatal effects of his rashness. A Snake had come in to devour the Child, which the dog flew upon and killed; in the doing which, he overturned the cradle, and some of the blood fell upon the child. When the farmer, there-fore, discovered his error, in having killed the preserver of his child, he paid the last sad token of his affection to him, and had him buried here: from whence the place was called Bedd Gelert or Gelert's grave.

We got meat for our dinner here, and good ale and wine; and after dinner walked down to the

Pont Aberglaslyn.

This is about a mile and a half from Beddgelert; the first half mile is through part of a pleasant vale; then, on a sudden, it contracts, and the mountains rise perpendicular to an amazing height, and the shaggy and venerable goats appear browzing on their almost barren sides, looking down with fearless contempt upon the insignificant and wary treaders of the desolate vale; through which

> the wildly-winding brook
> Falls hoarse from steep to steep.[13]

At length the pont Aberglaslyn opens to the sight. This is a strong stone bridge of one arch, built over this rapid stream, which forms, just at that point, a fine cataract, falling about 9 feet perpendicular.[14] Here we stopped to contemplate the amazing scene, and were much diverted by watching the salmon in their efforts to gain the verge of this labourious fall. How often and fruitless were they repeated; but one, larger and stronger than the rest, made a furious attempt, gained the top, and swam instantly up the opposing stream. This bridge joins the counties of Carnarvon and Mer-ioneth. I cannot help observing here how comprehensive and expressive the welch language is, and how the very names of the Towns and Situations convey an idea of the Places themselves. *Pont* signifies a bridge, *aber* a river, *Glas* green and *lyn* water, thus *Pontaberglaslyn* means the Bridge over the river of green water.

We returned to Beddgelert, supped, had a good night's rest; and after breakfast the next morning set off for Llanrwst, with our dinner in our knapsack.

To Llanrwst

our road, for about five miles, was the same we had come the day before, by the sides of the river and Lakes; afterwards we struck over a pass in the rocks to the right, and got into another vale, leading to Capel Cerig. Soon after we entered this vale, we got sight of a river which ran for some way, till it emptied itself into a lake just above Capel Cerig; our road was paralel to this, but some little way from it. About two miles short of Capel Cerig our road lay nearer the river, and we made to the brink to eat our dinner: a fine cascade presented itself, and we stepped from stone to stone, till we got upon a small rock in the middle of it, and here we sat down and dined with the waters roaring and foaming down on all sides. It was grand and awful. We eat our short repast and proceeded to

Capel Cerig,

a small village situated pleasantly upon a river, and not far from a fine Lake. The Houses are much the same as those at Llanberris, and are pleasantly intermixed with trees. Here is a picturesque bridge over the river. From the meadows just beyond the village, where the Hay makers were at work, we had a very fine view of the Snowdon hills, the top of Snowdon was at that time clear. We here enquired and were directed our way to Raiadir y Wenol, a fine waterfall which we had heard much spoken of, and were determined to see. Our road was, as usual, by the side of the river, but I think more sublime than any of the kind we had yet travelled. Each side of it was well wooded and the ground wild and craggy. Every now and then the river was shut out from our sight by the thick wood, then it again opened and discovered a steep precipice at the bottom of which was perhaps a fine cascade, or a rude torrent foaming over an uneven mass of rude rock. We next got into some corn fields, in which the corn stood <amazing> high, and there lost our way, but soon recovered it again by directing our course toward the river. We continued this road about two miles and a half, and at last reached the Waterfall,

Raidir-y-Wenol.

Resistless, roaring, dreadful, down it comes,
From the rude mountain, and the mossy wild,
Tumbling thro' rocks abrupt and sounding far;
Then o'er the craggy valley spreads again,
"And rolls its torrent", till again, constrain'd
Between two meeting hills, it bursts away,
Where rocks and woods o'erhang the turbid stream;
There gathering triple force, rapid and deep,
It boils, and wheels, and foams, and thunders through.[15]

The whole fall I imagine to be about 150 feet, but it is divided into several smaller ones, which form a pleasing variety and contrast in their course. Some fall in large and entire torrents; others more like torrents of rain, boiling up again from the lower bed, in green and white foam, from the dark and dingy waters. This fall is so surrounded by rocks and wood, that it is difficult to get a full view of it at once, the best is from a point of the crag in the bed of the river immediately above it; and there are various others from different points, both pleasing and grand. From hence we struck up the side of the mountain, and got into a path which lead us to

Bettus y Coed, or Bettus in the wood.

Here we got to a village larger, and situated in a more extensive and fertile vale, than any we had seen since we left Carnarvon. Here is a fine bridge, whose arches rest upon the solid rock, which forms the bed of the river, the water running only through one arch in a fine fall. From this village we have a pleasing view up the vale. The boundaries of which were fine culti-vated hills, with rocks peeping out from between, and the whole vale en-riched with small villages and some Gentlemen's Houses. The river at this bridge is the continuation of that from Capel Cerig, and Raiadir y Wenol; we followed it from hence, a pleasant walk of two miles, to

Llanrwst.

Here we found the best room of the Inn at which we put up, occupied by a party, who had come from Bala, 22 miles, to celebrate a wedding, with dancing, &c. They did not seem to dance with much spirit, as between each they rested for some time, before they began another. We found ourselves somewhat fatigued when we first got there, but we put on our clean linnen, and got some tea, when the party gave up the room to us, and we found ourselves sufficiently refreshed to enjoy the evening. Before supper we read from our book, which we found a great entertainment to us, at several places on the course of our Tour, as welch books were the only ones to be obtained. We supped between eight and nine and had the Harper to play to us: by far the best I ever heard. The high and grand notes were bold to a degree, and the lower ones, so exquisitely soft and harmonious, as I never remember to have heard equalled. The bridge at Llanrwst deserves particu-lar attention, it is a most elegant structure consisting of three arches, the design of Inigo Jones. The Town has little to recommend it. The next morning, having got our breakfast we set off, taking our dinners with us, for Denbigh.

Our road this day was over high hills; we had done with mountains for the present; but it was not so pleasant as any part of that we had hitherto come. We passed through Llansannon, about ten miles from Llanrwst, but did not stop there. Soon after we were out of the Town upon a hill to the left we saw a fine House belonging to Mr York, the situation is rich and pleasant. We walked on some way farther, and got under a large bridge of one arch to eat our dinner. The third rural, and I must say truly pleasant, dinner of the kind we had made on our Tour. From hence our road began to grow pleasanter, till we again got into the Vale of Clwyd, and reached Denbigh about five in the afternoon.

Denbigh.

Denbigh is situated upon a hill in the fertile vale of Clwyd, the town is in-different; but above it stands the fine, though small remains of a once noble and extensive fortification. From the top of this hill we had a good view down the vale, but we had seen it to so much greater advantage, when we first entered it above S^r. Asaph, that our present view would not bear a comparison with the former. We were up the next morning at six, in order to be at Flint before high tide, to be able to get over that day to Park Gate. About ten miles from Denbigh, we stoped at a small public House to get our breakfast. Upon our entering the House one of the most hideous objects I ever saw presented itself to our view. An old wrinkled Hag, seated upon the stairs, combing her long grey locks which hung over her face. We walked into the parlour, such as it was, and ordered our breakfast. Presently a decent, neat and well-looking old woman came to us; and, upon farther looking, I saw it was the same, who had so much disgusted me, when we first entered. Her hair was now neatly rolled up, a clean linen cap on her head, and the wrinkles were objects of respect rather than aversion, so great a change had her *tighting* herself wrought in her.

At this village we saw a curious and simple forge, for hammering iron. A rapid stream ran by it, which turned a mill, and the mill blew the bellows of the forge and worked the hammer at the same time. There were only two men employed at it; one heated the bars of iron in the fire and rolled up the tempered bars when it was hammered out; the other was solely employed in holding the bars, and directing them for the stroke of the hammer.

From hence we had an hot and brisk walk to Flint. From the hills above Flint we looked back and had a charming view, heightened by pleasing reflections, of the country we had travelled through. The top of Snowdon unveiled was superior to all. We saved our time to a minute at Flint, for we got there just as the last boat was going to set off. And had a pleasant but rough sail to Park Gate, where we arrived in time to make ourselves comfortable before dinner.

Thus ended the first part of our Tour, which I believe, unlike most others, ended to the entire satisfaction of both parties. Indeed every favourable circumstance united to make it agreeable: the weather, excepting the rainy day at Bangor, and the early morning in which we designed ascending Snowdon, which is at all times, and to all People, an uncertainty, was uncommonly fair and pleasant. Of my companion it is impossible to say too much in his commendation; any thing I could say would ill express the esteem I bear for him; and I believe there never was a pleasanter person on every account to take a tour of this kind with. I am certain more pleasantly planned tours have failed in this article of a companion, than in any other. And I take this, of all others, to be the most difficult point wherein to suit oneself. I am clear that the party, especially for walking, should not consist of more than three, and I rather think only two. To find three of the same temper, and mode of thinking, and who will mutually give way to each other, is more difficult than to find two; I therefore decide for only two: for, unless a strict harmony and mutual wish to oblige is observed, the time, which was to have been spent in pleasure, will be passed in quite the contrary extreme. For myself, I will say our Tour even exceeded the high expectations and pleasing ideas, I had formed of it: and I hope, and have some reason to think, it was not unpleasant to my friend.

With respect to our walking, I must say, that I had fancied much pleasure from the novelty of the mode of travelling before we set off; and had no reason to alter my opinion afterwards. It certainly is, especially in a mountainous and hilly country, the best and pleasantest way; as there are greater opportunities of seeing the country, and we found we could travel quite as quick as was necessary for us. Indeed, in some of the parts we travelled through, a wheel carriage had never been seen, and the only conveyance we could have got would have been welch Ponies, and I had far rather trust to my own legs than these animals; though I believe they are very sure footed and safe. We were likewise free from the restraint, to which a Carriage, Horses and Servants necessarily subject one. Our avarage distance each day was about twenty miles. And, as we took our usual rest, and eat and drank with great temperance and caution, we were well able to go through with it. There was one circumstance which tended much to keep our feet in order for walking: we always washed them with salt and water at night, which took off any tendency they might have to inflammation; and was besides a real luxury in itself. I never but once had my feet blister; and I prevented it being a farther inconvenience to me, by running a piece of woollen yarn, through it with a stocking needle, and cutting it off close on each side. These are two precautions with which it may perhaps be useful to any future pedestrian traveller to be acquainted.

Part 2.

On Friday August the 10th about 3 o'clock we left Park Gate in a boat, and had a pleasant sail over to Flint.

Flint,

though the County Town of Flintshire, is very small and the Houses indifferent. There is no market here, and the Assizes are held at Mold. The Ruins of the Castle, built by Hen. 2nd, stand close by the water's side, & are very noble; much of the outward Walls are still remaining, and are likely to remain a monument to future ages of the strength of these ancient fortifications. There are two Towers remaining, one to the south east, the other to the west, whose walls appear now able to stand the shock of contending armies: were armies such in these days as in those wherein this fortress was built. It was "within the rude ribs of this ancient castle"[16] that the unfortunate Richard the 2nd was first made Prisoner by the Usurper Bolingbroke.

A New Gaol has lately been built here upon Mr Howard's Plan:[17] the building is handsome.

As we were on our return home, and pressed for time, and had our baggage with us, in our second tour we went for the most part in chaises; and frequently found our superior style of travelling attended with superior inconvenience. This was the case at Flint, for notwithstanding we had ordered a chaise here some days before to be ready for us, yet the Horses were gone out to Harvest work, and we had above an hour to wait before we could get off. We at last got our chaise, and had a tolerable pleasant stage to Mold, where we arrived about nine o'clock. At _Mold_ there is nothing worth notice. Here we supped and at six o'clock the next morning set off in a chaise for Rythin. Though the distance is but 9 miles, 10..6 is always charged for this stage, the roads being indifferent and up and down tremendous hills.

Before we came to Rythin we crossed the Bwlch Penbarras (or pass whereon is the camp of Varus) a hill so tremendous that we got out of the chaise and walked down. From hence we had another delightful view up the Vale of Clwyd to Denbigh, S^t. Asaph, and so on to the sea. It was rich to the extreme, but did not surpass the first view we had of this charming valley. At the bottom of the Hill we got into our chaise again and were soon at _Rythin_. This town, as well as Denbigh, S^t. Asaph, and many others of less note in the Vale, stand upon small eminences; it is of little extent and dirty. There is a good church, and a good school. We breakfasted, took a fresh chaise, and set off for Llangollen. We passed over hills & through valleys, much as usual, till we came to Bwlch-y-Rhiw Velen,[18] which for the fearfulness of the descent surpasses anything we ever saw. It was cut in the side of the mountain, in some places scarce room for two carriages, in some places there were old & rotten rails at the side, in others none. We were hardy enough to go down in the chaise, and got into the pleasant Valle Crwcis. In this stands the Abbey, formerly a house of Cistertians, founded in the year 1200. It is a fine ruin, and being situated in a romantic manner amongst woods, forms a most picturesque object. The Vale of Llangollen joins the Valle Crwcis, through which we proceeded to

Llangollen.

The situation of the Town and country about Llangollen are the most romantic I ever saw; the town when compared with many others in Wales, is large and clean. And the Inns good. We dined, and after dinner walked up to the habitation of the female Hermits,[19] about a quarter of a mile from the town, and were highly delighted with the situation and simple elegance of the house and grounds. Lady Elinour was seated under a tree in the Garden, reading. Thence we ascended the high hills to the South immediately above the town; and here description will fall short in attempting to give an adequate idea of the delightful and romantic prospect before us. In the lowest bottom of the valley stands the town of Llangollen, the river

Dee running close to it, and, as it proceeds to the South East, rolls its rapid and *black* stream[20] through a thick wood. Above the town, and more under us, we saw the hermitage the effect of which was heightened by distance. The hills on the other side were rich in corn and pastures, and finely contrasted by the high barren mountains rising above them, and on the top of the highest of these stands the ruins of Castell Dinas Bran; a situation formerly famous for the command it had of this, then, grand pass into the country. We descended, and returned to the Inn, where we drank our tea, had the Harper to play to us, and afterwards walked out to see the Bridge. The Bridge is neat, and stands upon a rock, which forms the bed of the river. Just here, there is a cascade, which is small, when compared with some we had seen, but outrivalled them in romantic elegance; the river, as it rushes along over it's strong bed, perpetually forms cascades, and retires from the sight into a thick and flourishing wood. Here I left my friend, and again went up to the Hermitage, with my pencil and paper, to take a last look at that Arcadian spot, and sketch it for my future pleasure. As I was returning I saw at a distance, on the other side of the water, a vast croud of People, and, as I then imagined, a mountebank and his merry companion; I hastened to my friend, that he might be a witness to this curious scene, and we soon joined the throng; where we were so pestered by children, who knew no other English than "Pray, Sir, give me a penny?" that we turned

The home of the Ladies of Llangollen, with Dinas Bran in the background, sketched by Plumptre in 1792

51

back; but as we were retreating the men on the stage struck up a welch song; this was too much for me to resist, and I resolved to brave the attack and enjoy the humour of the scene. I returned, when a man with a wooden bowl applied to me for halfpence, which was a collection for the performers in the Spectacle I was about to witness. At a little distance from the thickest of the croud, a woman of a better appearance was seated, who was earnestly intent upon what was passing before her. I went up to, and addressed her, and, being answered in English, enquired what was going forward? She informed "It was an *Anterlude*, what we called in English a Stage-Play", and when I told her that I was unacquainted with the welch language, she explained it to me as it went on. The stage was about 3 yards square and 2 from the ground, being only a few boards raised against the end of a house, upon posts driven into the ground for the purpose. There was nothing of a scene or hanging, and a ladder, set up against one side of the stage, was all the contrivance for their "Exits and their Enterances".[21] The Prompter sat upon the stage during the whole of the performance, and read the whole of the play, which was performed by two men only, who changed their dresses in the house, according as occasion required. When I first went, one character was dressed as an old man in a long great coat and slouched hat, with a humped back, and a mask, which was painted upon a flat piece of leather; he was answerable, as I understood, to the Pantaloon of our Pantomimes; the other was dressed as a woman, after the welch fashion in a man's Hat, and a long blue Cloak or Coat; he soon went down, and appeared again in his own cloaths, but did not stay long, and when he was gone the old man died. Both of them then appeared as merry Andrews, and ended the Piece with a song, some of which we had before in the course of it. The purport of this Tragic-comic-operatic Drama was to ridicule the methodists, taxes, horse-racing, &c. and was a great favourite with the lower class of People, as their frequent and very loud bursts of laughter, sufficiently testified, but clapping with the hands is not customary with them. As I was unacquainted with the language, the jokes, which I imagine were coarse, were entirely lost upon me, but the spectacle altogether afforded me great pleasure; it gave me a perfect idea of the rude and early ages of the drama, and I imagined myself a witness to the performance of the father of the Drama, and of the ancient Greek Interlude. I went to the house, and asked if the performers had a book of the play to sell me, they told me I could get them in the town; but, when I enquired in the Town, I was referred to the *Philosophers* who lived in the country, and wrote, printed and sold them themselves. While I was making my enquiries, a Philosopher came in. Ye Lovers of Wisdom, Sages of Greece, had ye peeped from out your graves at that moment, and seen how vilely your own merited titles were abused, you would have shrunk back in anger, and never stirred thence, unless this good man had dug you up again, for digging was his profession. He lived 5 miles off, but he would fain have had me let him bring me one the next morning, or any I liked, and I would with pleasure have complied, had not the hour fixed for our departure been too early for him. So I returned to the Inn, informed my friend of what I had seen, we supped to music, and then retired to bed.

The next morning we were up at six, and set out on foot for Bala; having given directions for our luggage to meet us the next day at Oswestry. The morning was delightfully fine, and we had a pleasant walk of 10 miles, to Corwen, a very small Town, where we breakfasted. We put into the first Inn we saw, but it happened not to be the best; not that I think the best, especially for travellers in our way, is by any means to be generally accounted the most agreeable. I had far rather have the best room at the second Inn, than a second best or perhaps inferior room at the first. At the first, perhaps, they are getting up in the world, their house is established, and they dont care whether you come or not; but, at the other, they have a rival who takes in most of the company, and for what falls to their share, they are thankful. I merely mention this, as the sign of the other was "Owen Glendour", and though "good wine needs no bush", yet I always have a kind of wish to visit those houses, whose doors are kept by old acquaintance. But we were very civilly treated at the house where we were, and, when our host knew our business, he gave us some information for our travels: among other things he told us we could get some of the Gwynedd for our dinner at Bala, a fish which is only to be met with in the Lake there. We left Corwen, and set off for Bala, 12 miles. The road was very pleasant, but the day was hot. When we were yet some way from Bala, a man overtook us, and seemed as if he wished to join us. We spoke to him, but he could neither speak nor understand English. So we walked on, he walked on; we slackened our pace, so did he: a companion of this kind not being very pleasant, we resolved, if he would walk with us, that it should be a good pace, so we set our best legs foremost; but it was too much for him, he walked and run, and sweated, but to no purpose, we were too much for him, we distanced him, and got warm into

Bala.

The Town is small, neat, and airy, and the situation, being at one end of the Lake, very pleasant. Here we dined (at the Lion) and enquired of the Landlord our best route to Pistil Rayder and Oswestry. We told him we thought of going to Llandrillo that night, but he said it was too far being 12 miles, and was, besides that, out of our way; that we must wait and take a guide the next morning over Bwlch Brwan to Llangunnog. We made up our minds, therefore, to pursue his plan; and after dinner walked to the Lake. Bala Lake, or Bala *Pool* as it is generally called, is about 3 miles long, and 1 & ½ broad; it is the largest Lake in Wales. The River Dee takes its rise near the Lake, and is said to run through it, but that the waters do not mix. I believe it is a well known fact that the fish certainly do not; the Salmon of the River are never found in the Lake, nor the Gwynedds[22] in the river. We enquired for this Gwynedd, but could not get any; nor was there a boat on the Lake, which we expected, and had promised ourselves a Sail. There were formerly 2 kept here, one by the master of the Inn, the other belonging to S^r. Watkyn Williams Wynn,[23] but a flood had washed them both away. The Lake was unfortunately low in water, so that we did not see it to the greatest advantage. It is surrounded by rocks, the bottom of which are skirted with wood, and above these rocks Cader Idris (or the Giants chair) though above 20 miles off, appears most conspicuous. We returned to the Inn, and had our Tea; and afterwards went to lounge about the Town. We got to a mount (called Tomen-y-Bala) at the end of the town, whereon were many People,[24] amongst whom was a School master; we fell into conversation with him, which naturally turned upon the route we intended taking; when, to our surprize, we found, that all our Landlord had told us was merely to keep us at his House; that Llandrillo was only 8 miles off, and our best way to Pistil Rayder. We immediately returned to the Inn, payed our bill, and set off; our Landlady first kindly offering us a glass to cheer us, which we refused. It was after six when we set off, the Evening was calm with only a gentle gale stirring, the road was through a most delightful valley, and the thoughts of having thus unexpectedly forwarded our journey, all tended to make this the most pleasant walk we had during our whole tour. Thus we went cheerily on, till we arrived at

Llandrillo,

just before it was dark. We got our Suppers, and engaged a guide to take us to Pistil Rayder the next morning; then went to Bed. It is a small and mean Town: but it suited our convenience, and that was sufficient. At 5 o'clock the next morning, our Guide called us, and we set off with him. Stop one moment, gentle Reader, to look at our Guide. He was full six feet high, had a very black face, and his black hair was cut *yew tree* fashion close round his head, so that he looked as if he had a black coif on; he had a small Hat, a striped Jacket, blue breeches, stockings without feet and no shoes. He had a large stick in his hand, and took most immense strides with his long legs. As soon as we left the Town, we began ascending, and continued ascending, with but little intermission, for near two hours, being almost the whole time in the clouds, which were dripping with rain; path we had scarcely any, and the ground was a peet bog, so that we walked without shoes and stockings. Our Guide entertained us with his conversation; he told us the story I have related, in the first part of our tour, relative to Beddgelert, and many other things which served to divert the melancholy way. We came to a rude keep of loose stones; here, says he, a man was buried, who lost his way and perished in the snow. He told us it was an accident not unfrequent in those parts. Dreadful disaster! It brought to my mind Thomson's fine description of a man perishing in that horrid situation.[25] He looked for some dew berries to shew us; but could not find any, the bad spring had blighted them: they are a kind of wild strawberries, which grow in these Alpine regions. Here were foxe's holds and raven's nests; it seemed a retreat for horror and desolation. Sometimes the clouds opened and shewed us a yawning precipice beneath, with a frowning Lake at the bottom, or the still more dreary prospect of shattered rocks; then shut again, and left us only ourselves: happy at all times is society, but in these scenes of remote and desolate nature, doubly dear. We had at length got almost to our Journey's end, and began to descend, but it was so steep, that it was not without difficulty and fear of danger we reached the bottom. We gradually emerged from the clouds, the chearful rays of the Sun peered upon us, and cultivated nature smiled from the bottom of the valley: *Pistill Rayder* soon opened full upon us. At the first sight, I will own, I was much disappointed with it's appearance; but, the nearer we got to it, and the more we saw of it, the more our admiration grew upon us; till, at last, it appeared the perfection of sportive nature. The water falls 80 yards perpendicular; at first it comes over a ridge of the rock, slow and with seeming reluctance; as if it dreaded and shuddered at the horrid precipice it was to fall; but, as soon as it is over, it dashes down into a bason, formed in the rock about half way, from that down again to the bottom, where is another bason, and then it runs off in a stream. The water dashing from the top, fills the air with a mist, which, when the sun shines upon it, refracts it's colours, and makes the air appear as if studded and sparking with every brilliant of the East or rather I will say, (as some readers perhaps will not permit me to stud the air with gems) that it makes a very beautiful rainbow. We had our breakfast from a neighbouring Cottage, which we eat in a small room, just by the fall, built by the Gentlemen of the country, for the purpose of receiving strangers and visitors to this wonderfull fall. The simple elegance of Pistill Rhayder formed a fine contrast with the awful grandeur of Rhayder-y-Wenol, the cascade near Llanrwst, seen in our first Tour. After breakfast, we dismissed our Guide, and set forward for Oswestry. The day was sultry in the extreme, and our way along sandy roads, the heat of which blistered my feet, and rendered it painful to me to walk; my friend was in a better plight, and chid me into patience. We passed through Llanrhayder, and the vale of Llangedwyn, in which is a large & fine house belonging to Sʳ Watkyn Williams Wynn. When we were about 5 miles from Oswestry we inquired our way; and, afterwards, from a wish of cutting it shorter, lost it. A circumstance bad enough at any time, but then most cutting. We however were set right again, and a mile stone presented itself to us, which my friend says I read in the most pathetic tone possible "four miles to Oswestry"!! However we at length reached the wished for place, and were happy to rest ourselves. We had walked 30 miles the day before, and 26 this day, made 56 in 2 days; a long Journey on foot; but it was more the hot day and sandy roads that affected me, than the distance. I was too lazy to shave myself, so sent for the Barber. In he came. "Sir, shall I have the honour to take off the superfluous part of your face"? The man was a character, we humoured him, and he gave us it in full. Mr James Howell (his name) is a character well known in Oswestry, as well as other places. He has a very theatric turn. He was once in want of money when at Bala so he gave out "a Lecture on Heads". The company assembled, he pocketed the money, and made off, but was forced to return and refund: and, if I recollect my story aright, they read him a lecture on Prisons. We eat a refreshing and heartening dinner, and after it, set off in a chaise for Shrewsbury, 20 miles. We got there too late that night, and were too tired to see, or be seen, so after a short time went to bed. The next day we called upon 2 Cambridge friends, of the same College with ourselves, who shewed us the town and everything else worth seeing. The Town is very extensive, and some of the streets good, the Situation is pleasant, and the walks by the side of the Severn a great advantage to a place of the kind. But as descriptions of all the places we saw, and most particularly the Towns, are described in one author or another, it is needless to dwell upon them. The new church S^t. Chads[26] was almost finished, and was to be opened the Sunday following. There is a good Assembly room. The bridge over the Severn is handsome, but the finest we saw was at [*blank space*] just then finished. What most pleased me, of all that I saw, was the House of Industry,[27] in which 330 People, men, women, and children, were employed in spinning and the various processes of preparing wool. We saw them all at dinner, upon beef and beans, in one large Hall. The regulations do honour to the Committee, and every possible care is taken to promote cleanliness, and with that Health. The expences of such an undertaking were, and still are, great; but they every year diminish and in time it is expected the profits will more than clear them. It is a most glorious institution! On Wednesday we got to *Colebrook dale*[28] to breakfast. We designed to have entered this curious place the Evening before, but could not get a chaise. The effect of it in the dark is, I am told, and as I am well convinced it must be, far greater; the gloomy woods, sounding waters, and gleamy fires, giving it an effect, like that poets tell us of in their descriptions of the Shades below. The Iron bridge is an amazing work of art, but is calculated rather to surprize, than please, and seems more for curiosity than use. I think this will be known only by fame, when a stone bridge of the same expence would not have been the worse for the time it had stood: but it serves to shew the power of human art. Bentell Furnace was not a new sight to me, I had seen Iron founderies before. From Colebrook dale, we took a chaise and got to Donnington to dinner. This is the Living of a Gentleman we got acquainted with, during our stay at Parkgate, and who insisted on our visiting him on our way home. We were received with that cordiality voluntary friendship never fails to shew and prove. And there we spent a most pleasant 3 days. From Donnington we rode one morning to

Boscobel, to see the oak, commonly called the Royal, or Charles's oak; but the original is not standing, and what is now shewn, is only from an acorn of that tree. Near this is the House formerly belonging to the Pendrells; where Charles for some time resided in disguise, after the battle of Worcester, and when the pursuit after him was warm, thought the oak a safer retreat during the day. On the Saturday morning early we left Donnington, and passing through Walsal, Birmingham and Coventry, reached my friend's house, near Leicester, in the Evening.

A
JOURNAL
OF A
TOUR
INTO
DERBYSHIRE
IN THE YEAR 1793

[*Editor's note.* The summer after his Welsh trip Plumptre set out, again with John Dudley, on a walking tour round the Peak District—'a more civilized country', he remarks in explaining their methodical choice of clothes and equipment. It had certainly been longer established on the traveller's map of Britain. Wales was largely discovered in the late eighteenth century, but the 'Seven Wonders of the Peak' had been formalised into a list by Thomas Hobbes and Charles Cotton a century before. It consisted of one man-made wonder, the Duke of Devonshire's mansion at Chatsworth, and six natural wonders caused by freaks in the local geology: the Peak Cavern, then still embarrassingly known as the Devil's Arse; Poole's Cavern; Elden Hole; Mam Tor, the 'shivering mountain'; the Ebbing and Flowing Well at Tideswell; and St Ann's Well, the source of Buxton's original fame as a goal of pilgrimage and its later prosperity as a spa. Plumptre and Dudley dutifully visited all of them except the Ebbing and Flowing Well, and in obedience to the custom of the day added to their itinerary Dovedale, praised by Dr Johnson, and Kedleston Hall, built for the Curzons by Robert Adam in the 1760s.

Late eighteenth-century taste did more than tinker with the original list of Seven Wonders. Cotton and Hobbes had heaped jocular abuse on their natural curiosities, proposing them merely as grotesque foils to the man-made glories of Chatsworth. Travellers like Plumptre reversed these judgements of nature and civilisation. He casts a cold eye on the formal grounds of Chatsworth and Kedleston but, with a little help from *Paradise Lost* and *Macbeth*, finds an experience of the Sublime at Poole's Cavern and, particularly, the Peak Cavern. Industrial sites like the Speedwell mine (and, elsewhere, collieries and ironworks) can provoke the same 'mixed emotions of terror and admiration', though not the mills and factories he waves aside without much interest.

Plumptre's descriptions of the Peak Cavern and the Speedwell mine are among the most vividly detailed accounts to be found anywhere in his journals. Yet by themselves they do not typify his impressions of a region which was also 'a more civilized country' in the sense of being more commercialised. 'The effect must be more grand with only a few', he laments even in the Peak Cavern, sounding a note of disappointment any modern tourist can recognise. Elsewhere, the guides, innkeepers and other tourists he encounters make this a journal as much about people as about places. In his observations we can hear a battle between the candidate for holy orders, practising homilies for future sermons, and the aspirant playwright, seizing with relish on a comic episode or fragment of dialogue that would work well on the stage.]

The Gentleman with whom I took my Tour in North Wales, in the long vacation of 1792, and myself, were so much pleased with our excursion, that we resolved to take another on the same plan the ensuing year: we agreed to set off from his house in Leicestershire, and go through Derbyshire to the Lakes in Cumberland and Westmoreland; but circumstances obliged us to defer our purposed expedition, till we thought it too late to go so far north, and be out so long, as would be necessary to complete our plan: we, therefore, resolved upon taking only a more complete tour through Derbyshire, which, had we gone to the Lakes, we should have hurried over and seen imperfectly.

We had the experience of our former Tour to profit from, and were resolved to make our use of it, not only in respect to more important articles, but also in minutiae, and that as far as concerned our dress and appearance on our journey: this was more material than on our former tour, as we were to travel in a more civilized country, and be at places of greater public resort than any in north wales. For this purpose we had short blue coats, or rather Jackets, but in other respects made in the fashion; and here, for once, *fashion* coincided with *reason*, the large lapelles being convenient to button over in case of cold or rain; our Breeches were nankeen, with gaters of the same, which came up to them; and, to complete our dress, we had Scotch plaids, which in cold or rain wrapped round us, and in fine weather tucked up and hung at our backs without the least inconvenience. Thus was our dress at once handsome, neat and light; yet serving the double purpose of being airy in fine weather, and a safeguard from cold or wet in more intemperate changes. Our former knapsack was covered with goatskin, for the sake of looking handsome, and contained our usual change of raiment.

Thus equipped, we left Humberston, on Tuesday August the 20th. after breakfast, and had a pleasant walk, through Mount Sorrel and Loughborough, to Kegworth, where we dined. After dinner we set off for Derby. At Cavendish Bridge we crossed the Trent, and entered Derbyshire. I must not take my leave of Leicestershire without observing upon the beauty and richness of the country. It is delightfully varied with hill and dale, well wooded and a fertile soil. There are other counties more romantic and more pleasing for the visits of travellers; but, altogether, I do not know a county in England I should prefer to this for living in: though hilly, it is not too much so to be of inconvenience in draft[1] to farmers & travellers; and is free from the unpleasant and unwholesome marshes of a flat country: the air is remarkably healthy. There is a want of water in many parts of Leicestershire to complete the beauty of it's Landscapes.

Some way on from Cavendish Bridge we met a party of Drunken women returning from Harvest-work. No shameless rout of Bacchanalian women ever behaved with more indecency than did these; swearing and using every indecent term they could think of. Alas! that there should be any of a sex formed for modesty and grace, so far forget themselves, so forget even the dignity of human nature, as to intoxicate themselves, and riot thus shameless with bacchanalian revel in the broad face of day.

When we got to *Alveston*, a village two miles short of Derby, we wished much for some tea, we were dry, and had eat some onions at dinner which did not agree with us. We went into a neat looking public House, and called for tea; which, after waiting some short time, we got; my friend began to grow very ill, I gave him some tea but he could not drink it; he grew worse and worse and was at length quite sick: the night came on and, ill as he was, I judged it by no means adviseable to attempt to go on to Derby. I asked Mrs Sherwin, the Landlady, if she had beds for us; she said she had none. My friend was still very sick, but said he thought he could get on to Derby, and Mrs Sherwin kept comforting and talking to him. "Come, Sir, you must not let your spirits fail you, it will never do to be so low when you are sick, take a little more brandy and water. Brandys a very good thing for Sick People, I think its better than any medicine in the potecaries shop. My poor husband's much troubled with the gout, I give it him, when he's ill and it does him a deal of good". But neither her consolation nor the brandy and water had any effect towards making him better, so that I was resolved we should not go on if it was possible to procure beds. I still persisted in my request to Mrs Sherwin for them, and she still persisted she had none. I told her I observ'd there was another public house over the way, perhaps she could borrow beds for us there. She said no, that the people of the house and she were not upon good terms, and she could not do it, but I might go if I liked it. I went, but to no purpose; when they found from whence I came, they said "they had no beds for us, and Mrs Sherwin might get us beds in her own house". When I returned I found Mrs S. at the door: I told her I had met with no success, it was impossible for us to go on, and if she could not get us beds, I would make one for my friend on the bench in the kitchin, and sleep upon chairs myself. She began to question me about who and what we were. I told her we call'd ourselves gentlemen and were on a tour. "Call'd ourselves Gentlemen! a strange way we had chose for *Gentlemen* to travel for pleasure". I assured her it was the real case, and at length, after much entreaty, she said she had one bed in a two bedded room, but two labourers slept in the other. I ask'd my friend if he would like that, and we agreed it would be better than sleeping below all night. So I desired to see the room, and went up stairs with Mrs Sherwin. When we got into the room, she began "Here's the room, Sir, the two men sleep in that bed, and yours is in that press and I and my husband sleep in this room", shewing me one through it, "but the men" continued she "won't meddle with you, or if you have got any property with you give it to me, and I must be answerable for it, if its an hundred pound". While she was running on in this way, I said "we had not much money with us, only enough to pay our expences on the road,—but let me see the bed". "Let you see the bed?" replied the lady with much anger "I don't know why you should be so desirous to see the bed, there are neither bugs nor lice in it, it is as clean as your own, though perhaps its not so fine. Ay you may look about the room, theres neither looking-glass, nor toilet, but its as clean a one as yours for all that. You Gentlemen indeed and travel in this way. If you had stopped at Cavendish bridge, they'd have put you into one of the boatmen's beds and you must have been glad of it. Come to an house indeed and find fault in this way, you ought to be glad to get even clean straw to lie upon". She run on in this strain for about twenty minutes whilst I strived to pacify her by gentle words, saying How much obliged I was to her for accommodating us even in this way, that it was not to find fault or from a doubt of the cleanness of the bed that I desir'd to see it, but merely on account of my friend who was ill. She at length let down the bed, put clean sheets on and I got my friend to bed. How I came to be so unfortunate as to rouse this good Lady's indignation, I cannot tell; for, till I asked to see the bed, she had been very civil, notwithstanding she seemed rather suspicious. At one time she seemed quite tender and full of compassion towards my sick friend; but, whether I had hurt her honour in doubting the comfort and cleanliness of the bed, or whether she had been taking some of the fine *medicine* she had before spoken so much in praise of it, and it now began to take effect, I will not take upon me to determine. The People below (which consisted of the 2 labourers who were to sleep in our room and others who had come in) were not silent while Mrs Sherwin and I were at words upstairs, they kept talking together, and my friend heard them say something about "*Sharpers*". However, having got my friend to bed I made him some warm gruel; in the mean time the labourers retired to rest, and I soon followed their example. Presently the Landlord and Landlady followed, the Landlady locking our door as she went through. Misfortune seemed to attend us, for a drunken man, who wanted to get still more drunk, came knocking at the house door for liquor. However Mrs Sherwin would not regard him; and, after some time, he went away. Thus, after a day of fatigue, and an Evening of difficulty, we at last got some rest, and rose in the morning refreshed, and my friend well enough to pursue our Journey. We had some gruel, then paid our bill, and set forward. Thus ended our adventure at Mrs Sherwin's at the wheel at Alveston.

It is a pleasant walk from Alveston to Derby. On the left hand, just before you enter the town, is *Osmaston Hall*, the seat of S^r. Robert Willmott. The front of the House is stucco'd and large and handsome; the Grounds are very indifferent.

Of *Derby* we saw nothing more than in passing through. China manufactories we had both seen before, and silk mills we were to have a better opportunity of seeing afterwards at Nottingham; we thought it, therefore, needless to stop, and got on to *Keddleston* to breakfast.

The Inn at Keddleston is a public House for the reception of company who come for the benefit of the waters. The Situation is pleasant, and the accommodations seem'd to be good. There is a village about a mile off, Quarndon, where there is another spring equally famous with the Keddleston water.

After breakfast we dressed ourselves, and then walked down to Lord Scarsdale's House. In our way thither we saw the spring and baths. The water is very clear and fine, it is a chalibeat, the taste much like the Harrogate water. The baths are too small, and even small as they are, the spring does not always afford sufficient water for a change every day. The situation of the House and the grounds are very pleasant, and much has been done to render them so. Cottages and trees have been remov'd, hills levell'd and canals dug. The ground lies beautifully in hill and dale, well wooded and a fine piece of water running through the Park. The only thing to find fault with here is the formality of the cascades, the water falling down regular steps like nothing in nature; and since they have such beautiful specimens of nature to copy from in this respect, the want of a natural taste is unpardonable.

House.

The front is very grand; the body is very noble with a fine portico supported by [*blank space*] pillars, and a flight of steps up to it. The wings are at some little distance and join'd to the main body by corridors. We entered the House at the Servants' Hall, by a door under the Portico, put down our names, and were then shewn up into the Grand Hall, where the Housekeeper joined us. Of all the Housekeepers I ever met with at a Noblemans House, this was the most obliging and intelligent I ever saw. There was a pleasing civility in her manner which was very ingratiating, she seem'd to take a delight in her business, was willing to answer any questions which were ask'd her, and was studious to shew the best lights for viewing the pictures and setting off the furniture...

When we had seen the house, we walked about the Park for some time, and then returned to the Inn and dined at the ordinary.[2] The company was not very good. After dinner we set off for Ashbourn. The country was not very pleasing and the afternoon was hot. We stopped at Hullan Ward Gate to get some tea, and, while we were drinking it two bloods[3] stopped in a post chaise, and came in to the room where we were. They talked much stuff. Of what quality they were, I will not pretend to say; but they certainly were neither Gentlemen nor men of sense. I am rather inclined to think they were apprentices broken loose from some London wholesale warehouse, as they had all the impertinence and folly of those of that description who attempt the characters of Gentlemen when unable to sustain them. I have often met with these kind of Gentry, and as often wondered at the airs they have given themselves, and I know not how to account for this temporary attempt at bearish Gentility, unless it be either that they think they are so far from their shops as not to be known, or their releasment from the yard and desk with a few guineas in their pockets, gives their ideas too sudden an exaltation, and to look down on their former station makes them giddy. However, they paid their bill with an oath, agreed to depart with a damme, and set off cursing the Postboy. We set off soon after them, and had a pleasant walk, in the cool of the Evening, to *Ashbourn*, which place we reached soon after nine, getting in by moonlight. We put up at the *Green Man*, had a good supper and a comfortable night's rest.

The 22nd. The morning was wet, and prevented our going before breakfast to see Sir Brook Boothby's grounds,[4] which were close by. After breakfast we walked about the Town, which is not much worth seeing, the situation is pleasant. The day beginning to clear we set off for Buxton by Oakover Hall and Dove Dale. *Oakover* is about two miles from Ashbourn, and is much visited on account of a very fine Painting to be seen there: a Holy Family by Raphael[5] which is exquisite indeed. It is said that this picture was found in an old lumber-room, and was about to be parted with, when its value was discovered. It is reckoned worth £2000 ... The House is old and not a very good one, and the Garden quite in the old style. We were informed that the fine painting above mentioned was left by the late Mr Oakover to the family, with this condition, that it should be shewn to whoever came to see it.

The morning being rainy, though at times fair, we had not a very agreeable walk, but every untoward circumstance attending it was amply compensated by the pleasure we experienced when we reached *Dove Dale*. At the entrance of Dove Dale (or, as the beginning is sometimes called, *Bunster Dale*) stands *Thorp Cloud* to the right, a fine craggy mountain. The Dale here is tolerably broad, and the mountains less wooded than when farther advanced. You go on for some way, when the Dale takes a turn to the left, and then, I believe, it is that *Dove* Dale begins. The scene is now very grand. To the right are the high barren mountains of Derbyshire, and to the left those of Staffordshire covered almost entirely over with wood. The river Dove runs thro the narrow valley between in a rapid stream, sometimes through wood or rushes, and at others has its course impeded by small islands, or falls down in small cascades just sufficient to vary the scene and give a murmuring sound of waters thro the valley. On one side only is there just sufficient room for a footpath. As you proceed up the Dale the scene grows more sublime, vast pieces of rock rear their heads perpendicular to a great height and appear like the ruins of some stupendous fabric. It seems as if this had been the residence of nature, and here she had held her court. And those, who have seen the artificial cascades and parteres of Keddleston and Chatsworth, would think she had fled from the country, and left only her own habitation a ruinous monument of her own taste.

The impressions which this scene must almost invariably make on the minds of people are very grand; but ours were rather spoiled by our recollection of a Lady who, when she entered Dove Dale, burst into Tears.—Delightful state of sensibility! which, if a sparrow falls to the ground, can shed a tear upon the moving spectacle; or melt into childish weakness at the sight of a grand scene. But, when a near relation dies—puts on *becoming* mourning, and skips off sorrow to the tune of Morgan rattler[6] with an apothecaries prentice, or leers it away in delightful oglings from a side box at one of O'Keef's farces.[7]—The recollection of this rather discomposed our gravity, and—Insensible wretches!—we entered Dove Dale laughing: but our ideas soon refined, and the scene made that impression upon our minds inseperable from grand objects.

We went on above two miles, till we came to some cottages where we inquired our way to New-haven and left this charming spot to traverse a dreary country. The situation of *New Haven* is upon the top of a bleak Hill, and I hardly think any consideration, but that all-powerful one of making money could ever have induced any one to fix upon this place. But it is a convenient stage between Ashbourn and Buxton, and so served our purpose, as it already has done, I make no doubt, to many, and will to many more. The Evening was very rainy and the road dreary. We got wet to *Buxton* between eight and nine. We took up our abode at the *Grove*; to which place we had been recommended by our Host at Ashbourn (Mr Wood), who said that, as we were on foot, we should not perhaps wish to go to the best house. If we did, we must go to the crescent, but his Brother kept the Grove; and, if we mentioned his name, he would be sure to treat us well. And his brothers behaviour to us fully justified his character of him. We got our suppers, and the next day, *the 23^d*, staid all day at Buxton.

The Situation of Buxton is very bad: it is in a bottom surrounded by barren Hills, which attract the clouds and involve it in almost constant rain. But its salubrious waters make it resorted to by the sick, and the accommodations and amusements make it agreeable to those who come with the sick. The taste of the water is very fine, being warm and possessing all the spirit of cold water. The Baths are very convenient. The *crescent*[8] is the grand house for accommodation: It is a large handsome stone building, having 27 windows in a row in front, and a piazza at the bottom where the company walk in wet weather. It was built by the Duke of Devonshire and is divided into three different Hotels. In this building also are the assembly rooms and a large coffee-room. It is the peculiar priviliege of those who go to the Duke's House to bathe before nine o'clock in the morning. The other Houses had joined and made an artificial warm bath for the accommodation of those who wish to bathe early, but it is not equal to the other baths. Behind the crescent are the *stables*, built of stone in a circular form, with a piazza round for the company to ride under when it rains. I should guess the circus to be about 60 yards in diameter. The Houses are The Old Hall, the White Hart, the Eagle and child and the George, besides private Lodging Houses. We dined at the ordinary. Our conversation of course turned upon what we had seen and what we meant to see. One of the men at our end of the table talked much about his love for travelling, and his fondness for novelty, declaring he would go forty miles to see a joint stool, had he never seen one before. He wished us to make a party with him to Castleton, but we declined it. Another man, an Irishman, was giving an account of his having seen the Peak Hole and the expence it was to the party. He said he waited three days at Castleton to get a party to go in. That they then had the Cave lighted up with £3 worth of candles (which, supposing them to be penny candles, would be 720) and had a guinea's worth of gunpowder (which at [blank space] a pound would be [blank space] pound, and almost enough to blow up the rock, and at least must kill every soul in the cave). This shews how Travellers will lie, even when they must know what they say is impossible. We soon after dinner left these gentry and went to see *Pool's Hole*. This curious subterranean cavern is situated at the foot of a mountain called Coitmoss, about a mile from Buxton. There are several mean Huts about the mouth of the cave, where a number of old women live, who furnish people who go in with candles, and are themselves the guides. The entrance is through a very narrow low passage, so much so, that one is obliged to bend almost double to get in, the way is also very wet, but, soon after you enter, the cave is spacious enough. There are a number of curious petrifactions or incrustations formed by the droppings of the water, which ouses through the rock, into curious forms to each of which they give a name to what perhaps it has some slight resemblance. There is Pool's chair—The saddle—the turtle—Tripe—The flitch of Bacon—the organ—the toilet—The fount— the dark Lanthorn—the Lion—the beehive—and Mary Queen of Scot's Pillar, which it is said she named herself when she visited this Cave. There is also a place called his [sic] bread and cheese shelf. The way is very indifferent, much up and down, and in one place the guides desire you to lean towards the rock lest you should fall down a chasm, through which a stream of water runs. The women told us that the length of the cave was 669 yards. I think it could scarce be so many feet. You return a different way back; and, at one place, a light is left which, when you have proceeded some way farther, is seen through a rude archway in the back and has a very fine effect. I think that this scene would make a very fine subject for a candlelight painting.[9] The rude and dark cavern with the cut in the back and light seen through it, our three guides "so withered and so wild in their attire", seeming "not like inhabitants of earth",[10] and our two selves in our scotch plaids, all upon different crags of the rock, must make a very picturesque appearance. These good Ladies are never satisfied, so it is best for a person to give what he thinks is right, and not to regard their grumbling. When we returned from the cave, other women came to us with Derbyshire diamonds (small hexagon & pentagon pieces of spar) which they wished us to purchase, but we did not buy any. These women allow such a certain time, I forget how long; and, if the visitors do not return when that is expired, they come in with fresh lights lest any accident should have happened. From the Cave we went up the Hill and saw several curious Huts formed partly in the mountain and partly from the refuse of the lime kilns, which abound here, and which in time form into a mass almost as solid as the rock itself. From Buxton and the hills at a distance these huts and lime kilns have a pleasing and odd appearance, looking like so many tents pitched on the side of a hill, that a person might think there was a camp. In the Evening we went to the Assembly rooms to see the rooms & company, the waiter would have had us gone in, saying our dresses did not signify, as it was an undressed night, but we declined his offer and only went into a small room at the end, where we saw but were not seen. The room was very handsome and well lighted up, and the company appeared very good. We supped at our own house, and went in good time to bed.

The 24th. The morning was wet and we could not set off so early as we intended. After breakfast it held up and we set off for Castleton. Our way lay thro *Fairfield*, a village with a few trees about it, and from thence to *Peak in the Forest*. The weather was showery; but, when the rain came on, we let down our plaids and were kept dry. About a mile from Peak in the Forest is *Elden Hole* on the side of a Hill. This tremendous chasm has now a wall round it and a door to prevent men, or cattle from falling in. As we approached, we found the door was open, and a man at work mending the wall, who, as soon as he saw us, locked the door, in order, no doubt, that we should unlock it again with a *silver* key; but we were even with him, and got upon the wall to look into it and cast stones down. As soon as he found he could not get anything from us by shutting us out, he opened the door again and flung down several large stones, but his civility (or rather forced officiousness) could not move us any more than his rudeness: we did not give him a single half-penny. The depth of this chasm is not known, it has been attempted to be fathomed by a line of 884 yards, but it did not reach the bottom. The stones when thrown in were heard for a considerable time, and the noise died away by degrees. I thought that I heard them fall into water, my friend was of a different opinion. Many dreadful and wonderful stories are told of this place, such as of people being let down and coming up frantic, of cloths which have been thrown in being driven up by the strong current of wind, &c. &c. But the most horrid is one of a guide who undertook to conduct a traveller over these mountains, when he murdered him, and threw his body into this chasm.

The human mind (unless hardened by misery or cruelty) always revolts at the name of murder, and even shudders at the idea of an enemy murdering his antagonist; but when he, to whom another looks up to for safety, to whose direction, to whose honour he entrusts himself, forgets those great bonds of society, and murders, for a trifle perhaps, the one he is bound by every tie human and divine to protect, the thought is too horrid to reflect upon, <and one rather supposes it the work of some evil spirit in the shape of man, than of that being, whose supreme delight is in protecting his fellow creatures, and whose happiness is reflected alone from their's.>

From hence we proceeded to *Mam Tor*, or the shivering mountain. The earth of which this mountain is composed is of a dark colour and crumbling nature. The people in the neighbourhood say that it is continually crumbling down, but that its size never diminishes. There certainly is a lesser mountain at the bottom of this which appears to have grown from these shivers, whence this is called Mam Tor, or the mother mountain. Its perpendicular height is said to be 123 yards. We had a fine view from the top of this mountain of Castleton and the village of Hope in Hope Dale to the north east. Below us were the lead mines, and to the North west E Dale sloped down to the larger valley between two high mountains. A stream ran along it, and the trees planted on its banks waved along with it and shewed it's zigzag course. We went down to the lead mines and saw those at work without, and then went on to Castleton. When we got to *Castleton* we inquired about seeing the Peak Cave, and were informed that a party from Buxton were going in and we might go in with them. From what the lying Irishman at Buxton had said we concluded it would be an advantage to us to go in with a party, so we ordered our dinner to be ready against we returned, and set forward. A gentleman and two Ladies were gone on before, my friend and I next follow [sic] with the guide, and the large Party from Buxton followed us. Thus the company who went in were three seperate Parties.

The Peak Cave.

The way to this cave is by a pass between two rocks which grows narrower and narrower as you approach the entrance, when a huge rock rises 84 yards perpendicular, which has on one side a tower, the remains of an old Castle[11] which formerly stood here. It is just on the brow of the rock, and its near situation to so dreadful a precipice fills the mind with terror. A few trees and bushes are here abouts. The Entrance to the cave is in this rock, a circular arch 14 yards high, about forty wide and near an hundred long. The first sight of this is very striking, and the objects which present themselves unusual. There are two or three small huts without the entrance, and one just within the cave mouth, the whole of this first cave besides is taken up by boys and girls employed in making ropes. From the top of this hangs a large piece of petrefaction in shape somewhat like a flitch of Bacon, which resemblance give it its name. It is not so good a one as that in Pool's Hole. The old women who live in these huts furnish lights for the visitors to the cave, giving each one, when you pass through a narrow entrance at the end of this first cave and bid farewell to daylight. The Guide goes first and explains as you go on. The first place you arrive at is called the bell house, and from thence you get to the *River* about 15 yards wide. This is crossed in a boat, in shape like a tub, and will only hold one person, or two, if they are not very large. Some of the Ladies of the party were afraid of crossing the River and returned. The rock through which the boat passes is so very low, that you are obliged to lie upon your back, and are desired by the guide not to open your eyes: he wades in the water & pushes it on ... The effect upon landing is very grand, you are in a large cavern called the Cathedral, 90 yards long, 70 wide, and 40 high. You look up to the top in one corner and see a number of candles burning, which give a gloomy light sufficient to make "darkness visible",[12] and give some idea of the rude appearance and dimensions of the cave. Beyond this you come to another branch of the same river, which you cross upon the Guide's back. From this to a dropping well called *Roger Rain's House*. Then the chancel, 19 yards long, and the Devils Cellar, where it is customary for those who are fond of drinking, to drink what they have brought with them for that purpose. The walls are entirely scrawlled over with the names of those who have been so *devilish jolly* here. Here you go down steps, 150 feet, and come to another *river*, which runs from the end and looses itself through the rock here. This river you step over 7 or 8 times before you get to the end. Some little way farther, you come to three very regular arches in the rock, near which is a hanging rock, and a curious snake and other fossils on the side wall. The last cavern has a circular top and is called Tom of Lincoln. A little beyond this the footway ends, when there is 17 yards farther of water, this has been cut out of the solid rock and they still continue the work at times. The whole length of the cave is 750 yards. While you are returning, a man, whom the Guide takes in for that purpose, bores a hole in the rock and blasts it with gunpowder,

> whose roar
> Embowel'd with contagious noise the air,
> And all her entrails tore.[13]

The effect of this was very grand, the shock in the air was perceptible, and you could hear the roar all along the cavern till it died away. The effect of this was somewhat diminished as the servants of the party from Buxton had let off a pistol before. They were also hooping and hollowing about; and the lights and noise of so large a party took off much from the horror and solemnity of the scene. The effect must be more grand with only a few. In your way back, when you get to the chancel, you hear all at once voices over your head begin singing Psalms. You look but can see nothing. Soon a woman appears above with a light and you see a number of children in surplices, with tapers, which they light and go on singing for some time. The effect of this is astonishing. Nothing particular takes place till you get to the bell house again, where you put out your lights and the guide shews you daylight through the narrow way:

And now at last the sacred influence
Of light appears, and from the walls of Heav'n
Shoots far into the bosom of dim night
A glimmering dawn; here nature first begins
Her farthest verge and chaos to retire.[14]

In sudden thaws, or after great rains, the river overflows, from the passage in the rock not being large enough to let off the water as fast as it comes in. Sometimes it suddenly fills the Cave, and is attended with much danger, if any one is so foolhardy as to go in at the time. S[r]. J. Lowther, the present L[d]. Londsale,[15] went in once while the water was rising, with a party. The guide told us he was much in liquor, the party, on seeing the danger, returned, but S[r]. J.L. would go on, and was with much difficulty prevailed on to return at the instance of the Guide upon the rapid swell of the water. Within five minutes after they were out, the cave overflowed.

On our return from seeing the Peak Cave, our Guide told us, that, if we were fond of sights of the kind, there was a *Lead Mine*[16] not far off, which was well worth our notice. We assented to his proposal, and returned to the Inn to get our dinners; and, in the mean time, he went and brought one of the Miners to conduct us. The miner told us it was usual to take brandy on account of the cold; we took some, therefore, with us in a bottle, and set forward to the mouth of the mine, where we saw great quantities of lead ore ready prepared for smelting and the people employed in their various departments. It was four o'clock, the time the miners come from out the mine: the women, we observed, wore breeches. Here another Miner joined us, who was also to be the companion of our excursion. He was one of the stoutest men I ever saw: the very picture of health, well proportioned, and his muscles seemed of Herculean strength. It does not appear, from what we saw, that working in the mines is, as has been said, prejudicial to the health of either man or woman. They offered us miner's dresses, but, as we had our plaids on, we thought ourselves proof against wet, dirt or cold, and therefore declined them. The two miners then put on their dresses, and my friend and I set forward with them.

We entered a hut at the side of the hill, where our guides provided themselves with lights, which they carried in their hands by sticking several in a lump of clay, and then proceeded down steps for near fifty yards, till we came to a canal. This navigation is through a cavern cut in the rock, seven feet high, and four wide, the water about three feet, the length is 1000 yards. The miners have five guineas for every two yards, which they work by blasting the rock with gunpowder. We entered a boat, and my friend and I had each a chair to sit upon, our guides sitting one at the head, the other at the stern. When we had gone 600 yards, we came to a large natural cavern in the rock, where there was a most dreadful roar of waters; we stopped here to see a waterfall from an artificial dam, to keep up the level of the water through the navigation. One of the men pulled up the sluice, and the roar, added to the solemnity of the scene, was dread and awful. Hence we went 250 yards to another fall, nothing to be compared to the former: this joins the other after running some little way, and the joint stream runs under ground till it finds its way into the Peak cave. The whole course of this stream is wonderful; it loses itself underground about four miles from Castleton, on the Manchester road, runs through this mine, and afterwards through the Peak Cave, whence it again emerges to light, and takes its course through Castleton, Hopedale, &c. By means of this stream, there is a constant current of air through the mine, which keeps it free from any noxious vapours, which would otherwise be dangerous to the miners. One hundred and fifty yards farther brought us to the end of the navigation, when we chained our boat to a rail; and, with each of us a light, proceeded upon planks, laid upon rafters over the stream, for two hundred and fifty yards farther, stoping almost all the way. At the end of this board-way, we got to a small cavern, and there stood upright to rest ourselves. The Miners here told us, that, if we went farther, we must climb up the rock by rails fixed into the side: that many went no farther than this place; but, if we were not afraid, we might proceed. We told them to lead on. We climbed for ten yards up the rock, by rails sometimes a yard asunder; and at length got into a large cavern dimly to be seen by our candle-light: the dashing noise of a waterfall, to be heard and not seen, added to the terror of the place. Here our guides again asked us if we would proceed, telling us it was forty yards, climbing up the same manner we got hither, to the shaft they worked at. They looked in our faces (as they told us afterwards) to see if we were frightened, but we were determined to go on; and, with much labour and difficulty, got to the end of our scrambling, which was sometimes through holes in the rock just big enough to admit the body. Here we saw the waterfall which dashes with a large stream from the top to the bottom of the cavern. From this place we went on slanting up the rock ten yards to the place they worked at. We stopped to rest and take some of our brandy, which we found refreshing, and the miners explained the whole process of their work. We each worked out a piece of ore, as a memento of our expedition. The air here was unpleasant, the smell of smoking and of gunpowder, used in blasting the rock, being not yet gone off. There was another way out, by climbing one hundred and fifty yards farther to the top of the hill; but, as the way lay through another proprietor's mine, the miners never go by it, unless insisted upon by strangers; and, as we were somewhat fatigued with the exertions of the day, we judged it best to go back as we came. At the top of the cavern, the place we left off climbing, one of the men left a piece of candle alight, which he had brought for that purpose, and we went down, a miner accompanying each to direct our steps in the retrograde motion. We soon got to the bottom of the cavern, and our guides told us to look up. The sight was dreadful: the candle, forty yards above us, appeared like a star, and afforded a dim light just sufficient to give an idea of the danger we had braved. The cavern was sloped like a Bee-Hive, the way to the top was by the stakes fixed into the sides sloping inwards, sometimes by ladders, many of the steps of which were nearly worn through, and only a slight ballustrade, so that one false step, or the breaking of a rail had dashed us lifeless to the bottom: but all danger was now passed, and we congratulated ourselves that we had escaped it. The miners frequently go up this way *without lights*. They told us that there never was but one accident happened in this mine, when a man was drowned owing to his own groundless fears. We returned to the boat, and set forward again for daylight in high spirits, singing "God Save the King", "Rule Britannia",[17] and a variety of songs, in which we all joined; the miners, (one of them in particular) having very fine voices. At the large cavern I first mentioned, we left another light; which, when we got to the end, (600 yards) had a most beautiful effect, appearing like a star with the beams playing upon the water. We, at length, after two hours absence from it, got to daylight again, highly satisfied, and pleased with our excursion, and returned to Castleton, with the mixed emotions of terror and admiration.

Sunday the 25th we designed staying at Castleton till after morning service; but, upon inquiry, found that there was not to be any. The shops too were open. I am happy to say this was the first total neglect of all decency on a Sunday that I ever met with, but am sorry to be obliged to record it at all, and of any place.

After breakfast we left Castleton for Chatsworth. Just beyond the first mile stone on the [*blank space*] road there is a very fine view into Hope Dale and of Castleton. As we went through little Hucklow, a woman standing at a cottage door, I suppose from seeing our knapsack, asked us if we were Soldiers? We answered "God save the King", and passed on. The road from hence to *Middleton Dale* was uninteresting, and I must own I was much disappointed there. It is a pass between the rocks for about two miles upon a constant descent. The road takes up the whole, or very nearly the whole of the dale, and the rocks are bold, and in some places prettily planted with brush wood. But it wants water, that great and almost essential beauty to all views. We got to *Middleton* about one o'clock; and when we inquired about dinner were told there was a nice piece of roast beef which another person had bespoke, and we might dine with him. We assented to the proposition; and, before dinner came on table, another gentleman in a one Horse chaise, with a black servant, came to the Inn and

71

begged to join us. We all sat down to table, and the conversation turned upon what we had seen, and what we were about to see. We were very cheerful and pleasant. The Gentleman who last came in (whose name was Smith, as we learnt from a Bill upon the back of which he wrote a direction for us) advised us much to go to see *Router Rocks*, an old Druidical remains ... When we had given this gentleman an account of our tour, he said he "applauded our spirit, and envied our execution". After dinner we took an hearty farewell and each set off his own way.

We had a pleasant but hot walk to *Barslow*, a village prettily situated on the Derwent; and from thence to *Edensor* or *Chatsworth*. We went to the House after tea; but, as it was late the Porter said we should see it next morning early. We walked a little about the Park, and returned to the Inn.

The 26ᵗʰ we were up early; and, at seven o'clock, went to the House, which, to say the truth, is little worth seeing. Chatsworth was formerly one of the wonders of Derbyshire, from its being a fine spot and magnificent House in the middle of a dreary waste. But the whole country is now cultivated, and there are so many houses, which exceed this in magnificence, that it is only to be regarded with the gardens as a curious specimen of the old taste. The House is a Square and built round a Court, each front is different, and that, the *design* of which appears to have been the handsomest, has some gross defect in the architecture, so that it is purposely hid by other buildings and trees. Some of the rooms are large and handsome, but nothing striking ... The waterworks are worth seeing once, and that I think is the utmost to be said of them. Those who have never seen any thing of the kind before, curiosity tempts them to see, and is perhaps scarcely gratified when it has. The devices are many of them childish; and, as the water is only set playing at particular times, you do not see them in their best state at once, but have to wait for them to be set going.

There is a large stone temple with many flights of steps up to it, when you get there the man turns the cocks, and water gushes from all parts of it and falls down this formal flight of steps. It is a trick sometimes play'd, I believe, to get a person into this temple, when water spirts up from beneath and all about him, and wets him completely. There is also a tin-tree, which, as you approach it, the leaves spirt out water. A single fountain throws water to the height of 90 feet, and another fountain with Sea Nymphs, Dolphins, Horses &c., each spout into the bason. On the Duke's public days these waterworks play the whole time.

After breakfast we had a pleasant walk by Rowsley bridge and over Stanton Moor, from whence we had a fine view up three different vallies, and Birchover, to *Router Rocks*.¹⁸ I have seen few places that I have been more struck with than this Druidical remains. The scenery described in the opening of Mʳ Mason's Caractacus is well expressive of this place:

These cliffs, these yawning caverns, this wide circus,
Skirted with unhewn stone: they awe my soul.

These mighty piles of magic-planted rock,
Thus rang'd in mystic order, mark the place
Where but at times of holiest festival
The Druid leads his train.

There is a cottage built by the side of these rocks where a man dwells who shews them: they are fenced in by a rude kind of fence. Something of the grand and rude appearance of this pile of rock is spoiled by regular artificial doors made to these seemingly-natural caves, and a summer house built of *hewn* stone on one side. The man explained the place in his rustic manner. He took us into the caves, and next shewed us the *rocking-stones*. <They are the greatest curiosities of the kind I ever beheld.> It was by these that they put their prisoners to the test of their innocence:

> behold yon huge
> And unhewn sphere of living adamant,
> Which, pois'd by magic, rests its central weight
> On yonder pointed rock: firm as it seems,
> Such is it's strange and virtuous property,
> It moves obsequious to the gentlest touch
> Of him whose breast is pure; but to a traitor,
> Tho' e'en a Giant's prowess nerv'd his arm,
> It stands as fixed as Snowdon.

Our Rustic told us with some shrewdness, that this was what they tried their criminals with, but that "they could bring 'em in guilty or not just as they pleased, it was only putting a wedge underneath, and it would not move, and then the man was murdered". There are three of these rocking stones, all of which are easily moved, notwithstand their immense bulk and weight. The smallest weighs 8 ton, and the other 2 60 ton each. One of those, though I call it a stone, is in fact a combination of four or 5 piled upon each other, but by moving one of them gently it gives motion to the whole mass. There is a chair with arms to it cut out of a solid stone, and on the highest rock is a bason cut in it, I suppose for the purpose of holding water at their religious ceremonies. About a mile from this place, on the top of a hill, are 9 stones in a circle, which are called the 9 Ladies, this I fancy was the place where the Druids sat in Judgement. The man, seeing our knapsack, I fancy took us for Pedlars, and asked us what we dealt in. We told him small goods; but he did not offer to become a purchaser. We proceeded by Darley bridge, and over the meadows to Matlock bridge, and next to *Matlock bath*, but as we designed staying only one night, and were informed the houses there were all full, we went on a mile farther to

Cromford, where we dined, and took up our abode for the night. In the Evening we walked up to the Bath and drank tea there.

As soon as the traveller gets over Matlock bridge he is struck with the very grand appearance of the Dale. To the right are high sloping hills tolerably well cultivated. To the left, the river Derwent rolls over a bed of rock, sometimes forms a bed of deep dingy waters, and sometimes falls down in cascades. Above this the rocks rise perpendicularly, in various wild and beautiful forms, well varied and shaded with wood. The *great Tor* soon presents itself and appears high above the rest, like the monarch of the Dale. The Bath next presents itself, a busy scene of houses and company and shops for the sale of the Derbyshire petrefactions, worked up into various and beautiful articles for ornamental furniture. A mile farther you pass through a narrow cut in the rock, and at once come upon Cromford. After our tea we ferried over the river and went up what is called the *Lover's Walk*, a pretty shaded walk winding up the side of the hill; we crossed over this hill, and came down to a new House building by S^r. Richard Arcwright.[19] It is built of stone, in the form of an old castle, with turrets and battlements at the corners, and has a very odd appearance. At Cromford are S^r. Richard's cotton mills; but, as we were to have better opportunities of seeing others at Nottingham, we did not attempt it.

The 27th we had a pleasant walk thro *Critch*, *Pentridge* and Ripley to [*blank space*] a village about 6 miles from Nottingham. Here we stopped to get our dinner, and were much entertained with a woman who sat in the room with us. She was sister to our Hostess, and was come upon a visit to her from Loughborough. She entertained us with her remarks upon her sister's broad and provincial manner of speaking. She was a curious specimen of affectation in low life. From hence we got to *Nottingham* to tea, where we remained till the 31st.

The *Castle* is very Grand, and the view from it rich and beautiful; but we had been so much used to mountains and more Grand and wild scenes, that this specimen of luxuriant and cultivated nature pleased only from its contrast. The Cotton and Silk Mills are curious and wonderful. But for one, who does not perfectly understand their principles and effects, to attempt a description would be absurd and presumptuous. We walked one Evening to the top of a hill not far from the Town, to see what is call'd the *Shepherd's Maze*. This, I fancy, must be the *quaint* maze mentioned by Shakspeare in the Midsummer night's dream . . .[20] These mazes, I imagine, were made by the shepherds for the convenience of running in to keep themselves warm. This is contained in a space at most not above 30 yards square, yet is so very winding as to be a mile from the place at which the person enters, till he has run it through to the end.

On Saturday the 31 we put an end to this delightful tour, by getting well home to Humberston.

A JOURNAL
OF A PEDESTRIAN TOUR
BY THE CAVES IN THE WEST RIDING OF
YORKSHIRE TO THE LAKES
AND HOME THRO PART OF
NORTH WALES
IN THE YEAR 1797

[*Editor's note*. In the years following his election to a college fellowship and his ordination, Plumptre could still spare two of his summer vacations for travel. In 1796 he set out on his first visit to Scotland, boarding the packet boat from London to Edinburgh in mid-July for a walking tour into the Highlands as far as Inverary; he made the return journey through the Lake District and the Peak District, arriving back in Cambridge by the end of September. Most of the next summer, from the end of May until the middle of August, was passed in another walking tour that took him to a similar combination of old and new scenes: the West Riding of Yorkshire, the Lakes and north Wales. Both were ambitious expeditions—the first about 1500 miles and the second about 600 miles—and both confirmed his love of wild, natural landscape, particularly the scenery of north Wales and the Lake District. Yet neither issued in the carefully prepared journals that had recorded his tours with John Dudley. Instead, he celebrated his arrival in the Lakes in 1797 by beginning his comic opera, *The Lakers*, published the following year. Soon after his return he took up the duties at Hinxton, which increasingly preoccupied him.

For both 1796 and 1797 we have only the memorandums he took on the spot, though he called his notebook for the latter year a 'journal'. Three episodes from this 1797 tour, at least, are worth preserving. The first records his only visit to the Craven district of the West Riding, where geological freaks like Malham Cove and Gordale Scar were gaining the same popularity with tourists as the subterranean marvels of the Peak District. The next shows him at Llangollen, making the acquaintance of the Ladies whom he had glimpsed in 1792 and would visit again in 1799. The last also shows him pausing on the route he had travelled with Dudley in 1792, this time to give a much fuller account of the industry at Ironbridge—in its way, as capable as satisfying contemporary taste for the Sublime as Malham Cove or Gordale Scar.]

The West Riding

[*11 June, Bradford*] Set off at 7. Pleasant walk to Bingley up and down hill. Views fine.

From Bingley walked by canal side 3 locks at ye first rise, and 4 more higher up, then level till Gargrave. Canal winds by hills side in beautiful windings on ye left hand, for some way wooded to water edge and fine tufts of golden broom—sometimes varied by a fragment of a rock, a foot bridge, or open field with cattle or a corn field. To the right in the valley is

75

the winding Air, at one time Town of Keighley at a small distance. Hills bending in a fine sweep beyond, a wood winding round the farthermost. Hills that terminate the prospect blue with the gloomy day. Prospect at about 8 m. from B^y. changes to a more open range of hills on ye left. Kilwick church 4 m ½ from Skipton a little below ye canal a very pretty object. Flasby fell before us with 1. peaked and two more $\odot^r$. tops a fine object. Valley to Skipt^n. not so rich and beautiful. Skipton not to be seen till you come almost close to it, hid behind a hill. Heard the bells.

Skipton. Church and castle. Fair for Cattle at Sk^n. 1 every fortnight.

Left Sk^n. for Malham. Along Settle road to Gargrave turnpike (passed by side of Flasby fell) and turned off by lane to right for Malham, 7 m. 3 m. from M^m. ye village of Airton prettily situated on a hill above the Air. Kirby (burying place of the Lamberts of Calton Hall) 1 m. from M^m. and ye parish church. As I descended hill from Airton saw cove at distance.

Got to M^m. ½ p. 6. Met with Thos. Hurtley, who published ye account of Malham.[1] Not at all intelligent. I do not think he wrote the book himself. This afternoon showery.

[12 June] Rose at 8. Morning wet.

M^m. div^d. into E. & W. by a rivulet which runs from the Cove and joins the sources of the river Air which come underground from the Tarn. This part of the dale called Kirby-Malham-dale.

Craven not much wooded. Are trees but ye fine pastures are inclosed by stone walls.

Set up at ye Buck, John Brayshay's, his ears stick up, 66 years of age. Married at 44. Has a son 21. The youngest 4. 9 children. His eldest bro. W^m. thought like the Marq. of Granby.[2] Did keep Inn, but given up.

A riot in ye house evening before. B^y. lamented y^t. his wife was not at home as she would have kept 'em in order and turned em out of house.

Set off little bef. 11. to Cove about ½ a m from Inn. $\perp^r$. rock 288 feet high. Shelves in various places with grass and shrubs growing upon it. From ye middle it rises in a $\odot^r$ form on each side. From bottom a stream issues which comes from Tarn, and runs in winding stream to the sources of the Air, a little below Mal^m. Trees grow all along by side of it and it turns a Cotton Mill before it gets to Mal^m.—Stand under rock and look up. See it project over. Many swallows build about it. Hawk's nest by one of ye shelves (ye highest) taken for ye purpose of catching moor-game. Fox driven down from a lower shelf. Story of hare found having taken to a place under stones where a human body was found, no one missing.—Echo.—B^y. said y^t. people come for herbs. Put 'em between papers & screwed em down. C^d. not think for what unless for printing cotton. Hurtley's view a good one upon ye whole.—Returned to Inn, set off with Joseph Brayshay, boy 14, for Gordale. Air rises below Mal^m. in 2 places from Tarn, is joined by Cove & Gordale becks.

As you get into Gordale the rocks rise very fine on each side in broken abrupt precipices and fragments, interspersed with loose stones and grass. Yew growing out of fisures. Stream runs thro dale.—Gennets Cave, or Jenny's hole.—Wind round ye rock and come into vast amphitheatre of $\perp^r$ 100 yards or overhanging $\odot^r$. rocks of grey stone forming immense pillars with here & there a tree from $\perp^r$. Some dead from want of soil. A cascade oppos^t. rushing from chasm down yellow lime-stone rock.

Climbed up by side of cascade to a 2nd. amphith^e. Less y^n. y^e 1st but not less picturesque. Thro a $\odot^r$ chas^m. oppos^t. rather to ye right, water falls down foaming along ye rocks of y^s. dreadful chasm. Hurtley's view pretty correct. As you ascend, look back. The view tremendous. To measure with the eye the left hand rock from top to bottom, most astonishing.

A man killed here, after a dog in pursuit of hare. Had been at cocking at Kirby, was maddled.[3]

Flowers here:[4] cowslips, primroses (red bell (bog ranunculus) such as in Clare Hall garden), violets, bird's eye (pretty pink flower with yellow eye), orchis (or crowfoot), yellow Heartsease (or stepmother), Lady cup (small yellow flower with 5 pointed leaf, bell shaped).

Crossed over fells to Malham water or Tarn. Fine piece of water in ye midst of ye tops of mountains all craggy. No wood. Mr Lister's plantations but small and of no growth. Hall stands too much exposed. Small farm near it with trees much prettier. Followed ye stream to where in 2 places it sinks into ground. Over fells to Settle road. Came to lead & calamine mines. Tarn seen from road almost as well as at side. Not a tree till came to Settle. Lines of ye Country very fine. Misty so y^t. c^d. not see distant prospect.

At Golden Lion at Settle met with a Traveller who took me in his Gig to Ingleton ("gave me a *side*"). Passed by Giggleswick, Tarn, to left. Scar, and ebbing & flowing well by road side. Could scarce perceive ebb & flow. (See Marshall on the Management of Landed Estates,[5] p.90.) Came down hill by new road. To r^t. a Cave in rock. Did not stop to see it. Country better. Some few trees. Passed a funeral. Hearse 2 wheels 1 horse driven by boy in black great coat!

Settle no church, Giggleswick Parish Church.

Afternoon cleared up and was very fine.

Got to Ingleton soon after 6. To Bay Horse, Hartley. Traveller left me after tea.

For an account of this mountain and its caves: see Catcott on The Deluge, p.343.[6]

[*13 June*] Rose at ½ p. 6. At ¼ p. 8 set off with my Guide Willy Wilson (alias Law) formerly a soldier in the 66th. for Inglebro. He was 68 years of age.

About 2m from Ingleton we got into a narrow romantic glen which led to a small cascade called Yarlsby force. There is a long narrow piece of rock which is rather inclined to the horizon which reaches cross from rock to rock and from behind which the water dashes down. There are several ash trees grow near. I stoped to take a view and my guide went to the top, as he afterwards informed me to be an *object*. (Came to a scar above. NB I forget what this mem^m. means.) As we ascended we came to an old root of a tree. My guide remarked that "it had been there ever since Noah's floods affair".—Men sheering sheep—others digging turf—fine views as we ascended but the day began to be more and more misty. In 2 hours and ½ arrived at top.

The top of Ingle^bro. appears in the form of 3 terraces. The middle is formed of limestone, the top and bottom of grit. Round the middle terrace there are many holes like funnels.—Guide said "some hold a dispute that they were made by the Danes", as lurking places.—The top said to be a mile round. I think not so much. About 60 years ago there was 1 year a single match rode here—one 5th. of Novr. when guide was boy, a bonfire, with 5 barrels of tar, at which he assisted. On the top a beacon and several Danish ⊙^s.

View: to N.W. Whernside. E. Pennygant. S. Pendle. Saw up Vale of Lonsdale to Lancaster &, beyond Lancaster & Cartmel Sands, Isle of Walney, Langdale Pikes, &c. &c. Descended to spring at 2nd. terrace, thence to Fold's Foot at the 1st from the bottom. A most tremendous chasm to look down. Descended it, looked up: a fine front of irregular rock, overgrown with moss and plants:[7] rose-of-the-root (or as he called it rhodum root (or rhodium root)—such a *smell* as guide never see'd before), Saxafrage, white & purple stone crop, hurtle berries, grass upon grass (or viviparous grass), bog nunculus (or ranunculus), stinking rhamp (white flower 6 male 1 female). As we descended saw at little distance to left, Catum's wife's hole: shaped like funnel, turf. Near which is a fine spring, and for which reason in shooting season parties dine there.—Passed under another rocky front on N. side of Ingle^bro. called the Arx, less fine y^n. Folds Foot but grand.

Came to Meir (or Mare) Gill, a (or many) long chasm (or 's), trees growing over. Water at bottom, great depth. Sides of chasm overgrown with moss and plants. Black trout. A natural footbridge over one chasm.

Some way above this, a Cave called Foxe's hole, where there are damps[8] that no one dare enter in. Some colliers came to explore it, but y^r fire, a very large one, went out and y^y. returned.

Came over Salter's kill fell. Vast beds of limestone rock—guide's opinions of ye cracks—explained by rain after heat of sun—he thought *fire*. Y^t. y^se. mountains were once afire like ye mountains in Italy. Met here two men (at Salter's kill open hole) shooting hawks. One a schollar, the guides reflection thereon: had he been such he would have given up his time to Botany.

Came to Weathercote Cave.

1st. cave. Hear the water but do not see it. Look down immense hole: to cavity at bottom. Descend a little and to right, is a cave shaped like an oven. Rock supported by pillar. Clear stream of petrifying water runs thro. A small hole runs thro top like a chimney. Here M[r] West's dining table and chair.[9] Descend thro arch into a 2nd. cave of oval form. A fall of about 30 yards in front dashing down, cave filled with the spray. A large stone lies across chasm of ye rocks before ye mouth of ye fall. In great rains a river rushes down ye r[t]. hand side. In floods the cave fills to top. It is surrounded by a wall, in which holes are left to let out ye overflowings. The rocks on each side of the fall overgrown with very dark green moss. The fall is seen to great advantage from top. Trees grow round and over both the holes.—Paid a shilling.

Dined at cottage. Dressed eggs myself. Waited on by ye neathanded Nanny Moor.—Rookery before Cottage.

Ginglepot little below—no water in it. Chasm which you look down. Trees about. When full it overflows and runs along ye stony bed of ye glen.

Hurtlepot. Hole or pit, with water at bottom very black, but no cascade. Black trout here. The rocks which form this are very intire having very few cracks in them. Muddy & slippery as go down. Never overflows. Overgrown with trees. Stinking rhamp, very offensive.

Chapel in Dale.

Over side of Whernside to Yordas. Rotten stone & pumice-stone. Guide went to solitary house for light. Few trees about. I went to cave, met man shepherding. Told me of a flood which drowned some of his sheep in lesser cave. Sq[r]. entrance to Yordas. Go thro some sheep-folds to it. To right hand in rainy weather, before you enter, a cascade.—Vast pieces of pendent rock from top of cavern. Entrance not so fine as I expected from guides account, who set it up above Peak.[10] Yorda could not "jut thro with turban on". Entered with lights. Climbed over immense stones to Bp[s]. throne. Canopy of vast petrefaction incrustation. A large peak'd pillar opposite to it.—Wound round 7 pillars and thro narrow winding place, water at bottom, to interior cave, shaped like cone with part of one end cut off to stand on. Cascade here.—Noise. Lights. Guide like fiend, 2 front lower teeth projected over upper lip. Immense height. Claud glass.[11] Infernal regions. Rover,[12] after staying behind & making noise came to me like yell of furies.

When came again into large Cavern seen better from custom'd to ye lights, seen best from middle with ye lights kept behind ye pillar opposite Bp[s]. throne. As we returned to r[t]. went in Yorda's bedchamber. This goes into another cave or rather pit which overflows in floods, as does large one nearby, where sheep were drowned. Fills always very rapidly. Yorda, a Giant.[13]

Thro Kingsdale a bed of a river winds in a very ~~tine way, which has no water in it except in floods. It spoils much land. Was to have been cut straight, but dispute arose, and was not done.

Kelds head. Head of a river at foot of $\perp^r$. rock, which comes from

Yordas. Runs in even flow without any commotion. Did not at all remind me of S^t. Winifred's well.[14]

Thornton Force in narrow glen about 1 mile above Ingleton. There is much wood on the r^t. hand side & some scattered about on the left. Above the fall the water rushes very finely over a rocky bed. In one place it disappears sinking into the rock till it again comes to light in a smaller fall to the left of the great force. Water dashes in spray down the rock, the face of which is overgrown with plants and trees from the fisures. It is seen best from a little distance. A little below in the bed of the river, an <immense> fine piece of rock rises up in shape like a dolphin. The glen continues fine all the way to Ingleton. Some slate quarries in it. Went by Village of Thornton to public house at Thornton Church Stile (got there at 6), drank tea, walked to Kirby Lonsdale. Country mended. Fine evening. Went to Royal Oak.

The Ladies of Llangollen

[7 August] On the Llangollen road above Pontysylty to the left are immense lime rocks & kilns. Here is a very rich view of the Vale of Llangollen & Dinas Bran in the distance. Got to Llangollen ¼ past 4. In way was caught in hard shower & took shelter in cottage: woman could not speak English.

Hand at Llangollen only Inn. So full, no sitting room, was forced to dine in bed-room. Wrote a note to Ladies at the cottage.[15]

Mr P. of Cl. H. Camb. (on a pedest^n. tour) presents respectful comp^{ts}. to the Ladies at Llangollen Cottage & requests the favour of seeing the Cottage this Even^g. or tomorrow morning, whichever will be least inconvenient.
Hand Inn Llangollen
Monday Aug. 7. 1797.
To the Ladies at Llangollen Cottage

The Rev^d. Mr P. Llangollen.
Lady Eleanor Butler & Miss Ponsonby present their compliments to Mr Plumptre, and request the pleasure of his Company to Breakfast at ten o'clock tomorrow morning.
Llangollen Vale, Monday.

At 7. walked to Bridge & to Valle Crucis Abby.
Crossed over brook by bridge in grove, where were man & woman & children milking. Ruins very fine, trees growing within the walls, farm house built among the ruins. A neat room or 2 & garden by the side between Abby & brook.

Rained. Could not take sketches. Came home, drank tea.

No Harper now at the Inn. The blind one I remember, gone to live with a gentleman on the other side of Oswestry. Was a woman here last year, but is gone to live at Corwen.

[8 August] At 10 o'clock went to breakfast with the Ladies. In my way took a sketch of the Town and Castle Dinas Bran.

The Library—books in gothic arches, Gothic painted windows, Æolian harps, ornamented with pictures, and portraits.

Parlour (as well as library) plain blue paper, ornamented with view about Llangollen.

Garden. Chiefly shrubbery & lawn, all planted by Ladies, 19 years growth.

Kitchin Garden: at end a garden house, & place for frames.

The Farm & shrubbery. Bees. Hayrick. Field, barley. New planted trees, new garden. Cistern of water. Dairy.

A hedge of roses & lilies growing under beech trees, hedge of lavender.

Walked to Cottage in Valle Crucis, M^r & Mrs R. Smith, to hear M^r [blank space] Organist of Wrexham,[16] play upon the harp. The instrument very fine & his playing exquisite.

Mr Butler and Mr Eyres of Trinity Coll.[17] Camb. breakfasted at Cottage & accompanied us to Mrs Smiths. They went away at dinner time.—Dined at Inn.

Drank tea at cottage. Shewn the rooms above stairs. Miss Bowdlers transparencies.[18]—The glass of the gothic door[19] in library was illuminated.

Walked to Mrs Smiths and returned at 9 o'clock with the Ladies to Llangollen. When we set off the clouds in the E. above the mountains were illuminated from the moon below. The light increased behind the mountains, till the moon rose above in resplendent majesty and lightened all the scene. The reflection on the water behind the bridge seen thro the arches very fine. A solitary light in cottage window on the mountain side, very fine. "How far that little taper lends his ray, &c".[20]

The Even^g. so fine that I talked of going over the mountains to Chirk by moonlight, but the moon was soon overclouded, and put an end to my half formed scheme.

I had tied Rover up, and found him in stable, untied, where I left him.

At 10 it rained. But towards 11 it cleared again. Moon very fine greater part of night.

Day showery.

A return visit to Ironbridge

[10 August, Shrewsbury] Rose at 8. At 10 set off in a return chaise for Iron bridge.

Wrekin rising from level a fine object all the way, particularly whilst on the Shrewsbury side of it. It changed its form when past it, and not near so picturesque.

4 miles from Shrewsbury L[d]. Berwicks[21] a fine place. A main front with wings joined by corridors.

2 m. short of Iron bridge got out to see New Iron Bridge[22] and Bildwas Abby. Took 2 sketches. Ruins very fine—bridge not so handsome as the original one.—Passed the ground which slipped from its place.

The approach to Iron Bridge a singular scene: to the right are lime kilns burning close to the water's edge, whilst above them a hill rises with a swift ascent, covered with wood to the top. At the foot of this runs the Severn crouded with masts of vessels. On the shore are large piles of coals; the bridge in front. To the left rises a peaked hill with a summer house or temple at the top, the higher side cloathed with firs, the middle and bottom skirted with houses & trees mixed.

Went to Maid wood (or Bedlam) mine. Walked thro the burning coak, and up by iron road to mouth of the pit. Put on trowsers & smock frock & miner's hat, and tying Rover, descended, with a boy who came up to accompany me, in a chain fastened to roap & was let down by windlass 100 yards to bottom of pit. Went along the level some way, by iron roads very dirty and stooping. Got into carriage & went to end. The level 400 yards, went in carriage 160 of it. Saw the men at work. Candles. A man was killed in mines in March.

Came back stooping all way. Shewn a place where they had come to coal. Several different ways to different shafts—2 kinds of ore or stone: cross stone & penny stone. A mixture makes the best iron. Men work for 2[s]..4[d]. p[r] day or 2[s]..6[d]. Some work by great.[23] Men work at night to get the refuse away. Work from 6 in Morn. to 6 in Even.

Might have come out foot way but preferred ascending.

Ventured to look up & down, & not giddy: going down only looked strait to wall. Glad to get on terra firma again. When up the boy slid down rope to bottom & rested to change legs & ease hands.

After dinner 2 oxonians on a pedestrian exped[n]. into Wales came in. Were going by coach to Shrewsbury. Coach came just as I began to get into conversation with them.

Walked up to the Temple. Walk thro shrubbery on side of the hill. In temple seat with a high back which turns round on swivel by Iron rollers.

Up the Severn had an extensive tho indistinct view of a rich vale cut into pastures & cornfields by hedges & trees, hills with gentle risings terminating the prospect: the Brythen in the distance. The new bridge and Bildwas Abby at little distance were pleasing objects. The nearer ground was hills richly wooded, with the Wrekin in the r[t]. hand distance. Below, the Severn with its boats & heaps of coals.

The view down the river had little vale or flat ground. The hills bounding this dale winding with the river, & shewing its course where the water was hid by the hills in the foreground. The bridge in front with the river, boats, furnaces and houses all intermingled with trees formed a curious scene, while, immediately below, the lime mine with its many mouths gaped hideous below: the horse at the windlass drawing up the load added life to the scene, & a blast from one of the mouths spoke like thunder.

To N.E. another dale, narrower, the hills well-wooded, and furnaces in the bottom upon the margin of a black muddy river. The gloom encreased, and rendered this a solemn & sullen scene.

Descended to the Lime mine. The Entrance very grand. 2 fine arches in the natural limestone rock, with huge rough pillars, seen down a very steep descent, the arches & pillars being inclined in an oblique direction.—Descended, had a blast of the rock with gun powder, but the effect not so grand as heard from the outside. The stench left behind very offensive. The [*illegible*] holes to other mines both above & below but not so fine.

Returned to Inn with an intent to stay all night, and see this scene by moonlight. But the cloudy & rainy Even^g. began to make me doubt the effect, and seeing a return Kidderminster chaise, I inquired about it, and the distance, and, finding it was going to Bridgenorth, I determined to go by Stone to visit my sister[24] and friends there. Left Colebrook Dale & got to Bridgenorth (raining the whole way) at ½ p. 8.

A NARRATIVE OF A PEDESTRIAN JOURNEY THROUGH SOME PARTS OF YORKSHIRE, DURHAM AND NORTHUMBERLAND TO THE HIGHLANDS OF SCOTLAND AND HOME BY THE LAKES AND SOME PARTS OF WALES IN THE SUMMER OF THE YEAR 1799

[*Editor's note*. 1799 marked the summit of Plumptre's career as a traveller. It saw his longest, most carefully planned tour and his longest, most carefully planned journal. The tour took four and a half months, from the end of April to the end of September, and covered 2236 miles—1774¼ of them on foot, as he noted with triumphant exactitude. His route took him north from his parish at Hinxton via York and the Northumberland coast to Edinburgh and the Highlands of Scotland; the return journey embraced the Lake District and north Wales before cutting across the Midlands to Birmingham. In advance, he studied itineraries from previous travel books, forewarned the various relatives whose homes lay along his route through England and Wales, and armed himself with letters of introduction to people in Scotland. During the journey he took detailed daily memorandums, of which two volumes survive. Afterwards he wrote a three-volume narrative, bound in vellum and graced with a title nearly as long as the journey itself, and clearly intended for publication.

Even in the selected version presented here, it shows how thoroughly his tour satisfied the appetites of the late eighteenth-century traveller. Scarcely missing a castle, picturesque garden, mountain or waterfall along the way, he added to the list of mere sights by hunting up local celebrities: Blind Jack of Knaresborough on his way north, the MacNab family in the Highlands and, inevitably, the Ladies of Llangollen in Wales. At the same time, he welcomed the chances of the journey that allowed him to share a meal with French emigré priests on the Durham coast, go down a coalmine at Newcastle, see Sarah Siddons on stage in Edinburgh, inspect Sir John Dalrymple's amateur soap factory at Oxenfoord Castle, and witness a Quaker meeting at Rhayader in Wales.

While taking pride in its extent and relishing its diversity, Plumptre planned the journey first and foremost as a Scottish tour to complete the foray that lack of time had forced him to cut short at Inverary in 1796. His interest was typical of a generation that would soon include first the poems and then the novels of Sir Walter Scott among its favourite reading. The mountains and lochs of the Highlands and the remote wildness of the Western Isles held an obvious lure for an age already in love with the landscapes of Wales and the Lakes. Scottish culture, too, had ceased to be viewed with the wary contempt that followed the 1745 rebellion. Travel books by Johnson, Boswell and Thomas Pennant, coupled with James Macpherson's pseudo-Ossianic translations, sharpened an interest that was moving beyond polite eighteenth-century curiosity about foreign manners towards Romantic fascination with the life of the folk. Plumptre himself regarded copies of Johnson, Pennant and

Ossian as obligatory travelling equipment; the complete text of his narrative includes an appendix debating the authenticity of Ossian and offering a little Ossianic tale of his own.

Yet Scotland did not live up to all this learned enthusiasm. As he travelled west through the Highlands towards the Western Isles which Johnson had made the goal of all travellers to Scotland, Plumptre's conscientiously admiring response to the scenery was joined by more heartfelt complaint about the bad food and the worse hotels, the impertinent curiosity and the greedy extortion. The lengthening list of his dislikes may enliven the narrative—travel literature always thrives on annoyance and even prejudice more than approval and compliment—but it manifests a serious disillusionment for which not even some of Johnson's strictures had prepared him. What had looked in prospect an adventure threatened in practice to become a lonely ordeal, made worse by his repeated failure to find a reliable guide to accompany him and by his growing worries about the inroads on his purse. Eventually, no farther west than he had got in 1796, he cut short his plans to allow himself more time south of the border in the Lake District and Wales.

He knew both regions well from earlier visits. Now they were made additionally congenial by the presence of fellow tourists doing the round of stations recommended by Thomas West's *Guide to the Lakes* or swelling the breakfast party at the Ladies' cottage in the Vale of Llangollen. In contrast to the loneliness of his Highland journey, he joined a community of taste united in admiration for the Picturesque as defined by writers like William Gilpin, Uvedale Price and Richard Payne Knight. His own interest in their work is shown not just by increasingly expert references in the narrative but by his pilgrimage to the estates of Price and Knight later in the tour and his visit to Gilpin in 1800. Amid the familiar and sociable atmosphere of the Lakes, spoiled only a little by an unsatisfactory reunion with his old touring companion John Dudley, he recovered his spirits and even the appetite for a little new adventure: exploring the lesser-known territory of Ennerdale and Wasdale Head, and wandering more or less literally off the map in search of Haweswater. In Wales he jumped at the opportunity to join a fellow tourist for a trip west from Llangollen to Dolgellau and the coast at Barmouth. Having proposed a tour to celebrate his discovery of Scotland, Plumptre ended it by affirming his rediscovery of how deeply Wales and the Lakes nourished his own sensibility and that of his age.]

Preparations for the journey

Having been prevented in the year 1796 from visiting the Western Islands and Northern parts of Scotland, after having gone as far on my way thither as Inverary,—I had directed my thoughts ever since towards the completion of my object, but without success, something having always occurred to frustrate my plans, and business seeming to grow upon my hands with time. In the summer of 1797 various causes prevented my taking a longer Tour than to the Lakes in Cumberland & Westmorland, and in 1798 my summer was passed in my own county, except in making a few visits from Sunday to Sunday near to home. The longer I deferred it the less likely I seemed to be able to put my plan into execution, and I therefore determined, if possible, to make one great effort for that purpose against the year 1799. With this view I arranged all my plans, and, some months before hand, began to prepare for the *great undertaking*. As none of my friends, who might have the same views with myself, offered to accompany me, it was necessary to think of some sort of Being for that purpose, that I might not go entirely unfriended over those desolate regions. But it is not every one, in these days of ease and luxury, who has either the ability or inclination to undertake a tour of some hundreds of miles on foot, and submit to the fatigue of carrying luggage,—who can contentedly subsist upon coarse fare, and hazard the dangers of the seas.

I turned my eyes upon a Gypsie Youth, whose life I thought had well disciplined him for such an undertaking. I knew I should have much prejudice to encounter in attempting to civilize one of a race which bear so bad a character, and the peculiar trait of which is generally held to be thieving. But as he seemed to wish himself to leave his idle ways, and was well known in the county, which his family constantly frequent; and had often been employed by farmers in hay and harvest work; I got a good character of him from them, and determined to take him into my service; thinking, if I could be the means of rescuing a fellow creature from a wicked course of life, and could make him a useful member of society, I was doing no more than my duty. I had some thoughts however of easing him of part of his burden by getting either an Ass or a pony to carry our luggage, and by which means I could have added some luxuries to the scanty wardrobe of a pedestrian. I had even fixed the day for his coming to me; but he, rightly enough, had in the mean time been inquiring my character as I had his; and hearing I had a brother in the army, he was fearful I should kidnap him for a soldier, and declined serving me. Of all characters I should have thought that of a kidnapper would have been one of the last imputed to me—but the suspicion was enough, and as mutual confidence was necessary, I took him at his word, and our negotiation dropped; though I believe he would willingly have renewed it afterwards.

My plans now began to be talked of, and a lad in my own village came to offer his services, as he "heard I was going into Scotland, and he wished to look about him". A real liking for the undertaking was a most desirable qualification in the person I wanted. I represented the journey to him, however, in the most unfavourable light, but he still seemed to wish to accompany me, and I consented to take him for a month upon trial. "The patch was kind enough". He could read and write, and was a good walker; but he was "snail-slow in profit and a huge feeder";[1] he had not much ingenuity or curiosity, and I found his wish to accompany me was more from a dislike to his former employment, of plowing and threshing, than from a taste for travel itself; and, as I found more plague than profit (for his living cost me as much as my own) at the end of the month, I relinquished my pretensions to grandeur, and let my servant return to his usual occupations in the barn and field.

My next idea was to have an attendant only for the time; or not to keep one longer, unless I met with one entirely to my mind; and I determined to try a Highlander. I had heard great accounts of the distance a Highlander would travel on foot in a day, of the spare diet upon which he would subsist, and was induced from the accounts I had heard to think I should meet with more information, a higher sense of religion, and greater fidelity in a Scotchman than an Englishman. I concluded therefore that I should get one at a reasonable rate to accompany me on my Tour in the capacity of packbearer, guide and interpreter, before I entered those districts where the Gaelic is chiefly spoken, and from whom, as we journied on, I might obtain some information respecting the manners, customs and language of the Highlanders; for I never could travel the same road with another without beguiling the time with conversation. I have always admired D^r. Primrose's rule "never to avoid the conversation of any man who seemed to desire it: for if good, I might profit by his instructions; if bad, he might be assisted by mine". (Vicar of Wakefield. ch.6. V.2.)[2]

As soon therefore as I had finally settled my plans in my own mind, I wrote to a friend at Edinburgh "to whose kindness I had been infinitely bound"[3] on my former visit to Scotland, and desired him to look out such a Person for me.

My intended route was thro the counties of Yorkshire, Durham and Northumberland; and by Kelso and Melross to Edinburgh; thence by Kinross, Perth, Dunkeld, Blair in Athol, Loch Tay and Loch Awe to Oban; to visit as many of the Western Islands as convenient, even extending my journey to S^t. Kilda, if I found it practicable; to cross the counties of Ross and Sutherland to Caithness, and to return home by the Eastern coast. It was an extensive tour and would have taken some time in performing; but a friend had undertaken the care of my church for as long a time as I wished to be absent, and I was happy to think that I left my flock under an abler shepherd than I presumed to consider myself.

When my intentions were known, I found not only my friends, but several gentlemen who had travelled in Scotland, with whom I had no personal acquaintance, all ready to afford me every assistance in their power, and I was favoured with many letters to facilitate my progress.

Not willing to go entirely unfriended, I took with me a companion, whose fidelity I had sufficiently tried in my last pedestrian excursion, and whose gentleness of manners obtained him a kind reception wherever we went: this was a faithful *Dog*. On the road I found much company and amusement in his ranging the country along with me; at my meals he was contented to sit by me and put up with his master's leavings, and at night he watched by my bedside, warning the profane to "stay their rude steps". I beg to interest my Readers in behalf of my faithful *Rover*, as he will make some figure in the following pages.

Mr Boswell, in his Tour to the Hebrides, has amused his readers with an account of the dress and equipment of his fellow-traveller.[4] It may perhaps be useful to future Tourists to know in what manner I was fitted out. As it was my intention to make many visits among my own friends and at gentlemen's houses in the course of my journey, it was necessary to have a second suit of cloaths and more linen, than if I had intended to stop only at inns. I therefore took a small portmanteau, sending it from place to place as occasion served, and when obliged to separate from it, I carried a change of linen and a few other necessaries in a netted bag, at my back, made like a shooting bag and lined with oilskin. This I preferred to a knapsack, which I had tried on a former occasion. It not only looked better, but was more commodious, as I could change the position of it from side to side, or even make it bear more upon the back. Besides this I intended my servant from Edinburgh should carry a suit of cloaths &c in a knapsack. Every thing I took with me was new; that, besides being handsome, it might stand the wear, and not trouble me with perpetual mending. My travelling coat, of a very dark grey colour, was made with lapelles to button over my breast, and up to my throat, to secure me from cold, and was short in the skirts that it might not be in my way in walking. A crab stick, which had formerly belonged to a great man in our family, was to serve at once as a support and a defence. Besides a sufficient quantity of linen (seven shirts and all other articles suiting) and three pair of well-seasoned shoes, I carried the following knick-knacks: A Grays glass and a Claude Lorrain,[5]—magnifiers for botany,—a small telescope,—a pocket compass and pedometer,—a sixteen foot measure of tape, made to roll round a winch in a small leather case, like a lady's pocket yard-measure,—drawing and memorandum books,—a small case with colours &c, a silver pen and pencil,—a pocket and pen knives,—a pocket knife and fork, a pocket pistol[6] and drinking horn. I had moreover Kitchin's and Brown's maps of Scotland,[7] and Mavor's abridgement of Pennant's, Johnson's & Newte's Tours in Scotland.[8] I had taken the trouble of comparing these with the originals before I set off, and had very little occasion to add to them. I made one improvement, however, in which I found much use. I had them bound with a few blank leaves at the end of each, into which I copied Mr Pennant's Itineraries, and made others for D^r. Johnson's and Newte's: besides shewing the distances, they serve as indexes to the Tours. To this small library I added the pocket Edition of Cowper's Poems, a book I shall never think I have read sufficiently, till I can retain it all in my memory: a book which breathes the finest poetry with true religion and morality.

I had fixed my day of setting out, at least five months before hand, for Monday the 29th. of April. The proper season of visiting the Western Islands being the beginning of June, and as that was my great object, and I purposed being a month on my way to Edinburgh, I thought it better to see the parts of England I should pass thro in my way thither, before they had attained their summer beauty, than to be at all out of season at the Western Islands. But various obstacles, among which the extreme backwardness and inclemency of the season was a very material one, presented themselves. I however overcame them all, got all my paraphernalia in readiness, and being obliged to defer my journey one day on account of College business, I at length set off. . .

From Cambridge to Little Stukeley

[*30 April*] A day of the month, as a pleasant friend observed, as far distant from the *first* as possible.

I had been engaged for some time to walk over to Stukely with Mr Edward Bayley[9] of Clare Hall, to visit one of his relations. Various accidents prevented us from putting our intention into execution, till at length we agreed to fix it for the day on which I was to begin my journey. When the time however arrived, indisposition prevented Mr B. from taking so long a walk, and he obligingly proposed taking me in a Gig, to which I assented as a matter of necessity, beginning my *pedestrian* journey, like the Irishman, in a carriage.

The road from Cambridge to Huntingdon exhibits nothing very amusing in point of Landscape even in the pleasantest seasons; but now all was dreary to the view, and distressing to the imagination. The morning was cold, and the wind in the N.E. Not a leaf appeared on the few trees to be seen from the road, the water stood in the hollows among the corn, and the shepherds standing by their flocks, seemed in mute wretchedness, to deplore the unkindliness of the season. . .

Such weather was little favourable to a Tour of pleasure, but Scotland, not England, was the object of my journey, and I set out in the hope of the weather improving as I went on. <Unpleasant, however, as the day was, we saw a large party seated under a hedge near Boxworth, and regaling upon bread and cheese; they were *sessioning* (or *processioning*) that is going the bounds of the Parish in procession.> We reached little Stukely about one o'clock, when our kind hostess regaled us after our cold ride with some most excellent elder wine made hot.

I had now the happiness of becoming personally acquainted with a family, whom I had before known only from their excellent character. Mrs B. is a Lady, who, notwithstanding great family losses, which she feels with all the fond regret of an affectionate mother, yet preserves that resignation and cheerfulness, which she knows to be the duty of a Christian, and makes her life a blessing to others, dispensing happiness to the poor around her. Charity like hers "gives not its alms to be *seen* of men"; but, tho no ostentatious display of bounty is to be made, yet we are to "let our light so shine before men, that they may see our good works", and the pen of the recording Traveller feels itself under a duty of publishing various modes of benevolence to the world, who often only want to be told *how* they may be useful, that they may "go and do likewise".[10]

In the corner of the room where we sat is a box, on which is written *For the Poor*. Into this several little forfeits established in the family, and wagers are always put; besides the occasional mites of visitors, and other contributions of friends, and some annual donations of the family. This money is expended in a variety of useful ways. Coal and turf are laid in, and sold out to the Poor at a cheaper rate. From 10 to 11 every Monday is the hour of attendance, and no credit is ever given. Each family may have one bushel per week (unless there are only two, when they are allowed but half a bushel) or turf in proportion. In this house nothing is ever wasted, but broken meats, & soups, and rice are given away, as occasion offers, or necessity demands. Mrs B. keeps also two complete sets of child-bed linen, which are lent out to the poor during their confinement. They may be kept one month, and are then returned clean. Besides these, there is a school established in the village by Miss B. of which she has the superintendance. At this 8 young girls are taught to spin by an old woman, who has 2^s. p^r. week allowed her for her trouble. They are supplied with wool by the stapler. The eldest, who is about 9 years of age, can earn about 3^d. p^r. day, and the youngest, who is 3 and ½, about a half-penny. To these I might add the giving away Bibles, prayer books, repository tracts, and numberless instances which goodness is ever ready in inventing to benefit our fellow-creatures. I have known even cards in this house turned to a good account, and have made one at a pool at commerce, which was to relieve a poor woman and a large family during her lying-in.

Our treatment here was in the true style of plain but elegant hospitality; we had plenty without profusion, and cheerfulness without excess. A variety of wines, and other articles of home manufacture, received an additional zest from the liberality with which they were set before us. The house and garden partook of the neat simplicity of the owner's taste, and I may mention, as a curiosity, that this house contains the second mahogany table that was ever made in this kingdom. In the Evening the sun came out, and the weather was more mild, "giving promise of a goodly day tomorrow".[11] I walked as far as Great Stukely church, which commands an extensive prospect, but the ideas excited by it, from the unfriendly season, were not of the pleasant kind. We passed the Evening in cheerful conversation, and at a reasonable hour retired to rest, where I found another instance of the Industry of the family I was with, in a patch-work bed and worked carpets.

The coach journey north

[*3 May*] As there was not anything in particular to arrest my attention between Stamford and York, I determined to take the Newcastle coach which set off between 11 & 12.

The country between Stamford and Grantham is prettily broken into hill and vale, having villages advantageously scattered about, and not deficient in wood, the trees however were as yet bare of leaves. But inclement as the season was we saw many sheep deprived of their cloathing. Today I saw swallows, the first I had seen this year.

About 8 miles we passed the *Ram Jam* house, so called from a particular kind of ale of that name brewed there. There are above [*blank space*] different kinds, which have different names according to their different degrees of strength: Ramjam, Stingo, Old Surley, Hock-me-jock, Staggering Bob, Knock-me-down, Strike-me-dead, &c. &c. There was much new inclosure about here, and the country seemed to be in a very high state of cultivation. Three miles farther we passed thro Coltersworth, where the house is still standing in which Sir I. Newton was born. We dined at Grantham; there were 4 of us, and we had two bottles of wine *for the good of the house*, for I am sure they were not for our good: we paid 4^s. 6^d. p^r. head for our dinner and left 2^s for the waiter. Against this latter piece of extravagance I remonstrated, as, besides its being more than a reward for his services, it was establishing a bad precedent, and he would expect the same from others, who could perhaps still less afford it, and if he was disappointed, might treat them with incivility. Considered in this light, however well a person can afford to lavish his money on waiters, postboys, and coachmen, as a member of society he is to consider the general good, and has not I think, a *right* to be thus over generous.

The town of Grantham is situated in a bottom on the banks of the river Witham. There is not I believe anything particularly worth notice. The steeple of the church is remarkably lofty. The Houses and cottages hereabouts are mostly built of a glaring red brick, and some of the cottages of red mud. Grantham had been a scene of rejoicing the Evening before, on account of The D. of Rutland arriving at Belvoir with his bride. About a mile and a half beyond Grantham, from the top of Gunnersby hill there is a fine view, or rather *stare* over a rich, but flat country. On a clear day Lincoln Minster is to be seen at a distance on the right. In descending the hill, Belvoir Castle is seen, surrounded by wood, on a lofty hill to the left, rising out of the plain.

We took up this stage a very decent looking female; and the company, particularly an officer began to talk indecently. When I saw a blush rise in the cheek of offended modesty, I could not forbear giving a look and sign of disapprobation and the conversation stopped.

At Newark there is a fine stone bridge of seven arches over "the silver and slow-winding Trent"[12] for so it is called by Shakspeare though in reality a very rapid river, and close to it, on the edge of the water, stand the remains of the castle, which makes a considerable figure in the history of the civil wars.

The country continues flat to Tuxford, which place we reached between 8 and 9, and as I wished to see the country, and particularly dislike travelling at night, I determined to sleep here. I passed the night at the Fox inn, a neat house, where I was treated with much civility. Tuxford is a small town, pleasantly situated upon a hill, and commanding an extensive view.

[*4 May*] The sun shone into my room by 5 o'clock. At 7 the High-flyer Coach came by, & as the morning was fine, I got up behind into the Guard's seat, which has all the ease & comfort of an open carriage upon springs. Besides a considerable difference in the expence, I have, from a boy, been unable to bear the confinement of a close carriage for any time, without suffering considerable inconvenience. It brings on what Shakspeare would call a *queaziness*,[13] and which I sometimes have not got the better of for a day or two. This, though frequently a real misfortune, has, in the consequence, been a source of pleasure to me, which has more than over-ballanced it; for to this I owe my first taste for walking, and it has opened to me pursuits, of which perhaps I should not otherwise have thought. A horse indeed does not subject me to that particular malady; but my anxiety lest he should not be sure footed and quiet, destroys that security of mind so necessary in viewing the works of nature, and giving way to the contemplations which they suggest. Thus I own walking has spoiled me for every other mode of travelling, unless when for the express purpose of getting from one place to another; for even the most pleasant conveyance of an open carriage hurries a traveller on too fast for observation and reflection.

About 3 miles farther we saw Lincoln Minster at a distance on the right over an extended tract of rich country. From Barton Moor the country becomes more flat.

The Guard being on the Coachbox driving, a poor, but very respectable man, from London was my companion in the seat. He was going to Retford, on his way to Gainsborough, to take his son from school to see his friends in London. His paternal care and affection formed a pleasing contrast with the neglect of the father of a boy in the coach, who was going to school at Thirsk in Yorkshire. He had been brought to the coach office in Fetter Lane by a Gentleman, not his father, and committed to the care of the Guard, who was to pay his expences and be repaid at York. Who the boy was the Guard did not know; he called himself one name, and was booked in another. He was a fine stout lad, about 6 years of age, in a coarse blue jacket and without a great coat, for want of which he had suffered much from the cold in the night. But that he was travelling in the coach, instead of the York Waggon, he reminded me much of Caleb, in Foote's Taste,[14] who went to school with D^r. Jerk, near Doncaster, where but poor ten pounds a year was paid for "Head, back, books, bed and Belly; and they say the children are all wonderful Latiners, and come up, lack-a-day, they come up as fat as pigs". A woman (servant to an officers

Lady) who was going on a visit to her friends at Doncaster, had taken care of him. With these I breakfasted at Retford.

Retford is situated on the banks of the River Idle, which divides it into E. and W. Retford. There are two good churches and a handsome Town Hall.

Leaving Retford the day clouded over. We passed the 1st. Regt. of Fencibles on their march to Doncaster. They made very amusing groups of figures, particularly the baggage-waggons, in our foregrounds as we passed along; and on the race ground just before we entered Doncaster we saw a regiment of foot exercising. There is a handsome stand on the race-ground. The approach to the town is pretty. On the left of the road stands a hill with an obelisk on the top and a walk leading to it. In the town the Mansion House is a good building.

Seven miles from Doncaster, close to the road, on the right hand side, stands Robin Hood's Well, covered with a neat stone building of Grecian architecture. The Guard told me of some bones, in a cave not far from the road, which had belonged to some of Robin Hood's Merrymen.

From Wentbridge we ascended a steep hill, and had a rich and extensive view from the top. All the views this day were in the same style, but with little to please in a picturesque light. Two miles short of Ferrybridge on the left see Pomfret, whose castle is known as a scene of blood on account of the death of Richard the 2nd and the executions of Rivers, Vaughan, Grey and Sir T. Haute in the usurpations of Richd. the 3d.

The coach stopped to change horses at Ferrybridge and I walked on. At Byram,[15] one mile beyond, I stopped to see the new Lodges built by Sr. John Ramsden; they are of stone, and the outsides are neat; but they are all outside, having no convenience within. They have neither cellar nor upper-room, nor even a cupboard; and the two rooms (or Lodges) being on different sides of the gate, the inhabitants are exposed to all the unseasonableness of weathers. The poor woman who shewed them to me complained of their inconvenience, and by the neat manner in which they were kept, proved she deserved a better place.

A *Lodge* is at all times but a piece of ostentation, and, unless it leads to a magnificent house, is certainly out of character. A neat cottage, shaded by a spreading tree, with woodbines canopying the door and windows, and a neat garden would be a more pleasing object, would harmonize better with the scene, and form a more comfortable habitation for people, who seem to be placed there to open the gate for persons going to the Mansion . . .[16]

Four miles from York we came within sight of the Minster, a very grand object, but not set off to any advantage from the surrounding scenery. We got to the York Tavern about half past 5, and finding there was a play that Evening, I had a mutton chop and half pint of wine, and went to the Theatre at 7. I expected to find York the London of the north, but was disappointed in most respects. The Theatre is shabby, and the performers were very indifferent. The play was the Dramatist,[17] by no means the best of M[r] Reynold's five act farces. The only character tolerably played was that of Vapid by M[r] Melvin. He seemed really to possess merit; but the author had done so little for him, that he seemed to think it necessary to do something for himself and greatly over-acted the part. The audience was thin and gave no applause till the crockery was broken in the closet, and Vapid came out with a bason on his head; such is the modern idea of wit & humour ...

I was so little pleased with the play, that I did not stay the Farce, but retired to rest at my noisy inn.

An extraordinary character

[7 May] I passed through Weatherby to Spofforth, where I called upon that extraordinary character, _John Metcalfe_, commonly called _Blind Jack of Knaresborough_. He was then 82 years of age, having been born in the year 1717; he is above 6 feet high and of a very stout make. When only 4 years old he lost his sight from the small pox, and has ever since been employed in pursuits, from entering into which it might be supposed his loss of sight would have totally incapacitated him. His early amusements were birdsnesting, climbing trees and swimming. Music he acquired of course, but Hunting, racing, horsedealing, cocking & card-playing appear almost incredible: he has even served as a guide from York to Harrogate, without the other party knowing he had a blind guide till he got to the end of his journey. The incident of his running away with his wife is no less curious; when a lighted candle placed in her window at night, was to be the signal for his approach: in this, however, he borrowed the eyes of a friend to assist him. He next got into the recruiting service, and followed the fortunes of Colonel Thornton in the rebellion of 1745. Since that he has been engaged as a common carrier, and has undertaken the making roads, bridges, houses and dealing in timber; his arms and a long staff serving for a measure, and making calculations in his own particular manner in his head. He has walked several journeys to and from London, and never forgets a way he has once been. When I entered the room where he was sitting and accosted him, he rose from his chair and said with a smile, "he never had the pleasure of _seeing_ me before", for he distinguishes people by their voices as accurately as others do by the sight, and will recollect people he has heard but once at a great distance of time. I sat with him some time and was much pleased with his placid and cheerful manner. There is a life of him published,[18] but he told me many anecdotes of himself, which I have not noted among my memorandums concluding I had them in the book, but they are not there, and I cannot now sufficiently depend upon my memory to relate them. When I mentioned the calamity of loss of sight he said "He thought Providence knew what was best for us, his disposition was enterprizing, and had his sight been spared it might have been worse for him". He has had 4 children, 19 grandchildren and 35 great-greatgrandchildren.

Antiquarian observations

[9 *May*] As soon as I got to Boroughbridge I turned into some fields on my left to see 3 remarkable stone pillars, called the arrow stones, or Devil's arrows. They stand on a rising ground and in a line nearly north and south, being about 100 yards asunder ... I took two drawings of them, one from the north, including all 3., the other from the E. taking in only the first. While drawing some oxen in the field approached me, I supposed objecting to my Dog; but a man near, calling to me "He's a runner", I drove poor Rover away, and while they were running after him, threw myself over the hedge, and was soon followed by my dog. Thus were my antiquarian observations disturbed, but in all probability they would not have turned to much advantage, as antiquaries differ much in their opinions about them. D^{rs}. Plot and Stukeley suppose them to have been of British origin, D^r. Gale Roman.[19] They are made of the coarse rag, or mill-stone grit, and were in all probability brought, from Plumpton, 10 miles distant, by means of which we now have no idea.

After my breakfast at the 3 Greyhounds at Boroughbridge, I walked to Ald or Old-Borough, the ancient Isurium of the Romans. At a house at the entrance of the village, on the right hand, is a curious tessellated pavement. It is not, however, seen to advantage, as there is a floor over it at the height of between 2 and 3 feet, and only a trap door lifts up to shew it. The man of the house was not very civil, and on my inquiry whether there was anything else to be seen, said there was another pavement, but not so good as his, and discouraged my going to see it. I went however to the house a little farther on and was shewn into a tolerable sized room, entirely floored with roman pavement. The pattern is not so good as that of the former, but it is well worth notice. In the same room is a large stone with an inscription.

At this house I saw a woman not much more than 3 feet high and to appearance old. I asked the woman of the house what age she was, and she answered "Older than she seemed from her height: she was above 20, but had had bad health". She seemed to avoid the subject, and I think the woman must have been much older. From hence I went to Studforth hill on the S. of the town, and formerly a Roman station, whence there is a very good view over the country. As I returned I could not forbear calling at the first house, and telling the man of his unkindness to his neighbours, in discouraging strangers from going to see their pavement; he formed a displeasing contrast to the Smiths and Hills at Knaresborough.[20] The man however gave me only abuse for my trouble; but I hope, on his cooler reflection, my admonition might have its effect in future.

Refugees

[22 *May*] The rocks and cliffs all the way from Hartlepool to Castle Eden Dean are worth the attention of the curious. About a mile and a half beyond Black Halls Castle Eden Dean opens to the sea. The sides are tolerably well covered with wood, which at that time was bare of leaves, the gorse however was in bloom. A small river runs into the sea. A few sheep and cattle were feeding here. The hills farther on rise finely on both sides, and open into different glens, the wood becomes better as it gets more sheltered from the sea breezes, and a mixture of evergreens, yew and holly, added much to the appearance. Turning round a hill I discovered a Cottage situated at the bottom of a hill, which divided two glens, or Deans, running obliquely to right and left; not knowing which was that up which I was to take my course, I determined to inquire at the Cottage, but was some time in getting to it, in crossing the stream and making my way thro the gorse; I at length however got into a path, which soon led me to the Cottage. I knocked at the door, and it was opened by a tall stout man in a blue jacket. I inquired my way and was answered in french. Three other men, of the same appearance, were seated at a table at dinner, and invited me to sit down with them. I now recollected to have heard that there were 4 French Emigrant Priests, living in a cottage in this Dean, and immediately concluded these must be them, however mean their appearance, and being willing to see a mode of life so new to me, I readily assented, not doubting that with their English and my French we should be able to make out a conversation.

The two eldest of them seemed to be about from 60 to 70 years of age, the other two from about 30 to 40. The two eldest were by much the most cheerful; the younger had the marks of sorrow on their countenances. On attempting to converse, I found that though they had been resident in England for some time, yet they knew scarcely anything of the language, and I did not know much more of French, and the accent in which we respectively spoke was a further impediment to our communication. I know not that I ever till this moment regretted the not being able to converse in French. They gave me to understand they could speak lattin, but I was so little accustomed to converse in that, and when pronounced with a french accent was so different to the language of our Schools, that it was equally unintelligible to me. However, partly in English, partly in French, in lattin and with *signs*, we contrived to keep up something like a conversation.

This cottage was built for them by Mʳ Mair,²¹ from whose Hospitality they enjoy a peaceful assylum in this delightful and sequestered spot. It consists of two rooms, each holding two beds. They cooked their victuals in the one in which we sat, the other was occasionally their house of prayer. Here is a press which contains their Altar, with a print of the Virgin, Chalice, paten, &c, &c. I could not help wishing, whilst they shewed me these things, that so much integrity and piety had been exerted in the protestant not the Roman Catholic cause. In the other room were their cooking utensils, lamp, &c. A hatchet lay in one corner of the room, with which they cut their own firing. They both brew and bake themselves. Their fare was simple and good: Soup made of herbs and sour, and mutton hashed with onions. The beer was brought in a pitcher with a wooden handle of their own putting on, and every thing shewed the marks of ingenuity. They brought nuts upon the table after dinner, and their hospitality extended even to taking care of my dumb companion. Dinner being ended they took me out to see their two gardens, cultivated by themselves, and bearing plentiful crops of peas, beans, potatoes and a variety of herbs. One of them had constructed a sundial.

Whilst viewing these specimens of honest industry, and pious resignation, I could not withold my secret approbation of the respectable manner in which exile is thus borne; for however more deserving of praise those may be esteemed, who (as Mr Burke energetically expresses it) "stay at home to watch by the bedside of their delirious country"; yet, when driven into a foreign land, and forced, in some measure, to subsist upon the bounty of others, how much better is it to pass that time in manly labour, and sober seclusion from the dissipation of the world; than, by joining in the vices of great towns, help to bring those same calamities on another country, which the same vices had occasioned in the country from which they have fled.

I ascended the hill above the cottage and had a fine view of the sea. After which I returned into the house, and, in taking my leave, would have made an acknowledgement for their hospitable entertainment, but they would not on any account accept it. On my pressing farther, they seemed to think they did not understand me, and thought perhaps I wanted change. I said no, and one then brought out the Dictionary, and I first looked out *accept* and then *entreat*, but to no purpose. They gave me to understand they were allowed sufficiently, and that was all they had a right to enjoy in their situation, and they considered I had done them an honour.

Descent into a coalpit

[24 *May, Newcastle*] I looked out of my window at 4, when it was very fine, but at half past 5 it was raining. However as *views* were not my object this morning, and the rain was not much, I got up and set off for Heaton Colliery, where I arrived about 7, and was received at the office by Mr Daglish with much civility. A flannel dress arrived for me to descend in, which was soon followed by my conductor. I put on the dress, which consisted of shirt, pantaloons, jacket and upper jacket and hat, and having tied up my companion, we set off for the mouth of the pit.

There are 4 pits at Heaton, the two nearest to the office are called the A and B pits; those farther, which I was to descend, the C and D pits. Both of the latter were at work, but the C. pit was soon obliged to give over for the day, an accident having happened to one of the workmen from the stone falling in upon him. I asked my conductor, If there was any danger in my going? he assured me none in the least. I made many inquiries after the poor man, but could not get any direct answer. I fear he was much hurt. We reached the mouth of the pit, where I saw the coals drawn up by steam engines, a basket, or *corve* as it is called here, going down empty as the full one ascends. A horse then draws it on a sledge to a large inclined iron sieve, down which it is thrown and sifted from the small coal. It is then put into waggons, holding a chaldron each,[22] and drawn by a horse along the railways to the waterside and then shipped for London &c. This coal sells for 20^s. the chaldron, the dust at 6, and as the coals we have (at least at Cambridge) is considerably above one half dust, they do not stand the Merchants in so much as 13^s. the chaldron, for which we now pay 45^s.

The basket was now taken off the rope and a chain-loop fixed in its place, in which my conductor and myself seated ourselves, having each one leg in it, and the other out; he held with his right arm round the chain and directed us with his left; my left was round his right, and I held fast to the chain with my right. We then began to descend, the pit is about 80 fathom, or 160 yards, and we were about a minute in getting to the bottom. We went too quick at first and rubbed against the other rope. I was fearful of knocking against the coals which were coming up, and mentioned my fears to my guide, but he assured me there was no danger. I shut my eyes till we reached the bottom, when we stopped suddenly, and I was held by a collier, who led me to a seat. I was quite bewildered with the quickness and novelty of the motion, and possibly some little apprehension, and the darkness of the place, the dim light of the lamps and the grim figures of the colliers had a very strange effect. I was not quite recovered, when a loud noise, like thunder from a distance, approached nearer and nearer. This added much to my astonishment, till I found it was a horse bringing the coals in a carriage with iron wheels along the iron rail-ways.

When recovered my guide gave me a candle and we set forward together, the way being high enough to walk upright. The first place we came to was a large cistern of water for the horses to drink at, adjoining to a stable for 12 horses: there are 5 of these stables, making in all stabling for 60 horses. There were however 63 down in the pit at that time. These horses are let down in nets, and never come up again unless when ill. We proceeded on our way: the shaft is cut into *headways* and *boards*. The headways are 7 foot wide and in length; the boardways are 4 yards wide and 18 in length; the spaces between are called pillars, and are left to support the strata above

from falling in. When a pit has been worked out in this way, they sometimes work these pillars; and as pits always fill themselves up again, either
by the upper part falling in or the under part rising up, it is attended with
great danger and lives are frequently lost. They begin at the farther end,
and, if aware of the stone giving way, retire; if not, are buried in its ruins.
In several places the roof was already propped by boards and pillars. There
are few varieties of stone to be seen in this pit. The *brown post*, *blue-metal
stone*, and *band stone* are the chief. In one place is a Crane, for lifting the
corves from the sledges to the carriages. They are brought in sledges from
the place where the coal is hewn, and a horse draws only one corve; but
when put upon the carriages, a horse draws 3 in separate carriages, one
behind the other.

We at length reached the place where the men were hewing the coal, but
there was not anything particularly worth notice. I held my candle up to
the top to see what the stone was, when my guide immediately pulled it
down, lest there should be any inflammable air, or fire damp, as it is called,
and it should take fire.* We returned, almost by the same way we came, to
the bottom of the C. pit, which had given over working for the day on

* [*Plumptre's note*] I had inquired of Mr Daglish before I descended if there was the
least danger to be apprehended from the fire damps, and he assured me none at all; I
was therefore perhaps less cautious than I ought to have been, and I could not but
think with horror afterwards of what *might* have been the consequence. Mr Hutchinson in his History of Durham Vol.3. p501 gives the following account of the explosion of a mine:[23] "Those who have seen the fire-damps circulating in the workings
of mines, describe it to be like the curling and undulating of smoke passing along the
roof: a particular appearance on the top of the candle, where it gathers, if diligently
attended to, is the most certain criterion by which the approach of that dreadful
vapour is discovered. Several explosions by this inflammable vapour have happened
in this century, but in the year 1708, the most considerable one of the century. On
Tuesday morning the 17th. of August, about 3 o'clock, a terrible blow was heard, proceeding from the neighbourhood of Chester in the Street, as loud and horrible as if a
magazine of gun-powder had taken fire, yet of a deader and flatter sound; the report
was heard remarkably loud, at the distance of 6 miles. It was soon known that the
noise proceeded from an explosion of the coal mines near Lumley; no account of previous circumstances could be obtained, not one person surviving that was at work at
the time. It was conjectured, that upon working the coals some cavity was opened
where this magazine of destruction lay, which, getting passage, broke out with
dreadful fury at the mouths of the pits. The number of people, which the over-men
said were at work, amounted to ninety souls at least; if any survived the blast, they
died in the chambers of the mine, for no one durst venture down to relieve them; and
no vessel could be let down, the mouths of the pits or shafts were so shaken and
fallen in: about 8 or 9 bodies were found on the surface, but all of them blown to
pieces, some wanting the head, and others the limbs: one carcase was blown so
directly from the shaft, which was fifty fathom deep, that it was found at a prodigious distance; how high it might be thrown into the air, not to be calculated. The
violence of the shock was such, that several houses at a good distance from the place,
were shattered with the force of it, and the gin which wrought with horses, was
shattered to pieces, and scattered abroad to a great distance".

account of the accident, and passing round by the stable, came to a place where there is an immense fire almost constantly kept up for the sake of airing the pit. The air comes down one side, the fire creating a draft, which brings the bad air up the other, part of which is taken off from the general current by a funnel. The current is very strong thro the pit, and doors are placed at different distances to check it. These are kept by boys, called Trappers, who open and shut them for the horses &c and have 6^d. a day each. There are generally about 100, men and boys at work in the pit at a time. One set work from one in the morning till one at noon, when they are relieved by another set, who work till one in the morning again. Belonging to this pit are 100 Hewers, who earn upon an avarage about 2^s.8^d. a day, these are always bound by articles for 12 months, and cannot leave their master without his consent.

There are also   65 Drivers, who earn from 16^d. to 20^d. p^r. day each

30 Trappers (or doorkeepers) 6^d.

15 Extra men, besides Overmen and Deputies.

We ascended at the same shaft by which we came down, having been about an hour and a quarter in the pit. The distance from the mouth to where they were hewing was about half a mile.

Thus ended my subterraneous excursion, and I was not sorry again to visit the regions of light and greater security. The sight had more than answered in respect to the extensive scale upon which the work was carried on, but had fallen short in the mineralogical part, in which I had expected to have gained much information from my guide. The variety of strata indeed are only to be seen in the shaft sunk to get at the coal, which lies inclined between seldom more than 2 strata of stone. But as these shafts are generally lined you see but little even of them. Whin stone is the hardest to work through of any, but a quicksand is more troublesome to get thro from its continually falling in. When they meet with this they make a kind of barrel of wood, sometimes of cast metal, and drive thro the sand, which keeps it from falling in, and then they scoop it out. Coal seldom lies horizontal but rises to the N. & E. and dips to the S. and W. When the stratum is broken off by the intervention of a rock or any other substance, it is called a *trouble*, or dyke.

When I returned to the office I undressed and washed myself, and then went down to Mr Daglish, who shewed me the section of another pit, called the *Restoration* pit, which is 135 fathom deep: another pit called *Bigg's main* is 193 fathom.

Morpeth

[*24 May*] As I was walking on, a gentleman in a *quaterace* (for so a carriage with *four* wheels and *one* horse is sometimes called) overtook me—looked at me—and passed by. As I make it a rule whenever I am in a carriage by myself—which by the bye is not very often the case—to offer a lift to any creditable looking person, however poor, whom I may see on the road going my way; I thought he might have done as much by me. While these reflections were passing in my mind, he slackened his pace, and when I came up to him, asked me, if I was going towards Morpeth, if I would take a ride. Thinking it bore the face of a pleasing adventure, I accepted the offer; and finding we were both travellers and going to Morpeth, we agreed to dine together at the Queen's Head. He was going on to Alnwick that night. This gentleman (whom I afterwards found to be Mr Hepburn Mitchelson, of Middleton, near Edinburgh—and proprietor of Borthwick Castle) had taken me, with my net bag and long stick, for the clergyman of the adjoining parish going fishing.

The entrance into Morpeth is pretty, the castle stands on a hill to the left; and you pass over a bridge, just below which there is a wear, which makes a good cascade. I here observed Mr Pitts effigy[24] as the sign to a public house, the first time I had ever seen him in such a situation.

When we arrived at the Queen's Head, I found my portmanteau arrived, and a letter from Mr Walter Trevillyan Junr.[25] of S^t. John's College, Cambridge (to whom Mr C. Plumptre[26] had written, informing him I was coming that way) desiring my company at Netherwitton, for as long a time as I could conveniently stay. I saw Mr Dibdin[27] upon the stairs, and on inquiry found he was to perform that night at the Town Hall. Mr M. determined to stop the Evening at Morpeth and hear him, and we dressed, dined, and then walked out to look about us. What remains of the old castle upon the hill is good, but not very picturesque, it is only a square Gateway without any accompaniments. The town is very neat and pretty. The Hall, which consists of a front built over a piazza, with a tower at each end, was built in the year 1714 at the expence of the Earl of Carlisle.

However trifling the anecdote may seem, I must not omit the mention of the civility of a young man, apprentice to Mr Wilkinson the Chemist. Having a bad headach, as I imagined from the sulphur in the coal-pit I had visited in the morning, I went to get something for it, when he advised me to take some pepper mint water, and to smell at æther or sal-ammoniac. When I inquired what I was to pay he said nothing, nor would he make any charge when I pressed it, and seemed scarcely to be pleased when I left an acknowledgement upon the counter.

At 8 we went to the town Hall, where the County Courts are kept, for they are held at Morpeth, tho the Assizes are held at Newcastle. On the bench sat a row of ladies; one of more dignified deportment filling the chair, and they looked like a bench of female justices. Had *Mary* (the name by which Mrs Wolstonecraft generally went with her devotees)[28] been alive, how would her heart have exulted at such a sight.

The Entertainment was the *Sphinx*, the *story* of which, as far as I can recollect, for I did not make any memorandum of it, was taken partly from

Mr Dibdin's own opera of the Quaker, and partly from The Flitch of bacon.

Recipes

[25 May, Netherwitton] We stopped for refreshment at a cottage, the construction of which declared the rough climate in winter, being made with an outer room for lumber &c before you come to what is usually called *the house*. Here also the beds were made in presses in the sitting room, a custom I do not like, as it gives both the room and the beds a close unpleasant smell. This cottage however was extremely neat, and we were treated with *Ned Cake*,[29] made of flour and cream, or new milk, about ¾ of an inch thick and baked on a *girdle*, or round piece of iron, over the fire; also another kind of cake made of peas and barley, about the same thickness, and baked in the same way; this is sometimes made with wheat and peas.

The Bread is likewise made here of what is called Misling or *Maslam*, which is wheat and rye grown together.

Also oatcakes, both hard and soft. The hard is only oatmeal, with a little water, made into a paste and rolled out thin and baked upon the girdle. The soft has more water and a little yeast, is made in smaller cakes and baked faster. It is generally eat buttered.

In Yorkshire they mostly bake two kinds of brown bread, of wheat with only the coarse bran taken out, one called day, the other night bread, from the different times in which it is baked. The Day bread is baked a shorter time and in smaller loaves; the night bread is made in very large loaves and baked in a slower oven and for a long time which makes it browner and moister.

In the scarcity in 1795[30] a lady of my acquaintance made very good cakes of 3 parts rice and one *bean* flour, sifted fine. Any kind of cakes may be made this way, with usual receipt, using this mixture instead of wheat flour.

Alnwick Castle

[29 May] Alnwick Castle, which has been for centuries the residence of the Percy family, stands on the E. side of the town of Alnwick, and with its towers, walls, battlements and gateways makes a most noble appearance. On the top of the battlements are placed stone figures of Warriours, Heathen Deities and Saints. The mixture is to be sure strange, and their situation unnatural; if they are designed as *ornaments*, they are awkward, if meant to represent living figures (as was often the case in old castles, to give them an appearance of being well manned) they should have been only warriours, and they should have been placed *between* rather than *upon* the battlements. In such a situation the effect would have been very grand, at present they strike me as being heavy and unmeaning.

Passing over a bridge to a fine double gateway, I knocked at the gate and was let in by a very pretty female, the Porter's daughter, who attended me about, her father not being in the way.

There are about 5 acres of ground within the walls which are flanked with 16 towers and turrets. There are three Courts, a small one contained within the Keep of the Castle, the two others surround the keep, and are enclosed by the walls. I was first taken to the stable, which is on the right hand side of the first court as you enter, a very fine apartment, large enough to hold 16 horses, and fitted up in the gothic, but a light and trumpery style. From the first court a fine gateway leads into the second, where a large Lion, the Percy crest, stands upon a pedestal in the middle. Here were some shetland sheep grazing. I was conducted cross this court to the Armoury Tower, where there is much armour but not arranged in any order. Amongst others was the helmet of Henry Hotspur, which I put on. At the foot of this tower is a battery of 7 pieces of small cannon. I next ascended a higher tower, called the Cook Tower which commanded a very noble view of the Castle and Alnwick Church below—An obelisk, called the Duke's Tower, on a hill at a distance, formerly a wild moor, but now rich in plantations of Larch and fir—"the heights of heathy Cheviot beyond"[31]—Alnwick Abbey, Mr Doubleday's, by the water side—a handsome bridge of 3 arches lower down, with the Lion on the ballustrades: about the bridge it is very pretty—follow the river to another bridge of one arch—a belt and clumps meet the eye at intervals in all directions—and Ratcliff crag, with an old building upon it, rises to the N.E. A little below this tower is a seat in the wall called Hotspur's seat, and just by it a place where the wall is newer, called the bloody gap, having been forced with much slaughter at one of the sieges. Beyond this is another Tower which I understood from my conductor was called the Evidence Tower—but I find no such name in Mr Grose's Antiquities.[32] She informed me that the Duke had an E.O. table there. Impossible said I! an E.O. table? yes, sir, an E.O. table.—!!![33]

We returned now to the great gateway which leads into the Keep, and on the right hand of which is the dungeon, into which prisoners were let down from the top, where there was an iron grate, the only entrance for air and light . . .

I had heard so much of the splendid elegance of the style in which Alnwick castle is fitted up,[34] that I must own I was greatly disappointed. Unversed in the principles of architecture, I judge only from my own taste, and I must own the *light* gothic ornaments made in *plaister*, and painted in *gay* colours, seemed to me to be trumpery, and to ill accord with the massy, rich and sombre appearance of the outside.

I was next conducted into the *library*, a large and handsome room, and in my opinion the best in the house; while viewing this, the maid opened the door, and said This is the *Chapel*. I immediately turned that way, and the first glimpse presented a thousand pleasing ideas to my mind. I pictured to myself, or rather thought I actually saw before me, a spacious oblong apartment, lying East and West, with a large gothic window of painted glass at the E. end, representing some interesting story in sacred history, a handsome altar of marble under it, the roof of beautiful gothic, the sides embelished with paintings of scripture history, and a marble floor inlaid.

I entered and walked toward the E. window (as I imagined) to inspect the painting, when lo! the Percy arms presented themselves to view: I cast my eyes down to look at the Altar, when I beheld a white marble sarcophagus, at each end were the Lion and Unicorn in white marble.

Shocked at seeing a tomb instead of an altar, I inquired of my conductor, and was informed that it was the S. window, the chapel lying N. & S.—Upon the floor lay a painted floor cloth, and the walls were painted with the *genealogies of the Percys up to Charlemagne*!!! Three Chandiliers hung from the cieling. The E. window is on the left of the entrance, and is small, with a chair and reading desk before it. Opposite to it is a circular recess, with a window; here the family sit on chairs with the Percy arms on the back. Prayers are only read here on Sunday Evenings; the family go to the church in the morning.

Never had I seen in any place so much to admire so much to condemn; but to see the *House of prayer*, turned into the *House of ostentation of the Percy family* filled me with indignation, and I left the Castle acquiescing in the remarks of Mr Pennant: "The Traveller is disappointed in the situation and environs of the castle, the ancient residence of the Percies, Earls of Northumberland. You look in vain for any marks of the grandeur of the feudal ages, for trophies won by a family eminent for military prowess and deeds of chivalry, for extensive forests and venerable oaks. The Hall of entertainment is no more; and instead of the disinterested usher of days of yore, the visitor is attended by a valet, eager to receive the fees of admittance".[35]

Crossing the Border

[*31 May*] Passed thro Cornhill, a small village with a church which has no windows either on the E. or N. sides. I observed the same afterwards at Ednam. I now found myself in the neighbourhood of Scotland in seeing two women digging in a plantation, and arriving at the Union Bridge, a very handsome structure, crossed the Tweed and entered Scotland. The banks of the river are very pleasant particularly a gentlemans seat, Mr Marjoribanks, a little farther up. At a public house at the farther end of the bridge marriages are performed, if the ceremony, performed in such a place, and by some blacksmith or alehouse keeper, may be called by that venerable name. I soon reached Coldstream and breakfasted at the New-castle arms; from the Inn window I observed the following curious notice over a shop door, "Travelling caps and *boys of all kinds sold here?*" But as I was not in want of a son and heir, I did not go in to cheapen one. Coldstream is a small place, and has nothing farther striking in it; I therefore left it as soon as I had made my meal.

Kelso market

[*31 May*] I reached Kelso about 3 and found it was market day, and from my window at the Inn, I had a good view of the market, which exhibited a curious scene. The market place is very spacious. The Tollbooth stands on the E. side, an oblong building standing upon a piazza with circular arches, and a high tower in front. The ruins of the Abbey are seen over some houses to the South. The stalls, covered with broad check, formed two rows, or streets, in the middle of the market place, crossing each other at right angles. The place was crouded by people in their holiday cloaths, very gay;—fine raw boned wenches, with red faces shining thro black veils (which were very generally worn) like a fire in a dark night. Soldiers added to the groups, and the drums and trumpet and bugle horn at different times added much to the cheerfulness of the scene. It was like an English fair, rather than a common market. The commodities sold are various kinds of cloth, crockery, ribbands, laces, &c; hardware, toys and a profusion of gin-gerbread &c. Also books, and some of them, I was sorry to see, of a Jaco-binical tendency. The shambles are in a different part of the town, and are sheds built round a court. The town is large, but not very neat. I observed several thatched houses.

Sunday in Galashiels

[*2 June*] I strolled before breakfast towards Galashiels' house (for so according to the custom of the country the Laird, Mr Scot, is called—or else by his name as Scot of Galashiels) in a pleasant situation in a sort of bottom surrounded by wood, or rather plantations. After breakfast I walked on the hills above, with my Cowper in my hand, but was driven back by rain. At 11 I went to Church, and found a great concourse of people assembled in the Churchyard some standing and others sitting down in their plaids in groupes, waiting the stopping of the bell. I desired, according to my usual custom, to make one in the party with my host and his family; as, in such a case, I consider myself "the Stranger within his gates",[36] and bound with him to attend at divine service, laying aside all the idle distinctions of this world, and "rich and poor meeting together" before that "Lord, who is the maker of us all". (Prov. [*blank space*])[37] The church was very dirty, dark and ill-fitted up. It is not the custom in

Scotland on coming into the church to say a prayer, nor to pull off their hats till the Minister comes in. This is surely making it an act of respect to the Minister instead of the Divine Presence.

The service began with singing a psalm—then an extempore prayer, and then the sermon from Math. 9.27 &c a pretty good one, but not without some repetition. Then another prayer, another psalm and the blessing. The Congregation did not stand up when the psalms were sung, nor kneel during the prayers, and the clergyman put on his hat before he went out of church. These are indecorums which I hope every Church of England man would not see unmoved. The Minister gave notice of a sacrament for that day 3 weeks, and gave a very good exhortation to attend it, particularly to the rising generation; he concluded with some advice to Infidels and sectaries, desiring the former to join in some mode of worship and faith, and the latter to consider well the grounds of their difference. NB. there were two Anabaptist meetings in this place.

When I returned to my Inn, I found my room occupied by a party. I wished to have dined with the family but they were not to dine till after the second church, at which time I intended to set off and proceed one stage on my journey. I was put into a dirty wet bedroom to dine on poor broth and the scrag end of a neck of mutton: worse fare even than what Rogero[38] enjoyed in the vaults of the Abbey of Quedlinburgh (see the Poetry to the Anti-jacobin). The Ale was bad and there was only the heel of a piece of cheese.

At 3 I went to Church again and heard a sermon on Luke 1, which had very little to do with the text. The Church was as full as in the morning. Mr Pringle of Torwoodlee and his family were there. The Minister gave notice of a Lecture at 5. It rained hard when we came out of Church. And on my return to the Inn, I found the family, who had not been to Church, had taken possession of my room to dine. They made no apology. A guest came in, a very civil plain kind of man. After dinner each had a glass of whisky, in which they would fain have had me join, but I refused, adding I thought spirits bad for the health. The guest said it was all *custom*. I said then it was a *bad* custom.

Prospect of Edinburgh

[*5 June*] Walking from Middleton I could see Arthur's seat and Salisbury crags rising above the town of Edinburgh. The Fifeshire hills beyond them to the right, a vast range of hills in front, above which the Grampians, with snow on their summits, towered aloft; the Pentland hills on the left, at the foot of which, among some wood, I discovered Woodhouselee, Mr Fraser Tytler's.[39]

Farther on, on my right, saw Borthwick Castle and village in a pleasant glen, and some way farther, the ruins of New Byre Castle, close to the road on the left, a single tower, standing on a mound with a ditch round it. A little beyond the 9 mile stone came in view of the Firth of Forth with all its grand and beautiful accompaniments; but the day not being clear, tho the sun now shone bright, it was not seen to advantage.

Passed Dalhousie Castle on the left, situated on a rising ground above a deep, rocky, wooded glen, with a river rolling thro it. So severe a prohibition against approaching the house or entering the grounds was placed against a tree near the gate, that I did not dare even to look over.

A little way farther I met a man who asked me "Any public news, sir, aboot?" "Wonderful good (replied I, knowing the curiosity of the scotch) there are above 30, 000 men risen this morning". — "For what?" — "To pursue their daily labour with pleasure, to earn their bread by the sweat of their brow, and lay down again at night I hope in content". I passed on. The noise of a drum next called my attention, and seeing a number of people at a distance with a flag, I inquired what it was, and was informed it was the Taylors and Stonemasons at an *Apron Play*,[40] but I could not get any farther information.

At the Turnpike I turned to the left that I might enter Edinburgh by the new Town. A gentleman near the Links, (an open field or green near the town) I suppose taking me for a fisher from my net bag, or wishing to *fish* out of me what I was, asked me "What sport I had had?" "Sir?" said I. — "What have you caught sir?" "I find, sir, I have caught your notice". And thus did curiosity often make my bag a source of merriment. I was more than once afterwards asked, if it was for game? — "Not unless you make game of it". — And sometimes the question was "are you going a *fuiling*?" (the scotch manner of pronouncing *fowling*, which sounds to an Englishman more like *fooling*.) When my answer was, "I hoped I was not upon a fool's errand".

The entrance to Edinburgh this way is very striking. Immediately in my foreground I had a party of gentlemen playing at golf. Beyond, on my right, the rock upon which the castle stands, a most stupendous mass of itself, and with a great mass of buildings upon it. This however is greatly disfigured by the new barracks, which are built in a heavy formal manner, and far out-top the other parts of the castle. The old town, with many fine and many new buildings in it, stretching to the right, the new Town in front, the finest series of regular and handsome stone buildings perhaps in the world; the Firth of Forth appearing on each side beyond it, and the whole view terminated by lofty blue mountains.

The Rumbling Bridge

[*12 June*] Being market day at Kinross I met a great many people both men and women going thither, and some leading cattle with a halter of twisted straw. I saw much flat marshy ground and great quantities of lapwings. On the left I passed Tally bull the ruins of a gentlemans seat among some trees. At crooked Devon, a village which has not its name for nothing, I left the Stirling road, and followed another, in a line with the River Devon, till I got to the Rumbling Brig. This is a bridge of a single arch joining two verdant hills, being thrown over a narrow, but tremendously deep chasm of above 100 feet, thro which the river "boils, and wheels, and foams, and thunders"[41] among loose fragments of rock. This chasm is evidently the effect of some convulsion of nature, the rocks in one place, below the bridge, answering each other. The glen widens above the bridge, the sides are overgrown with trees, and the rocks are inhabited by innumerable jackdaws, whose cries add to the horror of the scene.

> The screaming nations, hov'ring in mid air,
> Loudly resent the stranger's freedom there,
> And seem to warn him never to repeat
> His bold intrusion to their dark retreat.
>
> Cowper's Hope.[42]

There is neither parapet nor railing to the bridge, that it must be really dangerous to horsemen passing over. A horse unused to so tremendous a gulph yawning on each side of him, with the roar of waters and clamour of birds, might start and precipitate his rider, and perhaps himself, into the abyss. This bridge was built in the year 1724, to replace one which fell in the former year. I descended a sloping hill on the S. side, where there is a fine view of the amphitheatre of rocks below the bridge. They rise perpendicularly on the N. side with trees growing out of the fisures. The S. side is a verdant slope scattered over with trees and goss in a very charming manner: the water makes no great appearance, but the view into the chasm is very fine. I followed the course of the river about a mile lower down to the Cawdron Lin, a still more tremendous object. Here the water shoots in spray, or white foam, into a vast circular bason worn by the water in the rock, and thence immediately into a second, not in white foam, but in a black torrent. Having viewed for some time these efforts of one of nature's resistless elements, I descended a steep wooded bank to the bottom of the rock (for these are on the summit of a cliff) into a deep glen, where the rocks rise perpendicularly on both sides. About half way down in front, the water issues from a small cavity and falls in a spreading stream of white foam about 30 feet. Trees grow in excellent situations on the top and sides of the rocks, and there is a very fine foreground of rock and trees. The glen below this is delightful and well wooded, and beyond is a view of the mountains about Stirling.

Ossian's Hall

[*15 June, Dunkeld*] We crossed[43] the river at the W. Ferry, and followed the walks at the side of the Bran, which empties itself into the Tay at Inver, just below the ferry. The Bran is a most impetuous torrent rushing over a wild craggy bed. These walks are well wooded, but flowers and flowering shrubs intrude amidst Nature's wildest picturesque. The sight and sound of the water is truly grand; but at length reaching an open space in the wood, where regular flower borders are planted amid the crag, a neat circular building of stone appears opposite which is called Ossian's Hall.[44] It is necessary for the *ciceroni* to inform the visitor, or he would not imagine that a small snug building, at the edge of a small amphitheatre of trees, which comprehend a trim flower garden, was the Hall of "the King of Shells". Entering the building, which is neat and lighted from the top, opposite the door is a painting of the mournful and blind Ossian, and the Daughter of Toscar with her harp raising the lovely song of Selma. Whilst contemplating this, it is suddenly drawn aside, and discovers a most elegant room (of which the outside appearance of the building had given no idea) it is of an oblong form, with a circular bow at each end, that opposite the door being a window, with blinds over it. The walls are most elegantly painted and gilt, and are furnished as also the cieling with mirrors of different kinds. The blinds being drawn up discover a very fine cascade till then only heard. The view up the river is wildness itself; and the water coming in an oblique direction, and meeting an opposing fragment of rock at the edge of a steep fall, is precipitated in three streams of white foam down rugged rocks into a narrow chasm below. The height of this fall is not considerable, but it's features are truly picturesque. When the visitor has attended to this most interesting scene for some time, for it is few that will be soon satisfied, he sees it in a variety of different ways from the reflection in the mirrors in the room. In looking up to that which is in the cieling the water is seen as it were shooting impetuously *upwards*, a most novel and curious effect.

The room was so elegantly splendid and the effects so new, that I scarcely knew how to find fault. Yet I had rather have seen a ruder and more appropriate building in this place, and have visited this elegant cabinet in the Duke's own mansion.

A Scottish fiddler

[*16 June*] At Inver I saw the famous Niel Gow,[45] the fidler; — the father of Niel, now dead — Nathaniel, who lives in London — and John, who lives in Edinburgh. He is the father, or original composer of the present Scotch Reels. He is old and rich, I was informed worth £2,000, and has a daughter in Edinburgh, whom he allows £25 per annum, which she generally spends and calls for £25 in addition. Yet he himself lives with his wife in the same mean hut he always did, and dresses as a common peasant. He is very fond of drink, and generally comes home drunk from Balls &c where he plays. People send for him frequently to the Inns to play; but as I was informed they gave him a few glasses of whiskey, and half-a-guinea, for playing 2 or 3 tunes, I did not send for him.

Scotch manners

[18 June, Blair Atholl] I must beg my reader's pardon for here mentioning an anecdote, which I would more gladly pass over in silence; but as it is a strong characteristic of scotch manners, and was one of the circumstances which greatly tended to give me a disgust in travelling in the country, I cannot forbear noticing it. I had left my portmanteau and all my cloaths lying about in my bedroom, a place which I considered as mine alone during my stay there. But, upon my return, I found a table slopped with whisky, and chairs, where a party had been drinking, and upon farther investigation I found that in a utensil, for which there was a particular place of deposit on the other side the garden. I made some stir at this in the house, and I must say in justice to the waiter and my Landlord, they made every requisite apology. It was a circumstance however which I think no English traveller could think upon but with disgust, and that too happening at one of the principal Inns, on one of the high roads, and on the estate of one of the first Noblemen in Scotland.

Difficulties with guides

[19 June, Blair Atholl] Being arrived at the ne plus ultra of conveyances for a Portmanteau, it was necessary to stir myself for a servant,[46] and Mr M'Intosh not being able to find one for me, the waiter found a youth of about 20, Sandy Robertson, who came from some little distance to school at Blair, and was willing to go with me two or 3 days upon trial, at 3s. per day. I liked his appearance tolerably well, and no other offering, I agreed with him; first asking him what his parents would say, and he said, he had desired a lad who lived just by them to let them know, and the waiter said he made no doubt they would make no objection. I accordingly made up a bundle in my plaid, intending to get a knapsack made as soon as possible, and packed up my portmanteau, directing it to go back to Edinburgh to wait my return; and soon after 10 set off with my new companion. He seemed clever, but shy, and tho he spoke English tolerably well, yet when I asked him any question, which he did not clearly understand, or could not well answer, he seemed distressed.

We kept along the Dalnacardoch road for nearly two miles, and ferrying over the Garry crossed the moors towards Tumel bridge. In our way had a fine look back towards Athol House, with its woods and Ben-y-glo rising majestically beyond. Came to a small loch with no trees about it, but in a good situation if planted. The day was very hot and the cattle had taken to the water. A man here was burning the hether and cutting peat; the hether blazing along the water side had a very singular effect. We descended a little above the head of Loch Tumel, a very fine Lake, the mountains which bound it are extremely wild and picturesque and well sprinkled with wood. It is finely broken by promontories running into it, and at the upper end is a small Island crowned with wood. The many windings of the river above the Lake among wood thinly scattered are very beautiful. Schehallion rose sublime on the W. with snow on his sides. Huts with a very few trees about them are pleasantly scattered thro the vale. At Tumel bridge, where the high road crosses from Kenmore to Dalnacardoch, the bed of the river is very rude and fine. I stopped at the public house here and got some milk, while Sandy got some ale, and then we proceeded. The day was very hot, but there were pleasant breezes. Birch groves rose on all sides. Going up a steepish ascent in the road Sandy began to complain that his *head was sore*, he thought from the ale he had drank; he found the heat and weight of the bundle too much, and *"wondered* whether he would go on to Kinloch". He now began to think his father and mother would miss him. I remonstrated with him, that he should have considered all these things well before hand, and unless he went on to Kinloch, I should not pay him.

When we reached Mount Alexander, the seat of Mr Struan Robertson, who was building a new house with battlements, &c. on the site of the old one, the residence of the famous old Poet Struan,[47] Sandy said that house belonged to his forefather, and he would go and get something to drink at a hut close by, as he was very thirsty. As he had got my bundle I did not chuse to trust him alone, and was following him, when a man and his wife came out and asked me in: It was Sandy Munro gardiner to Mr Robertson. I asked if he could find me a person to take my bundle to Kinloch, and he said if I would walk in and take an egg he would see. Sandy said he could go no farther, and while an egg was getting ready, I walked to M^r R^{ns}. house, and into the garden to see the famous fountain, or spring, of argentine, so called from its throwing up small particles of mica with the sand, which gives it a silvery appearance. On the other side of the water stands cross mount, Mr Stewart's, and a little further on the house of Colonel Macdonald: the whole vale is very pleasant and has several neat houses in it.

Not far from hence is the great fall of Tumel, but for want of proper information, I did not see either that, or another fall on the same river near Faskally.

I had a very excellent dinner of eggs, oakcake and milk, for which my kind host and hostess would on no account take any recompence. Another bundle bearer arrived, John Macdonald; so I dismissed Sandy with his full pay, and set off again with John.

The view of Loch Rannock improved at almost every step. Came to the village of Drumhastle, which was washed away about 17 years ago, by the immense swell of a mountain torrent which runs thro it. The sides of the mountains are scarred with deep and rude rocky channels, which at times pour forth vast torrents.

From the last rising ground before Kinloch is a very fine view of the Lake, the mountains rising finely on all sides, and at the West end, at a distance beyond the immediate boundaries, rose two vast and many pointed hills with snow on their sides, the names of which my guide told me are Corryhabar and Buarchliah. The village of Kinloch with its bridge and kirk, and a few fine trees around the houses at the E end of the Lake, are in a very excellent point of view.

When we reached the Inn I agreed with John M^d. to accompany me for two or 3 days upon trial, at 3^s. per day; and he said he would go home for some linen, and be with me by half past 6 in the morning at latest.

I had now travelled considerably above 600 miles on foot, and found no inconvenience from it, till this day, when I got quite lamed, and walked with considerable pain. I had worn an almost new pair of shoes; these I had rather objected to, as too tight, when my shoemaker brought them home. But he assured me they fitted me, and I, very foolishly, gave way to his assertions, and now suffered for it. Like Achilles I was vulnerable only in my heel, which was considerably chafed.

The inn at Kinloch is truly Highland, tho it is 2 stories high; and I was put into a tolerable, tho a very dark room. No loaf bread was to be had, and only salt butter. Salmon was brought me with my tea, but it was not very fresh. I desired the chamber maid to take care that the sheets she put upon my bed were quite dry, and she answered, "yes, she would toast 'em well at the fire".

After tea I strolled down the street, if a few miserable huts on each side of the way may be so called, to the Lake; the evening was fine, and the sun setting gloriously behind the mountains at the head, gave a rich glow to the prospect. I felt a tranquility in this sequestered spot, which made amends for the unpleasantness of the day; for the misfortunes or roguery of Sandy Robertson, I know not which, had given me some uneasiness.

On the N. side of the Lake extends a large pine forest, at the W. end are the Barracks, but without soldiers, and on the S. side Carrie, formerly the Struan estate. The Lake is about 12 miles long and 3 broad.

This Country was formerly the most barbarous and its inhabitants the most savage in the Highlands. In all this estate in the year 1745 there was not one who was of age, that did not march with the Pretender to Derby, and their numbers were not less than a thousand. The Chief had been in 4 rebellions, was always attainted, and yet kept possession of his estate till the year 1745. On his taking part the third time in the rebellion of 1715 he was again attainted, and the estate granted to his sister. But he got possession of her person and confined her in a prison on an Island in the Lake, till, to preserve her life, she made over her estate to him, and in the last rebellion, he rowed up and down the Lake in his boat bidding defiance to the soldiers, who were in quest of him; and afterwards made his escape into France, where he died at the age of 90.

The Person who attended the Pretender over the mountains, after his defeat at Culloden, and never left him till he saw him safe aboard a French ship, was a Rannock man. He was very poor, and knew of the reward offered for apprehending the Pretender, but would sooner have lost his life than forfeited his trust.

On account therefore of the disloyalty of this part of the country, two officers and a company of soldiers were for many years quartered at the barracks at the head of the Lake.

There was no place of worship here or within some distance till lately, and even now that a kirk is built, service is performed here only once in 3 weeks.

Behind the inn are a few fine sycamores, an ash and an oak. At the door I observed a large stone with a conical hole in it, and on inquiring the use of it, was told it was a knocking stone, for beating barley to make broth with. It is done with a kind of pestle, which gets off the husk and ends, and leaves a round grain. The Inn was thatched with fern, with the root end outwards. The huts are sometimes covered with sods, sometimes thatched with hether, broom or fern.

[20 June] I was awake by 6 o'clock and lay in expectation of the arrival of my new guide; but expectation was in vain, and at length at 8 o'clock I got up, and began making inquiries after some one to carry my bundle to Kenmore. Most of the men were out at work, and those who remained at home, being the most idle and seeing my necessity were exorbitant in their demands: It was only 18 miles the longest way round by Aberfeldy, one man offered to take it for 3^s..6^d., but then he said I might go by Aberfeldy, and he would go the nearer way by Cashaville; but not chusing to to be thus imposed on I rejected his offer. My lameness was not any better, but I had changed my shoes; and I thought if I could pass this day in rowing upon the Lake, I should rest myself, and might meet with a servant before next morning. But when I came to talk with my host about a boat, he said I must pay 5^s. for the day, and have two men and board them. This proposal pleased me no better than the former, and I determined at all event not to submit to these impositions, but to leave Kinloch and be my own bundle bearer, if I could not provide myself otherwise. A peasant I had some conversation with in the village told me of the postman to Aberfeldy, who lived 2 miles on the road, who he made no doubt would take it for me the next day. I got breakfast, and at 10 set off lame, with my bundle under my arm, besides the bag I usually carried, and the day very hot to complete it. I had however another proof of Highland extortion before I left my Inn. For tea and breakfast, with only oatcake to eat, salt butter and no milk or cream, I was charged 1^s. each, and 1^s. for my bed, for which, at the same style of house in England, I should not have been charged at all, or at most but 6^d.

Thus it is that in Scotland the traveller is exposed to the alternate and distressing extremes of generosity and extortion. When you are upon a Scotchman's hospitality, he thinks he cannot do too much for you; but where it is his business to make money, he thinks he can never have sufficient, however unreasonable his charge. This certainly is often the case in England, but when it happens, you at least have comfort for your money.

Thus Poetry,[48] which succeeds the best in fiction, has been peculiarly happy in celebrating the simplicity of the honest Highlander.

Thus I left Kinloch Rannock with a heavy step but an exulting heart, and after walking 2 miles called at the house of Sandy Stewart, the Aberfeldy postman, but no one was at home. A little farther on, seeing a man at the door of a house, I inquired for a Carrier for my bundle; he said he knew of no one; but he soon followed me, saying he was going a mile, and offered to carry it for me. He looked honest, and what with the heat of the day and the pain of my heel, I was glad to accept his offer.

We stopped at a cottage some way farther where he said, if I would wait, he would see for some one to accompany me. What would I give? 2^s. to Cashaville.—He soon returned and said he could not get any one, but for 2^s..6^d he would go himself; and I accepted his offer. I begged some milk, but it was sour, and the woman of the cottage then offered me cream and water, but that was sour likewise. I offered her a 6^d. which she refused, and on attempting to put it into her hand, she put her hands upon her head and said *no—no*.

We crossed the hills by the foot road winding round the base of the mountain *Schehallion* or *perpetual storm*, on the side of which D^r. Maskelyne, Mr Reuben Burrow, and M^r W^m. Menzies, Land Surveyor, in the year 1774 erected a tent, and resided four months for the purpose of finding its attraction[49] and for astronomical observations. My guide told me he remembered it well, for he used to take cows and goats milk to them every day from his father, who was a farmer. The direction of this mountain in length is nearly east and west; its height above the surrounding valley, is, at a medium, about 2000 feet; and its highest part above the level of the sea, is 3550 feet.

I had a view of Loch Tumel and Ben-y-Glo, and passed within a mile on my right of Schehallion well, where, as my Guide informed me, the people round came on the first sunday in May to drink the water as a cure for the gravel.[50] The remedy seemed an odd one to me, and my guide could give me no farther information of the nature of the water, and I could not go out of my way to see it.

The sun was most scorching, I pursued my way with great pain, and began in my own mind, half in earnest and half in jest, to parody the Eclogue of Hassan or the Camel Driver.[51] The reflection of the sun from the road was distressing to my eyes. I should advise a green shade or green spectacles, to those who travel much on high roads in the summer. A cloud at length came over, and afforded some relief from the intense heat.

We got into the high road again 2 miles short of Cashaville, and descended into a beautiful glen, with the ruined tower of Castle Garth on the right, on the rising of a hill between two glens. A little farther on, close to the road side, is a small, but very pleasing cascade, on the stream of Haltnie, which rises in Schehallion and falls into the Lyon just below.

I reached Cashaville at 3, where I dismissed my guide, for he was not willing to wait and accompany me on to Kenmore; and I met with a civil Landlady, and got an excellent dinner of loaf bread, fresh butter, and eggs. Quite overcome with the toils and heat of the day, I fell into a profound sleep after dinner, from which I did not awake till 6, when my Landlady, not having been able to procure a man to carry my bundle, had engaged a woman; by no means an uncommon bearer of burdens in Scotland ...

When I reached the Inn at Kenmore I was put into an indifferent room, and not received so well as I could wish; and understanding that Mrs Mac Andrew the Landlady was an Englishwoman, I desired to speak with her, expecting she would be pleased with seeing a Countryman; but when she entered, I repeated to myself with Malcolm "My countrywoman, and yet I know her not";[52] for instead of the smile I expected to see beaming on her face, she appeared "a cold friend to me i'th' north",[53] and I did not find the *amor patriae* at all alive in her mind, and I was no better off than before.

The grounds at Taymouth Castle

[21 June] We were next conducted[54] through a dark narrow arched way underground to the Hermitage, an octagonal building, having a 3 sided sashed bow (if what is not circular may be called a bow) on one side. The walls of the room are covered with moss and shells, there are various wild animals (foxes, cats, badgers, &c) hung against them, and artificial fruit, and a mock basket just raised from the wall:—a couch of goat skins, with a case of sham books above it—the stools are covered with skins, and a mossy table has some curious plates. The windows are made of large square panes, with wooden frames painted white. So heterogeneous a composition for a Hermitage cannot fail to strike a person of any taste in *costume* with disgust. The whole is in much too modern and magnificent a style for the thing it is meant to represent; and what rusticity there is, is too much studied and artificial to impose upon the imagination even for a minute. It might make a vermine room for some sportsman, or suit a

London Hermit, but not one who had retired from the world and its vanities,

> Remote from man with God to pass his days,
> Prayer all his business, all his pleasure praise.
>
> Parnel.[55]

If it is to be an Hermitage, it should be such as a Hermit would have lived in; but if a building of more modern and elegant make is required, still let the costume be preserved, let it be a pavilion, a Temple, a tent, or a Knightsbridge room, but do not insult buildings by calling them names ...

The Temple of Venus, was the next place which particularly attracted our attention, a handsome building and not very unappropriate to the style of place—if a pagan temple can ever be proper in a Christian country. Why should we erect buildings to remind us of the Idolatry, ignorance and immoralities of the Heathen world, when the same taste and purposes might be answered in a temple, or a *school* of Piety, Justice, Temperance, Patience, &c where Statuary or painting might record illustrious examples of Christian Virtues. But there is a kind of received cant or mummery in gardening and decorating grounds, from which it is difficult to emancipate taste.

A penny wedding

[*21 June*] A penny wedding was celebrated this Evening at the Inn at Kenmore. When the bride and bridegroom are not in circumstances to treat their friends, the friends treat them, paying so much a head for their entertainment, the profits of which often leaves them a *pretty penny* wherewith to set out in the world. In former times when money went farther than it does now, a penny was the sum; from whence it had its name. But it is now advanced to 8 pence. The party met to supper at 8. and afterwards danced till 2 in the morning. I went into the room to see the dancing, which was very good, but it was too hot and close to remain.

These ceremonies are sometimes such, I have been told, as to be more like the ceremonies in a pagan temple of Venus, or Bacchus, than a wedding in a Christian Country.

The people of Kenmore appeared the most decent and neat in their dress and manners of any I saw in Scotland. Their houses are kept cleaner, and all exercise some trade; Lord Braedalbane seems to have

> Scatter'd plenty o'er the smiling land,

and the Traveller

> Reads his History in his People's eyes.[56]

Deliberation and determination

[23 *June, Killin*] I began most seriously to weigh in my mind, whether I should proceed on the Journey I intended when I set out, or rather return into England, to which I could most truly say,

Where'er I roam, whatever realms to see,
My heart untravell'd fondly turns to thee.[57]

On the one hand I considered the pleasure which I had long promised myself, in visiting the Islands and Highlands of Scotland, and to accomplish which I had twice made considerable efforts. I considered that I was to tread "that illustrious Island, which was once the luminary of the Caledonian's regions",[58] and which had been rendered still more celebrated in modern days by the visit of my illustrious countryman. I considered the new country, the men and the manners I was to see, and thereby lay in a store of instruction and amusement, that was to last me my life. I looked forwards in imagination to the lofty mountains, the gloomy caverns, the expansive lakes, the foaming torrents and the thundering cataracts; to the pleasure of exploring parts of Scotland hitherto unvisited, or at least

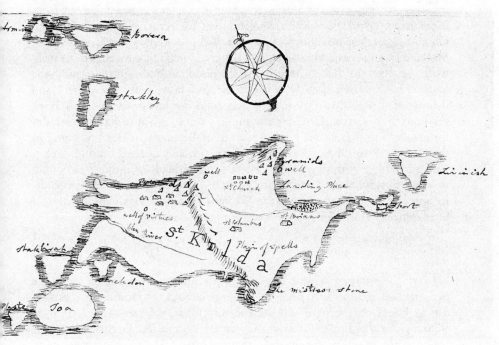

Unseen places: sketch map of St Kilda prepared by Plumptre in 1799

undescribed by Travellers, and to a voyage on the bosom of the Atlantic: On the other hand I considered myself as wandering almost alone—for my faithful companion could only speak to me by his looks—through countries where I was a stranger, their language at times unintelligible to me, where the accommodations were at the best indifferent, and often dirty, and where I was exposed to continual extortions, which I was informed would be still greater where I was going: I reflected on my treatment at Blair—on the little dependance to be placed on guides—on the savagery of Rannock, and the cold neglect at Kenmore: But then what need had I to mind accommodations, when, with the recommendations I already had, and with what in all probability I should farther receive as I proceeded, and the known hospitality of the Scotch, almost all the houses of the gentry would be open to me. Then again, on the other hand, such a method of getting on was ill suited to my plans and my turn of mind. When a stranger enters a gentleman's house, he gives up the command of his time. Civility requires that he should not make it an Inn—he must attend to the hours of the family, he must not go in at night and out again in the morning: the hours of breakfast and dinner must be attended to—the interval is too short to see much, particularly at any distance, and to a person travelling on foot, and to join the board of luxury was most repugnant to my ideas:—added to this my wardrobe would not afford the cloathing necessary to make the appearance, where a stranger is often judged from his outside. I had moreover strong motives for returning. A friend, with whom I had taken two journies on foot, had promised, if I returned out of Scotland in any reasonable time, and we could make it convenient, to walk with me over the Lake Country of Cumberland and Westmorland—the weather now too was bad; if it continued so it were better to return—and if it mended, I could enjoy it with him amid my favourite scenes. Having revolved these circumstances in my mind, I resolved not to hazard seas and unexplored countries, but when I arrived at Dalmally, instead of going to the Westward to Oban, to return by Inverary, and Lochs Lomond, Ketterin and Earn, to Edinburgh, and write to my friend to know if he would meet me at the Lakes. Thus I put an end to my second and in all probability my last attempt at visiting the Western Islands, and northern parts of Scotland.

St Fillans

[24 June] Wishing to see the wonders of S^t. Fillan's,—the church yard, the bed, the bell and the holy pool for dipping lunatics,—I inquired my way of a man I met on the road. He looked me full in the face, and I suppose thinking that (as D^r. Johnson would have said) that no Englishman in his sound senses could be travelling in that country, said "What are you going to duck?" I assured him no, and he directed me by some cottages to the river, which I forded and soon reached S^t. Fillans.

In the church yard is the bed, which consists of some beams of wood laid along within the inclosure of the old walls of the chapel, some fragments of which still remain. The bed is in 3 divisions. In the most northern one, at the head is a stone with a circular place for the head to go in.

Formerly a small hand-bell was kept in the church yard, laying loose upon one of the tombs, and was said from its Virtues to cure sore heads. Such were its wonderful properties, that it was affirmed, that if ever it was taken away it would come back again of itself. An English Traveller, at Tyndrum the former summer having a mind to put its Virtues to the test, sent his servant for it at night, and took it away with them. Nearly a year had elapsed when I was there, and it had not returned, and some *doubts began* to be entertained whether it ever would. That the whole history of S^t. Fillan, his well, the pool, and the bell are gross pieces of superstition, few people I should hope would hesitate to acknowledge. Indeed it seems almost too gross for the Highlands of Scotland, particularly in any place where there is a protestant Minister residing. But that the Traveller was very wrong in taking this mode of curing their superstition, supposing it to have that happy effect, I make no scruple in declaring. Yet I should be very sorry were he ever to think of returning it, as it would seem to give truth to the legend and confirm them in their errors. Near the church is a well, which is said to cure all disorders; but *the famous holy pool* is in the water of Strath Fillan, the same which afterwards runs into the Dochart. A point of rock juts out into the river, which divides it into 2, screening the one from the other. The women are dipped in that to the E. the men in that to the W. The times are May Day, Lammas and once besides. The ceremony is, after being dipped 3 times, the patient walks 3 times round 3 cairns to the N. of the pool,

> Thrice to thine,
> And thrice to thine,
> And thrice again to make up nine.

and drops a stone and some piece of linen, or wearing apparel, each time. He is then tied in the bed in the church yard for the night, and if he gets untied by morning (which is always attributed to S^t. Fillan's personal assistance when it happens) he will then recover. But I should think such a regimen rather calculated to distract than restore a man to his senses.

Scarcity

[*25 June, Tyndrum*] I had my breakfast at 7 and when I was about to pay my bill, desired the chambermaid to get me change for a 20^s. note; but silver was not to be had either at the Inn or in the village, though it can boast of a shop. I had only silver to give the chambermaid, and the Landlord desired me to pay the bill to the Landlord at Dalmally. I asked him if he was not afraid of my neglecting to pay it and he said, no, he trusted to my honour. When I told the Landlord at Dalmally that I had a bill to pay, (and I suppose it was very small compared with what some had to pay, for it contained neither whisky nor wine;) he said very well. "But how do you know that I tell you the right sum?" He made no doubt of my honour. It was very common at Tyndrum to leave the bills to be paid at the next stage, and sometimes, they could not then give change and it was necessary to leave it still farther till they reached Inverary. But they never lost the money. I am happy to find that such confidence is never abused ...

I reached Dalmally in time enough to escape the rain, which fell very heavily, while I enjoyed a nice peat fire in a comfortable room.

The Loaf bread which I had at dinner was stale and mouldy, yet I thought it better than oatcake. It had come from Perth 78 miles. There is a Baker at Inverary, from whence they get their bread sometimes, but often, when there is an opportunity of Carriage, he has none by him. Even at Kenmore the bread comes from Perth, and so likewise at Blair. There is a Baker at Aberfeldy, but his bread is not liked. There is no baker between Dunkeld and Inverness. I asked the Landlord why he had not an oven by his fire side, and baked his own bread. He said that barm (or yeast) was not to be had, as he did not brew. To this I could not at that time make any farther reply than by telling him the receipt for making the *Ned Cakes* which I had eaten in Northumberland, and I desired the waiter (who I believe was his daughter) to make me some next morning for breakfast, but she said she was not used to them and did not know how to make them. Thus it seems to be rather an aversion to trying anything new, than necessity, which drives them to such straights for bread and good substitutes for it. Biskits can certainly be made without yeast. But I know there are several substitutes for it, besides leaven, all which, tho possibly not so good, might serve the turn, and there are many receipts for cakes which might be made and baked in a camp or a Dutch oven in 20', a less time than travellers are often kept waiting to less purpose. It is an old but a very just general saying "Where there is a *will*, there's a *way*".

Inverary boasts of a Butcher, but he does not kill regularly, not above once in a month or 6 weeks. In the *season* the Landlord generally kills a sheep, and very often has not a call for it, till he is obliged to give it to his servants.

Amidst much stuff and ribaldry written on the window shutters of my room, I observed the following lines, which from the sentiments they contained, I thought worth transcribing into my Memorandum book:

Had I an hundred thousand pound,
   The happiest man on earth I'd be,

For doing good to all around
    Would give them joy but more to me.

I thought however the sentiment might be improved upon, and wrote the
following answer underneath.

Lament not, man, that thou art poor,
    Thy means of doing good confin'd,
The poorest has that heavenly power;—
    True treasure is a virtuous mind.

'Tis not how *much*, but *how* we give,—
    The widows mites, if well applied,
More worthy objects can relieve
    Than thousands lavish'd forth beside.

We all can pity, all can pray,
    And God will hear the righteous' prayer:—
A good example shews the way
    To Heaven, and gives us treasure there.

John McNab

[*25 June, Dalmally*] The rain continued the whole afternoon, and not
seeming likely to hold up, after tea I determined to walk out, and visit the
McNabs, mentioned by Mr Pennant and S^t. Fond in their Journies in Scotland.[59] Their habitations are situated on a hill a little to the S.W. of the Inn.
When I reached the cottage, I inquired for McNab, and he came to the
door and desired me to walk in, shewing me into a room, with a fire of
peat on the floor in the middle, the smoak ascending thro the chimney immediately above. There were windows both to the N. and S., a set of
shelves for plates in one corner, and a bed in the other. The family have
lived in this farm, and carried on the occupation of a blacksmith for 407
years, a wonderful thing, as they are not freeholders. He had only 4 years
then remaining of his old *Jack* (or lease) and he feared that Lord Braedalbane will then raise his rent, as he has been offered 3 times as much for the
farm, which John said he could not give. But I think his Lordship is too
good a Landlord to part with so old a tenant for a trifle. There are 4
brothers of them, the mother of whom was still living at the age of 99 and
had her faculties entire. Her mother lived to the age of 104. John, the
Eldest of the brothers, and in whose cottage I then was, was aged 78, and
was a bachellor, as likewise was his brother Malcolm, who lived with him,
both being farmers. Donald, the next, lives hard by, has had 13 children of
whom 4 sons and 5 daughters are still living; and Sandy (i.e. Alex*ander*)

who lives in a farm at a little distance, are both Blacksmith's and famous for making dirks and knives. The Lunos of modern days—see Ossian.[60]— Several of his brother's children were in the room with us. I was going to see Sandy, as I had understood he had got some reliques of Ossian[61] in his possession, but one of the servants told us, that he had fallen upon a knife, whilst sheepshearing, which had run into his hip and hurt him. John said, however, that he had nothing but what had been printed. He shewed me some old armour, which had belonged to his ancestors, a breast and back-plate, a target, a helmet, and an iron hat, which was round, with a flap turning up on one side, with a pipe to put a feather in. He mentioned M[r] Pennants having taken notice of the family in his book, and the visit he had from S[t]. Fond and his party: he said they were getting stones, with hammers, and collecting plants &c. I inquired after Patrick Fraser, the schoolmaster, who had accompanied S[t]. Fond to Oban, Mull &c. He took orders and went abroad to the E. Indies, and the climate not agreeing with him, he returned; he got well again, again went out and died. M[c]Nab said he was a *terrible* scholar.

He talked of the severe Winter and of the number of sheep lost in the snow. Upon which I mentioned the case of Elizabeth Woodcock[62] of Impington near Cambridge, and he was much struck with the story. Having the printed account of her case in my pocket book, which I had carried with me as a voucher, lest I should tell the story and any one doubt my veracity, for the account is truly wonderful; and thinking I could not bestow it where it would be more prized, I desired him to accept it. He seemed much pleased, and said "You'll stop here tonight". I answered "Yes". We talked on for some time, and after I had sat above an hour, got up to come away; when he said "Won't you stop all night: you'll be welcome?" I told him I had ordered a bed at the Inn. That I fancied I had misunderstood him when I said I would stop all night, thinking he meant in the place, at Dalmally. I almost wished indeed that I had accepted, as it would have been a curious peep into life, and I should have measured the pleasure I should have given him, by what I receive when any of my superiors, either in rank, fortune, or abilities, honour my humble cot with their presence. He ordered some milk, which was most excellent cream, and after some little time I returned to the Inn. He inquired my name and place of abode, of which I informed him; and he said he should call on me when he came that way.

An encounter on the road to Inverary

[*26 June*] Descended into a wild country, but with great numbers of sheep and cattle. At some distance rose the woods of Inverary and the mountains on the other side Loch Fyne, appearing of a most lovely aetherial blue. A single hut with a potatoe ground, prepared me for a few more farther on, and still proceeding saw a good deal of cultivation, and that even at some distance up the sides of the mountains. Within 5 miles of Inverary came to the Duke's woods, and at between 3 and 4 passed a largish square white house, before which a man was standing with a tobacco pouch in his hand. He accosted me with, "A good Evening", "A fine Dog", and "Have you got any Tobacco?" It seemed almost like Bays's question "Pray have either of you gentlemen got a piece of brown paper and a little vinegar about you"[63]—But I was happy in having some (for I liked the man's looks,) and taking out my pouch, undid a long piece of my roll, which I had carried to make friends with. He cried out "that is too much: when you come this way again I will pay you". I told him I never should come that way again. "Then (said he) I am sorry I have not a dram to give you". "Can you give me any sweet milk" said I. "Yes, walk in". I walked in to the house, and found his name was Donald M'Farlane, schoolmaster in Glen Array. This house was built for him by the Duke of Argyle, and is 2 stories high, with gothic windows and a fire place like an English house. I sat with him a short time and we conversed pleasantly. Donald was a bit of a wit and he gave me the following riddle to solve: "He had 4 sons, and each of them had 3 sisters. How many children had he?" I gave him likewise a pinch of snuff, and when I came away he insisted on accompanying me and carrying my bag. I said no. But he begged he might, as "it would give him plea-sure". I then acquiesced. We presently came to a public house, and he would fain have treated me with a dram, which I firmly, and I trust civilly declined. We soon turned into the Duke's grounds, at a white gate on the left hand conducted by the noise of a waterfall, over which an Alpine bridge is thrown, the most characteristic of any I had seen in Scotland. Donald told me the Duke talked of building a *better*. I hope it will end in talk. It is a truly picturesque scene. The fall is not high, but rich and varied in its numerous parts, the rocks fine and the wood in advantageous places. The bridge which crosses the top of the fall is a most happy object in the scene. It is backed by woods, among which larch appear, and these again by verdant hills. A large pool receives the water, and it is a salmon leap, but none were there at that time. I asked the name of it. Donald said it had none, but he called it Lin-nhe-gluta, or the Rumbling Pool. We walked thro the plantations to the Mill within a mile of Inverary, when I resumed my bag, took leave of Donald and arrived at the Inn a little before 6.

Rest and Be Thankful

[*28 June*] I left Carn Dhu after an early breakfast and pursued my route through Glen Kinglass. The mountains which bound it on all sides rise boldly from their bases to their craggy summits, bearing pasture with little interruption to their very tops. Their sides deeply furrowed and water, from the rain the night before, was pouring down them into the roaring torrent below. A few birch trees are scattered over the hills and frequently fringed the sides of these torrents. Birch is the natural growth of the country. If the mountains are defended from Deer and cattle and sheep they grow spontaneously. Vast heaps of stones sometimes lay by the road side and even on the road itself, which shew with what fury at times the water must descend. The clouds skimming along the tops of the mountains shewed at intervals the azure vault above.

Crossing the stream at a bridge and thro a pass to the S.E. entered Glen Crow in which is a small loch: the rocks above this rise more abruptly and their sides are chiefly crag. Ascending a steep road I at length reached the celebrated seat which bears this inscription on a stone at the back

Rest
and be thankful
1748
Repaired by the XXIII Reg^t.
1768

and hence had a look down into the other side of Glen Crow with its mazy stream and a few huts scattered through it. The rocks which enclose it are very grand. The seat is made of turf in the form of a semi circle, with a sort of terrace round it, with rude steps at each end leading to it. The 15th. mile stone from Inverary is just below. Here I rested thankfully[64] and the back sheltered me from the wind which blew rather cool from the pass, while my companion Rover sat on the top to enjoy it. The sun shone bright, but was not too hot. I took out my Ossian, and reading the poem of Carthon, came, very appositely, to the Ode to the Sun . . .[65]

A stream accompanies the traveller down the mountain, which soon, with its tributaries, encreases into a river. The road then turns thro a pass on the left and another part of the glen opens, as fine a specimen of rock scenery as I have any where beheld. The mountains themselves with their rocky heads tower aloft, and the immense masses tumbled from them which lie in the glen below, fill the imagination with fear and wonder. In one place where the road has been cut through a prodigious mass, the marks are still observable where it has been bored to admit the gunpowder to blast it: it is at once a specimen of the wonderful works of nature and of the labours of man. At length I reach the side of Loch Long, at the edge of which a little lower down stands the pleasant place of Ard Garton. Had the owners of this spot and Dunderaw &c any taste, they would improve the ground a little about their houses and make these Lakes much more beautiful. It is by no means so common in Scotland as it is in England for every gentleman of any property to have a pleasure garden or shrubbery, or even to make the ground about their houses neat. With the natural advantages of mountains and Lakes, what might not a picturesque genius achieve in these situations in the way of Landscape ...

I never experienced the different effect of weather on scenery so forcibly as today. When I passed through these glens 3 years before in the rain, I thought it the most desolate country I had ever seen. This day they were all grandeur.

The horrors of Glen Falloch

[*29 June*] The outside appearance of the Inn was not very inviting, and upon my entering and calling, one who I should have taken for a woman, "but that her beard forbade me to interpret she was such",[66] made her appearance, in what, in England, would be called a bed gown, being tied round her neck and coming down to about half way of her petticoat, long coal-black hair, twisted in a curious manner, and teeth which projected in front like the balcony to an Adelphi window.[67] Being tired and hungry, I asked what I could have to eat. "I suppose you want flesh". I said I did not care what, provided it was good of the kind, "Had she any eggs?" "Yes, and mutton ham. And some broth". "Then get me some eggs and ham & mutton broth ready as soon as you can; And shew me a room". I was shewn up stairs into a room, the walls of which were made of rough stone, and neither plaistered nor whitewashed; the glass in the window was very much broken, a 4 post bedstead without hangings stood in one corner of the room, and another bed was in the wainscot of the room. After some time the Sycorax[68] of the house brought me up a bason of broth and put it upon the table. I asked if she did not lay a cloth—she exclaimed—oh!—and laid one with many wry faces. I tasted "the gruel", which she had made very "thick and slab",[69] and I found it taste so strong of bad dripping, that my stomach revolted even at the taste, and I did not forget it the rest of the day. My dog however could manage to eat it, and I was glad to get him a meal. The Eggs next arrived,—but "Where is the mutton ham?" "We are so throng[70] I've no time to do it". "I think you might find time to oblige a hungry stranger". I ate my eggs however, and with some tolerable butter and oat cake and beer I made a meal.

I next had up the Landlord Reynold Macallum and found him almost as stupid and pigheaded as his sister, and all I could make out from him was, that I must have a guide over the mountains to Loch Ketterin.

A gentleman at Edinburgh had done me the favour to lend me Ainslies large nine sheet map of Scotland,[71] which was rolled up in a tin case and which I had taken the trouble of carrying in my hand, or under my arm, ever since I parted from my portmanteau. In looking at this I found there was a carriage road from Glen Falloch to Loch Ketterin, and came to this place under that idea; but upon inquiry, I found there was not even a foot-path, and the road was only *talked of*. I told the Hag I must sleep there that night. She said I could not have a bed. I had already walked 21 miles on a hot day, there was no other house within 10 miles and those entirely out of my way, I therefore said I must stop, and they must do their best for me, when the Landlord said I should have a bed.

I inquired for the schoolmaster, thinking he might be company and assist me among these savages, but there was none in the Glen. It is in the parish of Killin from which it is 21 miles. S^t. Fillans which is 10 miles, is a chapel of ease to Killin; and Arroquhar, 12 miles, is the nearest church the other way. Some masons, who I had seen on the road mending the bridges, now came to new rough-cast the house, in doing which the mortar was sent through the broken window into the room. I therefore walked out and took my way up the Glen and found it pleasant. It is prettily wooded and the river rushes over a craggy bed. The road to Tyndrum ascends steep, and turning towards the E. opens to a prospect of Ben More. I returned to the Inn and asked for a pen and Ink. The answer was "I've no pen and Ink"—and she shut the door. I read a little in Ossian, and after some time knocked, but could not get any one to answer. I went down and desired to have Tea.—"I am so thronged I cant get water yet".—"Why, the kettle is boiling on the fire".—"Yes, but I want that for something else".—I gave her a pinch of snuff, which made her somewhat more obliging, and in half an hour I got tea. When she brought this, I said to her "Mind that my sheets are well aired".—"You'll have no sheets here tonight".—"Why not?"—"They are all at the bleech: but I've as good blankets as between here and Glasgow".—Not being used to sleep without sheets, and not liking to sleep in my cloaths as one great source of refreshment to me is getting out of my bandages, and rest being of importance to me, for I determined at all events to proceed the next day I went down and asked the Landlord if he could not borrow a pair of sheets of a neighbour; when he said I should have sheets, and I afterwards found that they had them in the house the whole time. I agreed with a guide to conduct me over the mountains next morning. It was William Macallum, brother to the Landlord, but a much more "tricksey spirit".[72] At half past 9 I ordered my bed to be got ready, and a sheet, which was doubled, was produced, and put on my bed. I asked if it was dry? "Its as dry and as fine too as what you get at home".

"I should like (said I to the woman as she was making the bed) to breakfast at 7 in the morning".—"You'll not get it till 8". I was put into a double bedded room, one bed at the foot of the other, and who was in the other I did not know. He had a consumptive cough, which kept me awake all night. Had a Scotch stable or Cowhouse been like an English one, I certainly should have desired that in preference; but I saw no alternative, but to take it patiently. The beds in the room in which I sat were to be occupied by the masons. I packed my cloaths about me, had my crabstick by my side, and made my dog sleep upon the bed. Without his fidelity to confide in, I could not have endured it. However I bore it tolerably well, and being very much tired got some rest.

[*30 June*] I rose before 7 and thinking it vain to ask for bason and towel, washed at the brook, which ran near the house, and had this been the greatest inconvenience I had suffered at Glen Falloch, or anywhere else, I had travelled on contentedly to Johnny Groat's house.

My chumb[73] had left his bed some time, and I found him drinking whisky-and-water below. I entered into conversation with him, and found him to be the master of the masons at work on the road. He was a very civil, and seemingly good kind of man, in the last stage of a consumption, and I think by this time in all probability has coughed his last. I went to see after the people of the house, who were all snoring in their styes. I represented my case to my chumb, who roused them. They lighted a fire, I got breakfast, and at ½ p. 8, set off with my guide, tho the mist was upon some of the mountains and the day not very promising; but such was my dislike to the place, that even tho it was Sunday, I resolved to try my fortune else where, and hoped to meet with a church in my way.

Scottish curiosity

[*2 July*] Here an old woman overtook me with "a fine day", and understanding I was going to Loch Earn head, said she would bear me company. I gave her a pinch of snuff but soon left her behind.

The Curiosity of the Scotch is astonishing. A man makes no scruple of coming up and asking "Whats the news?"—"Where do you come from?"—and if you give him an indirect answer, he asks at once "Whats the name of the place?" If this question is answered, the next is "What line, or occupation, you follow", and so on. In former times, according to Ossian, it was reckoned a great breach of hospitality to inquire a strangers name or place of abode.

I was continually asked if the map I carried in a tin case in my hand was a *prospect* (meaning a prospect glass or telescope) and one man came up and asked "Whats the use of that thing?"

The Pedestrian: an Highland Eclogue[74]

Scene the savage country of Rannock: Time mid-day.

In silent sadness o'er the dreary waste,
The 'lorn Pedestrian with his Rover past;
A little tea his wicker bottle held,
But one thin biskit did his pocket yield;
A crabtree staff he held in his right hand,
In's left a map of Caledonia's land;
In tartan jacket was the stranger clad,

127

And round his shoulders hung a tartan plaid;
A change of linen, worn to near a rag,
Hung at his back in curious network bag;
The sultry sun had gain'd the middle sky,
And not a tree affording shade was nigh;
His panting Dog the burning road pursu'd,
And long and lonely was the tract he view'd;
O'er come with toil and heat, the weary man
Thrice sigh'd, thrice struck his breast, and thus began:
  "Sad was the hour, and hapless was the day
  When far from Hinxton cot I bent my way.

  Ah little thought I of the toil and heat,
The coarse, bad fare, th'extortion that I meet;
Yet, James, no longer wilt thou get such trash,
When thy light pocket's emptied of its cash;
Soon will they drain thy pocket of its share,
And thou must beg thy way from door to door.

  Thou mute companion of my toil, that bearst
My ev'ry hardship, ev'ry sorrow shar'st,
In vain thou striv'st such pleasing food to know,
As roofs more rich, or Hinxton cot bestow;
Here only *sewins* and thin broth are found,
And oaten cakes and porridge do abound.
  Sad was the hour, and hapless was the day,
  When first from Hinxton cot we bent our way.

  Ah hapless taste to visit men and scenes,
Which draws the Trav'ler from his own demesnes!
Is not the country round one's peaceful home,
Dearer than richer scenes for which we roam?
Yet, restless there, a weary jaunt we take,
To view the rugged rock and crystal lake.
Full oft we brave the cold and oft the heat,
And only in the end fine prospects meet.
Ah why was travel so attractive made,
So soon its call by easy man obey'd:
Why heed we not, whil'st mad we haste along,
The voice of Peace and Solitude's sweet song?
And wherefore think the wide-extended plain,
Verdant with pasture, gold with waving grain,
Why think we these less pleasing to the sight,
Than Rannock Lake, Schehallion's rugged height?

Sad was the hour, and luckless was the day
When first from Hinxton cot I bent my way.

Still hapless man! If Native here I meet,
And him with civil words and snuffbox greet,
Unlike to England, here expos'd I lie
To Scotch impertinent curiosity.
Perhaps I ask if th'place I seek is near,
The answer is—"Are you a stranger here?
Tell me the name o'th'place from whence ye come,
And what's your occupation while at home?
How like ye Highland places, Highland fare?
What is your business? What d'ye carry there?
Tell me. I wonder what can be its use?
And do you bring us any foreign news?"

Fatigued with heat and toil, and wanting rest,
I seek the Inn and ask for all their best.
Long do I wait, and when my patience's tried,
Tho bad their best, that best is yet denied;
The surly hostess scarce my wishes meets
To lay me on my bed a pair of sheets.
Sad was the hour and luckless was the day
When first from Hinxton cot I bent my way.

At nights dread hour the silent flea will creep,
If aught of rest I find, upon my sleep,
Or some gaunt gnat will hum my head around,
And wake to anguish with envenom'd wound.

Thrice happy they who never wish to roam,
Nor leave the calm delights they find at home;
Who does not travel, does not fortune tempt,
At least from strange unkindness he's exempt.
Sad was the hour and hapless was the day
When first from Hinxton cot I bent my way.

Ah hapless youth! for she thy love hath won,
The tender *Clara** will be most undone.
Big swell'd my heart and own'd the powerful maid
When fast she dropt her tears as thus she said
"Farewell the youth, whom sighs could not detain,

* [*Plumptre's note*] An allegorical personage, meaning *Clare Hall* and College business left there in agitation.

129

Whom *Clara*'s breaking heart implores in vain.
Yet as thou goest may ev'ry blast arise
Weak and unfelt as these rejected sighs.
Safe o'er the wilds no perils may'st thou see,
No griefs endure; nor weep, false youth, like me".
O let me safely to the fair return,
Say with a kiss she must not, shall not mourn,
O let me teach my heart to lose its fears,
Recall'd by wisdom's voice and *Clara*'s tears".
    He said and call'd on Heav'n to bless the day,
    When back to Hinxton cot he bent his way.

At the Theatre Royal in Edinburgh

[*11 July*] I dined at Mr Sulivan's at 3. and at ½ p. 5 went with Mr W. Cadell[76] to the Theatre to see Mrs Siddons,[77] who was to make her first appearance in Lady Randolph in Douglas. The Boxes and Pit at Edinburgh are the same price, and Mr Hill, the bookseller, at Mr Sulivan's desire, had given me instructions how I might get thro the boxes into the Pitt with great ease, and which we accordingly did.

The house is neat, but not what would be expected in the New Town of Edinburgh. The heat was very great and the audience called to have the green curtain drawn up. Upon its not being done, a man climbed on to the stage from the Pitt and went behind the scenes. He returned and said "he could not find the way to draw it up, and they would not shew him how". Upon some of the audience laughing, he took hold of the curtain and tore off near a quarter of it. This was applauded by the audience: such are the manners of the Edinburgh Theatre.

The subject of the curtain which is let down between the acts is a Pyramid inscribed with the names of Thomson and Home. The Genius of Scotland is represented standing between Tragedy and Comedy, attended by Music and dancing. On one side is a perspective view of the castle, on the other the College as it will appear when finished.

I had promised myself much pleasure in seeing Douglas, a play written by a Scotchman and founded on a Scotch story, performed in the capital, and the principal character sustained by the first actress in the world. But great was my disappointment, for even the *Costumi* [sic] were not preserved, and it did not seem to have the advantages of dress and scenery that it enjoys in London.

It is needless to say that the acting of Mrs Siddons was excellent; but in the smallness of the house there is an advantage in hearing, which is lost at Drury Lane. Her son, Henry Siddons,[78] performed young Norval, and well. The mother and son, acting together in their respective characters, certainly added to the interest of the piece.

Of the other performers I have nothing to say in commendation. The Glenalvon of Mr Woods,[79] is greatly esteemed at Edinburgh. But it appeared to me to be *acting* and not nature; he had too much strut and grimace. Lord Randolph and old Norval were very bad.

It is told of the Scotch, that when the Play of Douglas is performed, they exclaim "Where are ye now Wally Shakspeare". To compare Mr Home to Shakspeare is injustice to him. His compositions must shrink from the comparison. Scotland cannot boast a Shakspeare. But with Otway and Rowe[80] Mr Home's name may always be mentioned as one of the brightest ornaments of the Drama...

Mrs Siddons having left the stage for the night and the play being finished, I was not induced to stay the farce, tho Mr Woods was to play one of his principal characters; I was so little pleased with his Glenalvon, that I had no expectations from his Petruchio...

[*13 July*] ... I called on M^r W^m. Cadell, who made me stay dinner, and at ¼ past 5 I set off for the Theatre, and thro the boxes, got the first into the pit. The Play was the Gamester.[81] One of the best, and most interesting of our English Tragedies. The story is domestic and natural, and comes more immediately home to the feelings of an audience, as misfortunes they are all subject to either in themselves or friends, than the cares and troubles of greatness, to which, but few, in comparison, can ever be exposed. Tho written in prose, the rhythm of the sentences is so excellent as never to offend the ear, and the thoughts are always just, often moral and religious, and frequently poetic...

The Mrs Beverley of Mrs Siddons is one of her finest characters, and a true picture of conjugal fidelity. Her scene with Stukely in the 3^d. Act is unrivalled. Her manner of saying "I gave them (her jewels) to a husband". And her reply to Stukely's saying "he gave them to a mistress"—"No, on my life he did not" and then "Ill not believe it—He has no mistress;—or, if he has, why is it told to me?"—are all in the very first style of nature. But her answer, upon Stukely's declaring his passion for her, while "the lightning is flashing from her eyes,"—"Would that these eyes had Heaven's own lightning, that, with a look, thus I might blast thee!" was like a flash of lightning indeed.

In the last scene her look of despair, and her exclamation at going off after her husband's death, were truly piercing.

Mr Woods in Beverley was worse than in Glenalvon. He acted and mouthed and strutted, and yet the audience applauded him loudly. The applause to Mrs Siddons was always suppressed that no word might be lost. It reminded me of the Epigram upon Barry and Garrick:

Mark how the town received her different Lears.
To Barry she gives loud applause, to Garrick only tears.[82]

The rest of the performers were so bad that the audience hissed and laughed at them when Mrs S. was not on the stage. Henry Siddons did not perform.

It always strikes me as a great defect in a play, the performers, when the scene is out of doors, wearing full powdered heads, and their hats under their arms. It takes off from the deception, and instead of being a representation of *Nature*, it is a *play* . . .

[*15 July*] . . . I dined at the Hotel and by my usual management went to the play and got the first into the House. The play was the Grecian Daughter,[83] which is upon the whole a heavy piece, and the language inflated. The situations however are fine, and Mrs Siddons in Euphrasia was every thing an author and an audience could wish. She was dressed like a Grecian statue, in fine white linen drapery, with a girdle of coloured stones, and a circle of Jewels round her head. The loose-flowing robe was uncommonly becoming. Every look and every attitude was a fine subject for a statue. In the scene with Dionysius in the (5th?) Act, where Philotas gives the feigned account of Evander's death, her change of look from fear and horror, to exulting joy, her relapse to fear, and confidence again are wonderful, and her almost speechless gratitude to Philotas, when Dionysius is gone is truly touching. But her stabbing the Tyrant in the last scene is one of the finest pieces of acting I ever saw. After striking him, and his falling, she seemed filled with horror at the idea of killing a man, yet thankful for the deliverance of her father; and sinking upon her knees in gratitude, was quite overcome, and sunk to the earth. How far Mrs S. is justified in thus altering the situation, and indeed in some measure the character, I will not take upon me to determine. But if the author himself has seen it, he must allow it I think to be an improvement, and only lament, that the alteration must cease, with the improver, as no other actress now on the stage can equal the sublimity of the idea.

Young Siddons was good in Dionysius, and I saw Mr Woods in Evander with greater pleasure, perhaps from having heard that he bore a very good private character.

The play given out for Wednesday was the Stranger.[84] Had it been any other play, I should have absented myself with regret. But it is a Piece I dislike. And Mrs Haller, is, in my estimation, the worst character I ever saw Mrs Siddons perform.

Sir John Dalrymple

[*16 July, Edinburgh*] Sir John Dalrymple's servant called upon me early to say, Sir John[85] had sent the horses for me, and he would be ready to go at my time. I breakfasted with D^r. Tait, after which I dispatched some of my luggage to Cambridge, but my bundle from Kenmore was not yet come to light, and I began to think, I should never *ken* it *more*. I paid my bill and as I was coming away Mr Walker came to thank me for my favours. I told him I was not worth thanking, I was so bad a customer. He replied that I gave him my custom and therefore he was as much obliged to me as to those who spent more. This was civility, and his argument was good, tho I fear few in his line see it in that light. I should be happy to recommend Pool's and Walker's Hotels, for they are both kept by Mr W. as clean and quiet, and where all the people are civil and the provisions good and the charges reasonable.

Tho I did not like the idea of riding to Oxenford Castle, yet I did not chuse to seem to slight Sir John's obliging attention, and accordingly set off on my palfry attended by my squire. We passed the Drum, Lord Somerville's, on the right, then upon sale, thro Dalkeith, and observed Newbattle, the Marquis of Lothian's on the right, when thro Dalkeith.

Sir John was out when I reached Oxenford Castle, but I was received by Lady D. with the greatest politeness.

Oxenford Castle was the seat of the Viscount's Oxford in James the 6^{ths}. time, from whom Lady D. is descended. The old Castle was put into the present form by Robert Adams the Architect. It is a square, with turrets at the 4 corners, a wing on each side, a bow from the E. wing and another from the back. In front is a very handsome portico with turrets. The dining room is 40 foot by 28, the Drawing room 38 by 26 and the library which is over it is the same size. Here are some pictures by Jameson,[86] a scotch Painter, but school-fellow with Vandyke. They are pretty good.

On a visit of James the 6th. from England he was entertained here with his suite by Lord Oxford, and a temporary theatre was built near the house to act plays before him. James put Lord O. to so much expence that he was obliged to sell the greater part of the Estate, and all he got in return was two looking glasses, now in the house.

The Castle stands on a knowl at the edge of two glens and commands a very rich and extensive view. The Firth of Forth with the Fife hills beyond are seen from the top.

Sir J. returned by 4 and two Miss D's. made up the party at dinner.

After tea I rode with Sir J. to Preston Hall,[87] Sir J. Callandar's, close by, a scene of much magnificence and little comfort.

At supper I was treated with *hattered ket*,[88] a kind of curds and whey, a dish I believe peculiar to Scotland. At ½ past 10 the family retired to rest.

[*17 July*] Having made some inquiries of Sir John respecting his *fish soap*, he said I should see it made. Sir J. maintains a chemist, of the name of Crooks, a very ingenious man, who lives in a cottage at the gateway leading to Cranston Castle. All things had been prepared, and at 7 o'clock, my host still distressing me with his kindness in putting me on horseback, we rode up to Mr Crooks.

The discovery of making soap from fish[89] instead of oil, by Sir John Dalrymple, is likely to be of considerable advantage to many classes of society and most particularly to the Navy. Its costing 25 per cent less than soap made from oil is no trifling consideration; and its being capable of being made to wash with cold, or hard, or *salt* water, bespeaks an infinite superiority. In its present infant state it seems likely to answer every purpose of the black soap.[90] And when improved and divested of its unpleasant smell, which Sir J. hoped very soon to overcome, will rival the brown[91] and the soft.

At M[r] Crooks we found every thing in readiness. The process is very simple. A lee is first made of 3 parts potash and one lime. This is put into a boiler, and when boiling, the fish (what we that day used was damaged salted herring) is put in and stirred till the liquor is saturated, or will not dissolve any more. When cool it is about the consistence of the common soft soap and is fit for use. A Tin box of this Sir J. gave me home with me [sic], and obligingly gave me leave to set up a manufactory of it at Cambridge. In its present state, I fear, that, at Cambridge, we are too refined to use *fish soap*; and I urged its being a pursuit quite out of my way; when S[r]. J. observed that it was in any body's way to make £10,000. To this position I assented tho not to the means.[92]

A peep at life

[*19 July, Middleton*] I rose at ½ past 4 when the Dilly[93] arrived. The morning was rainy, and there was only one place vacant, which belonged to the gentleman with whom I had sat the evening before. I asked the driver to take me on the seat with him for one stage to Bankhouse.—No.—Will you take my portmanteau to Carlisle? No.—Another driver came, took the reins and drove off. I went down into the kitchin and had some conversation with the man who had driven the stage from Edinburgh (for the carriages on this road change drivers every stage) and he was very uncivil. I took him to task in a mild but firm manner, and made him more courteous. I went up stairs, finished dressing and returned to the kitchin fire, which was one of the most comfortable I ever saw. It is an oblong recess 7 feet by 4, a bench round 3 sides of it, and a window on each of these sides. The fire is in the middle of this in an iron grate 3 feet by one and one deep, with a hole below for the ashes, and a large chimney over it, round which is a shelf. The seats will hold 10 or 11 people and a bench or chairs may be set likewise on the 4th. side. It is a most sociable fireplace. Here I sat and conversed with some of the servants and read Cowper, till the family began to stir, and a fire was lighted in the parlour, and at 8 I had breakfast. The rain continued. My friend M[r] Mitchelson was absent from Middleton, or I had been well off. I amused myself however with writing part of a ballad.

Between 12 and one a gentleman's carriage drove up and a gentleman and Lady got out and the horses were taken off. I had dinner at 2 and on conversing with the Landlord, who was a very civil man, I found that the personages who got out of the chaise were servants, and were going on to Bankhouse. I desired the landlord to represent my case and ask them if they would take me on. He did, and they said they should be very happy to do it, but they feared their master would know it. I said I would not wish them to do anything at which their master would be angry, but I thought it was what any good kind of man would approve. They assented and I set off with them, and finding them very civil and even agreeable people, I desired we might pass the Evening together at Bankhouse. The gentleman had been at sea, had been in the action of the 1st. of June and was at the taking of the Cape.[94] The Lady quoted old scotch songs, had a book of hymns in her workbag, and both of them lamented their master's always travelling on a Sunday.[95] "A Poet (says D^r. Johnson in his Rasselas. ch.10) must be acquainted with all the modes of life. His character requires that he estimate the happiness and misery of every condition; observe the power of all the passions in all their combinations, and trace the changes of the human mind as they are modified by various institutions and accidental influences of climate or custom, from the sprightliness of infancy to the despondence of decrepitude". And thus, being one of those who attempt writing, I had an opportunity of seeing something of a line of life, to add to my stores in the estimate of the happiness and misery, the virtues and the vices of every condition.[96]

The house was extremely full, and I was put into a 2 bedded room with a traveller: at 12 other company came, for whom they were obliged to make up beds on the floor in another room.

Entering the Lake District

[25 July, Cockermouth] I was called at half past 6, but as it rained, I did not rise till 8. and the weather continuing wet after breakfast, I made my memorandums till 12, when as it seemed clearing, I set off, over Gillerbury moor, for Ennerdale. I lost my road and got to Eaglesfield the birthplace of Robert Eglesfield, confessor to Philippa, Queen to Edward the 3^d. and founder of Queen's College Oxford; where a very civil man put me into my way again for Pardsha gate; and passing Morgin Tarn and Lamplugh cross (loosing my way twice more) at length reached Ennerdale Bridge. The principal object in my walk was Knock Morton a high fell on the left. There are two public houses at Ennerdale bridge, which is about two miles from the Lake. Here I intended to have stopped and dined, and walked in the Evening, or the next morning, to the Lake; but a lad I overtook in my way, informed me that Jo Bowman, a statesman, who lived at Mire-side, at the edge of the Lake, "was a right honest man", and often accommodated gentlemen at his house who came thither fishing, or to see the Lake. I liked the idea of a private house better than an inn; and wishing to see something of the manners of the people in these parts, I resolved to go thither, but lost my way for the 4th. time, and got to the paper mill on the River Ehen, a good mile short of my destination. Thence I crossed the moor towards Waterside. The view from the foot of the Lake, or Ennerdale broad water as it is called, is as fine perhaps, and as much contrasted, as that of any Lake of the same size. Below is a fine bason of water, of a somewhat circular shape; the ground round the lower end wears the most beautiful features, while the upper end is environed by wild crags and lofty mountains. This may truly be reckoned one of the passes into the Highlands of Cumberland. On the left rises the mountain called Herdhouse, Bowness knot below it, and Windsor crag below that: Latterborough, with some little wood on its side, stretches beyond; in front, Pillar and steeple and the coves rise supereminent: on the right, Side fell or the Kings forest, formerly a deer park, and crag fell with Angling stone, a bold crag projecting into the water, below it. At the S.W. end of the Lake stands Craig, a white house amid a few trees, and on the N.W. on a rising ground, How Hall, belonging to M[r] Senhouse, once the residence of that family. An Island rises in this broad part of the Lake, in a very nice point of view, but it is only a small bare rock. It might however be easily enlarged, by bringing the loose stones from the side of the Lake, which would be improved in many places by their being removed. It should be both enlarged and raised, and with a little soil to set the trees growing, it might be planted, and would soon form a pleasing feature in the scene. If a stone hut were added for the accommodation of Fishers, it would form a delightful retreat. M[r] Price's Essays on the Picturesque would furnish some useful hints[97] on this head. A single stone also appears above the water in another place. The same advantage might be taken of this and another Island formed, still adding to the beauty of this interesting Lake. Windsor crag and Angling stone would be greatly improved by the addition of some trees.

The Island is the haunt of water fowl; the Lake affords Trout, Char[98] and Perch.

I had visited this Lake 2 years before, but the day was unfavourable and we saw it only in the approach from Buttermere by Flutering Tarn and from Windsor crag. I was even then much pleased, but did not see so much of it, nor to such advantage, as now. I find some of the names of the mountains different to what they were in my former memorandums:[99] those on the right hand are there called Iron Crag, Boater Crag, Ravlig and Angling crag. I then made my minutes from a peasant I spoke with on the spot, and now Jo Bowman was my informer.

I reached Mire side between 5 & 6, and entering the neat habitation of Jo, inquired If I could be accommodated for the night? and was answered in the affirmative by M[rs] B with much complacency. I was more tired and stiff this day than I had been since I set out; it arose perhaps in great measure from the roads being very greasy which made my feet slip about;

and possibly the little irritation of mind, which arises from loosing ones way, had contributed to my feeling the fatigue more sensibly. I was glad therefore to sit down in a large old fashioned arm chair, by a nice turf fire, and rest myself. My kind hostess was eager to prepare something for my refreshment, and on my chusing my favourite meal, tea was quickly prepared. Jo soon entered, and I found both him and his wife very plain good sort of people. They have two sons and a daughter. Jo is what is called a statesman, that is one who has a small estate of his own. He keeps 8 cows and about 900 sheep . . .

An Irish gentleman, during the troubles[100] in his own Country the former summer, had sought a refuge from the miseries of civil war in this tranquil spot. He remained with them some time, and boarded with them in their plain simple way. For this they charged him 7ˢ. per week. His chief amusements were reading and fishing. He had likewise a turn for agriculture. Had I not been limited to time, and had other objects in view, I should undoubtedly have remained here at least a few days: perhaps weeks would here have seemed no more. It is indeed a delightful retreat, near the water, and sequestered among trees. A neighbour of Jo's has a boat on the Lake, which he lets out at 1ˢ. per day. Such is the difference in the charges where extravagance has not taught men to lose sight of moderation.

I crawled down thro a pleasant shaded lane to the waterside in the Evening; it was still and soothing; the sun set was glorious.

I supped with the family on barley cake and butter, and milk with cream in it, a delicious repast; and as I always wish to conform to the custom of the house I am in, retired to rest at nine, for which my fatigue made me the more ready. I had a very comfortable bed and rested well. I had no fault to find, but that of the window not opening, which made the room close.

Pastoral simplicity at Wasdale Head

[26 July] At Gosforth I observed in the churchyard a stone cross about 12 or 13 foot high, with curious figures carved on it. Crossed the river Bleng, and winding over a hill, soon got into Nether Wastdale, but the Lake is not visible to the traveller till he is almost close to it. The view is rich, consisting of houses situated among wood and crag. The rocks which screen the water close the scene below and form a middle distance, the savage mountains at the head of the Lake the distance.

Reached Nether Wastdale Chapel and the public house a little beyond it, at past four. The Host and Hostess were out making hay, and only an old woman and superannuated man were left in the house. I got some bread and cheese and beer, for they had nothing else in the house, not even eggs.

I now found it would be near 6 miles to Wastdale head, tho Jo had told me it was only 3, and there is no public house there. It was too far to go and return hither, and indeed the place was so poor that I did not wish it.

137

In this dilemma it struck me that possibly I might meet with such another accommodation as on the former night; and on asking the question, the old woman told me "Any body there would give me a bed; but Thomas Tysen or Isaac Fletcher were statesmen, and I should get well off with either of them". As I came to see men, as well as scenery, and wished to compare men and manners in all stations and in all countries, and now in particular to contrast English with Scotch manners, I resolved to try my chance and soon after 5 again set off.

The way lay thro lanes for about a mile to the water's end. When arrived at it, the most savage of the Lakes lay before me, for I think it even surpasses Wyburn in that respect. It is about 3 m. long and ¾ of a mile broad. It is said never to freeze, and to be so deep, that a line of 50 fathom, at only a stone's throw from the side, near the head of the Lake, would not fathom it. The fish are Trout, Char & Perch: the farmer at whose house I lodged told me he caught a red trout of 14 [sic] weight some years ago. Salmon come into this Lake at the latter end of the year.

The mountains on the right rise almost perpendicularly from the water, those on the left slope more, rising in the most rugged forms, their names are Bell-rib, High-fell and Yeaborough in front Kirk fell, Great Gavel and Lingmel. Scafell and screes are the boundaries on the right, the latter extending with a steep shattered side for 2 miles. These mountains are more rude than those at the upper end of Ennerdale, with less vegetation and more beaten by storms. From the top of screes the farmers get their ochre wherewith they *rud* their sheep. The rains have washed down the loose stone, and the ochre streaks the grey side with red streaks. A few fields, nicely penciled out, appear at the head of the Lake. There is only one small Island, or rock, near the shore towards the lower end of the lake. The road runs just above the water, and is up and down crags.

Crossed a stream, called Nether-beck, at a bridge, which is one boundary of a small Vale, running up to the left, called Bowder dale. It contains 2 or 3 houses and a few inclosures. Over-beck is the boundary the other way.

Looking down the Lake from the head, the view is still very grand, still the same rude barriers rise on each side, and tho the rocks at the lower end are small in comparison, yet they are finely varied. At the S.W. corner is a kind of square terrace, resembling a Roman camp. I was not aware of it when on the spot, or I should have explored it, and I did not return that way.

Leaving the water Wastdale head opens to the view very soft and beautiful; it is a perfect flat at the bottom of the most rugged mountains, and extends about a mile, when the road ascends the steeps to Styehead in Borrowdale, and thence to Keswick ... The flat is divided into inclosures and is prettily sprinkled with houses shaded by trees. Lingmel beck waters the S.E. side, and Row beck the N.W.[101] It is much intersected by other small streams besides these, and parts of the meadows are very swampy. The scene was enlivened by Cattle and Haymakers: the long shades of Evening overspread the valley and the sides of the mountains, while the setting sun just gilded their tops: "The river, rushing over its pebble bed imposed a silence with a stilly sound" and all was serenity and delight.

The house of Thomas Tysen being rather nearer than Isaac Fletcher's, I repaired thither, and, on making my wants known, was welcomed in with much readiness and civility. I found my host and hostess plain good kind of people, who understood the true hospitality of letting me have my own way, and I had tea and went to rest soon after 9, where I found a very comfortable and neat room, even approaching to elegance: I had a bason with water and towel set for me, and the only fault I found with the sheets was that they were finer than I liked.

In this sequestered, and innocent spot, if innocence is anywhere to be found, there is neither public house, shop, nor artificer of any kind. They are obliged to go as far as Gosforth, 10 miles, to have their horses shod. It is 16 miles from Keswick and the same from Egremont, the nearest market towns; but as their soil produces little more than sufficient for their own use, the distance from a market is not of material consequence. Yet these friendly mountaineers, during the summer months, while the snow is off the mountains, keep up a social intercourse with the inhabitants of the neighbouring vallies. Mine host, had he not been detained at home by his own concerns, was to have gone this evening over the mountains (about 10 miles) to a sheep-sheering in Ennerdale.

Here is a chapel of Ease to Nether Wastdale, but it has not the right of burial. Service is performed every Sunday, and the clergyman resides constantly, having no other duty nor employment besides teaching a few boys. His stipend is about £30 per an^m.

At the same time that I would recommend this spot to the curious traveller, as well worthy his notice, I cannot forbear adding a *caution* backed by _entreaty_, that he do not introduce luxury, extravagance and vice into these retreats of pastoral simplicity. Let him put off and forget the dissipated world before he approaches them. Their difficulty of access has, as yet, secured them from the visits of the great with splendid equipages, and a dissolute retinue of servants; and the seducer, the drunkard, the common swearer and blasphemer, the gamester and the prodigal with their trains of Envys, Hatreds & Malignancies, are, I hope, as yet strangers to them: the lover of the Works of nature, as a humble pedestrian, will, I hope, alone traverse these delightful regions; should *Sin* overleap the barriers of this little paradise, and teach them vices,—the names of which they would be strangers to, but for their prayers to the Almighty to defend them from them,—tremendous will be his account at the last solemn audit: to his own burden of guilt will be added that of every one, whom his wilful or unguarded profligacy has corrupted.

[27 July] I rose at 6, after a good night's rest. The morning was fine, and I went to see the waterfall a little above the house. It comes from very rude rocks in two falls. The upper is a white sheet, and the lower, (which is perhaps about 15 or 16 feet) in a torrent of white foam sloping off to the right; while on the left, there are small trickling streams running into the same bason. A green hill rises above, and the right hand bank is prettily wooded with a variety of trees, round some of which the honeysuckle entwines and shews its elegant flowers, scenting the air with its perfumes. An ash tree grows on the left, and a very small mountain ash below that: the best place for viewing the cascade is from a large stone in the river just below. This Cascade is about the size of the lowest fall at Rydal, and is scarcely inferior to it in point of beauty: a little art would make it a formidable rival.

I insisted upon breakfasting with my host and hostess at their usual hour, which was 7, and the meal was neat and excellent. When we had finished, Thomas Tysen offered to set me on my road in his way to the hayfield, while his wife and servants accompanied the cart another road. The ale-bottle was produced, and on declining to drink so early in the morning, my refusal was received with complacency.

When about to depart I desired to know what I had to pay. "I was kindly welcome to what I had had". I pressed it farther, but they would not make any charge, nor would they accept money, when I offered it in the form of a present. Not having any other trifle I could offer, when I parted from my friend Thomas, I took a silk handkerchief from my neck, and insisted upon his accepting it as a memorial: he complied, with reluctance, adding "it was too bad".

Arrival at Ambleside

[27 July] The road in ascending Hardknot is very steep, in a zigzag direction and covered with loose stones. The traveller, unless the season is very dry, will be much amused with the mountain torrents. When near the top, look back upon a very fine view over Eskdale, varied with rising grounds, the river winding beautifully through it, and a very extensive view thro the mountains at the lower end, I suppose to the sea in clear weather, but it was now too hazy to distinguish it.

Descended by a road equally bad to a stream, the head of the Duddon, and crossing it, accompanied it to the top of Wrynose. Here are three large stones on the left of the road laid in a triangular form, called the 3 shire stones, each one standing in a different county; Lancashire, Westmorland & Cumberland meeting in a point at this place. Here is a fine view thro Langdale to Windermere. I descended a steep road covered with loose stones. This was formerly the great communication between this part of Cumberland and Westmorland, before the roads by Hawkshead & Keswick were made to Kendal, and the pack horses, with immense loads and their bells, used to toil up these steeps; they used to travel in companies, and a train of them winding up or down the ascent, with their tinkling bells must have been a curious sight.

The rocks at the head of Langdale are very rude, and there is a view up another branch of the vale to the left. Pass a rock rising up[102] in the middle of the dale, something resembling a Cap, a single tree grows on the side like a tufted feather. See little Langdale Tarn, and a conical hill, with a flat top, rising beyond it: the view is well-wooded and rich. I had not long descended before a mist came upon Wrynose.

I was now in a country with which I was well acquainted, but it was such as to please on frequent visits. The wood was suffering its periodical spoliation in several places as I proceeded towards Ambleside. The Charcoal heaps, with the curling smoak rising from them, and their screens of plashed brush wood to keep off the wind, and the figures employed about them, are interesting objects in such a scene. M[r] Gisborne in his Walks in a Forest has given a very pleasing picture of the whole process.[103] The wood sells upon an avarage at about £7 per acre.

Passed Colwith Force, and round the head of Elterwater, to see the *reedy* lake,[104] and thence by Skelwith Force to Ambleside, where I arrived about 6.

I went to my old lodgings, intending, if they were disengaged, to take them for a week, while I waited the arrival of my friend. But they were engaged and re-engaged[105] for the rest of the summer, and I found my worthy hostesses much incommoded by their lodgers, whose servants intruded into their apartments and occasioned them great inconvenience and trouble at their advanced ages. The great resort of company to this place renders lodgings scarce and dear, and greatly encreases the price of provisions. A wealthy gentleman from London and his lady last year occupied these lodgings, and sooner than not have every thing they wanted, gave 2[d]. for an egg, the same for a quart of milk, and every thing else in proportion. The consequence is the price has been raised to the inhabitants, several of which have resorted to this place as a cheap retirement, and moderation is changed into extortion. No longer back than 11 years ago my lodgings were let at 3[s]. per week, 4 years ago for 5[s]. I was the first, who, 2 years before, had given half a guinea; they are now new-papered and let at one guinea. Even 3 years ago a gentleman had a whole house, furnished, at 3[s]. per week.

Delicious Grasmere

[*29 July, Ambleside*] Had the morning been fair I intended walking to breakfast at Troutbeck and making a round of calls; but as it rained I determined to wait in the hope of the following day being finer. At 10 it held up, and I walked out, first directing my steps to Rydal, again to behold the

beauties of that place. Pelter bridge had been rebuilt and in a less picturesque style than before; the stones with which it is constructed are too
much shaped and the whole too much plaistered with mortar. The mellow-
ing hand of time, however, will improve it. The lower cascade must ever
delight. Passing the small but pleasing Lake of Rydal water, I came to "delicious Grasmere",[106] which for pastoral beauty surpasses all the others. It
has forfeited however its title to a part of the praise which Gray bestowed
upon it: "Not a single red tile, no flaring Gentleman's house, or garden
wall, break in upon the repose of this little unsuspected paradise; but all is
peace, rusticity and happy poverty, in its neatest most becoming attire".[107]
On the E. side of the Lake some little way up the side of the hills a new
built white house with a large garden wall stares the traveller full in the
face, and forms a most dreadful blemish in the scene. The lover of the picturesque certainly has no right to expect of the proprietor of such a place
that he sacrifice his garden and his comfort merely to please his eye. But
why may not both tastes be gratified? and, if the garden is wanted, surely a
natural and pleasing screen might be made of a plantation, a variety of
groups of trees, which should render the place in all respects more delightful to the owner and the visitor.

Windermere

[*30 July*] I passed the Parsonage near a row of Pines, and reached the Ferry
just as three gentlemen, whose faces were known to me at Cambridge,
were about to enter the boat. I crossed with them, and we ascended together to Mr Braithwaits summer house built upon West's first station.[108]
The building and the trim plantations of flowering shrubs about it, are in
much too finished and artificial a manner for the style of the place. The
building consists of an upper room, and a lower, where a person lives who
takes care of it. The room is a very good one and handsomely fitted up.
The chimney piece is of Kendal marble. The E end of it is 3 sided, with a
window each way commanding the delightful prospects described in Wests
guide. A picturesque cottage on this spot shaded by a few trees, had been a
more appropriate building and erected at half the expence.

The travellers I had joined having some idea of extending their Journey
into Scotland, I mentioned my being just returned out of that country.
Mr Pennants remark[109] that Windermere is *here* what Loch Lomond is
there, naturally produced a comparison between the two, and, as I was
talking with Englishmen, I made no scruple in giving the decided preference to Windermere, tho I do not consider it as the first of our Lakes.
Ullswater I think may claim the preeminence, and Scotland can boast of
finer Lakes than Lomond. The upper end of Loch Lomond, which I consider as the finest, is certainly deficient in wood. The Lower part is too

Windermere from the inn window at Bowness, apparently sketched in 1799

vast in extent, its Islands too large, and its barrier mountains too small for picturesque effect. The grand feature of the Scotch Lake is the vast mountain Ben Lomond, but the mountains at the head of Windermere, Fairfield, Langdale pikes, &c are equally grand in proportion to the scene, and more pleasing in their forms. The sinuous form of Windermere is much finer and its shores more pleasingly diversified with bays and promontories. The view down Windermere is far superior to that down L. Lomond.

Hawkshead and Esthwaite Water

[*30 July*] The Vale and Lake of Esthwait with its sloping hills, scattered woods and cottages; and the town and church of Hawkshead are very pretty, but he who sees it from the road above Belmount sees it to the best advantage. In no country perhaps is so much taste displayed as by the cottagers in these parts. The form of the houses and their chimneys, the porticoes to the doors, the climbing shrubs & trees planted against the house and partly shading the windows; sometimes taste is displayed in the variety of pattern in the lead work even of the windows themselves; and with high trees either overhanging or placed in advantageous situations near the habitations. Sometimes however false taste intrudes and a bright white, with red or blue, sometimes both, coloured coping stones, and blue slate, give it too trim and glaring an effect.

A wet walk from Ambleside to Keswick

[*2 August*] I packed up in the morning and then called at my old lodgings where my kind hostesses would fain have had me put a leg of dried veal into my portmanteau, which I declined, accepting instead what she called an Ambleside fruit cake, which had been made on purpose for me. I made another call or two and at 10 our whole party[110] set off to see the Rydal Cascades.

I had never before staid at the Inn at Ambleside, I can not therefore refrain from mentioning the civility of the Landlord Mr Wilcox and his wife. The house is very neat and quiet, nor are their charges, all things considered, very unreasonable. I was not charged for my bed, tho I had two rooms and no horses. It is true I had ordered my *half pint* of wine every day, *for the good of the house*. He only charged 1^s. per mile for the chaise, tho my friends had paid 15^d. from Manchester to Ambleside. The dearest thing is boat hire the boat to the ferry being 5^s. 2 men 3^s. and 6^d. for ale for them being in all 8^s..6^d.

Mr Wilcox I understand gives out that he does not wish people to *stay* any time at his house, those who come and go away again soon, answering his purpose best. And Mrs Wright at Low Wood complains that the gentry now never eat supper: "She does not understand it".

To my friend and myself who had seen the higher Cascade at Rydal in such full force on Wednesday Evening it appeared now comparatively tame. The lower had just the proper quantity of water, not enough to be turbulent, and yet sufficient to come in a thin stream over the point between the two divisions of the left hand fall.

A chaise waited for us at the bottom of the lane, and I now found the inconvenience of being attached to a party. My friend would have me go with them, so I rode on the seat with the driver, but the rain coming on and the plaid soon getting wet, I determined to take the Umbrella and try my chance on foot; but the wind was so high and the rain drove so hard against my back, that I was soon wet. The streams down the sides of the mountains were very fine: "Huge Helvellyn stream'd with tears". The rain suited the gloom of "savage Wyburn",[111] but destroyed the beauty of the Vale of S^t. John. Skiddaw and Saddleback were not to be seen, and but little of the view from Castle Rig. Finkle street hause[112] however shewed his impudent face thro the gloom.

I reached Keswick about 4 when Mr Wood at the Queen's Head[113] was so rejoiced to see me for the 3^d. time that he would shake hands with me.

It happened to be Lammas fair at Keswick, formerly a considerable fair for Leather, but now much declined, and the wet day had prevented the country people from assembling to shew their best cloaths.

After dinner we walked to Crosthwaites Museum[114] where I was sorry to find my old friend the Admiral in but indifferent health.

The Museum should certainly be visited by every body, but on a wet day it is really a very great acquisition to the place, and some time may be passed there very agreeably. He has all the views of the Lakes, his own plans of them, sells West's Guide &c. The coins, spars, specimens of wood &c &c, musical stones and the Chinese Gong or Loo are very fine; but he has many things which are trifling, such as 6lb of lead swimming in 4lb of quicksilver, a collection of tobacco pipes of all nations—16 different ways of spelling the proper name of Braithwaite—and 11 different names[115] for a small stream all in common use in Cumberland.

There is another Museum in Keswick, kept by Hutton, the Guide and Botanist, who has a very good collection of the Plants and fossils of the country. It is a great pity that the Admiral and he are bitter enemies. Though of the same trade I see no reason but they might agree well. Both Museums are worth seeing and each might do a good turn and recommend the other. The Admiral however has his likes as well as his dislikes. M[r] Pocklington[116] has been his friend, and he returns it by standing up for him and his taste on all occasions. He is very angry with M[rs] Murray for having spoken slightingly of it in her tour, and refused to sell that book as well as the Opera of the Lakers for the same reason.

The shores of Derwentwater

[3 August] Our party set off on foot after breakfast for Lowdore. The road was dirty owing to the rain of the day before. The first spot which particularly arrested our attention was Wests 3[d]. station,[117] to his account of which I know not that there is anything to be added. As we proceeded, a man on horseback passed us, having two pencils in his hat, emblems of his being a sketcher: he seemed a *kiddyish*[118] sort of a person. The Guide and Botanist followed him on horseback. As we passed Barrow Cascade Hall, he came out at the gate with the guide on a full trot and said to the guide "Its a pity there was not more water", and off he went again.

M[r] Pocklington in addition to his former misdemeanours against taste, has painted the latches and hinges of his gates, the nail heads and tops of the rails, scarlet and put a large brown J.P. on each gate . . .

When we reached Lowdore Kiddy was sketching on the wall below the bridge.

We proceed [sic] thro the wood by the bank of the mill to the bottom of the fall. It was finer than I had yet seen it, yet it would have been still improved by a greater quantity of water, as from the vastness of its features it requires a very great torrent to see it to any advantage. The man who shews it said that the former Evening all the stones were covered. After

The Falls of Lodore, apparently sketched in 1799

viewing it from the seat below, I climbed to a rock amid the cascade, where I stood while the waters thundered on all sides of me, and the spray enveloped me in mist. Two towering perpendicular rocks rise on each side, a wilderness of large loose stones lay between them, over which the waters dash in white, or rather tawny foam, not in an equable current, but shooting out at intervals beyond the stones over which they rush. Trees grow on the rocks on each hand, and some are even rooted in the stones over which the waters roar. This fall is about 171 feet . . .

We got a pastoral repast of bread and butter and milk at the *Hotel*, and my friend and I set forward for Watinleth. My friend being less experienced in climbing mountains than myself, would ascend the rock a little to the left of the waterfall. With great labour we reached the top, and got into this most surprizing valley in the bosom of the mountains, where

146

rude rocks, rising on each side, have precipitated fragments into the vale, where trees grow upon the rocks and in the meadows below, thro which the rapid river of Watinleth, the feeder of Lowdore, rolls its course. Near the village the shooting and roar of a waterfall caught our attention. We went to the side of the river, but found it must be viewed from the opposite side. Just below the bridge at the village is a pretty view of the small Lake or Tarn. It is bounded by rude crags and a promontory on the right breaks the sheet of water. The river & bridge occupy the middle of the foreground, a large pollard oak and rock are on the right, and a barn backed by trees, oak and pine are on the left. We crossed the bridge and then descended and viewed the waterfall from below it on the West side. The rocks are very fine both in form and tint and are advantageously wooded. A peaked rock stands up in the middle of the river. The water coming from the top meets from two different ways, falling in one mass of tawny foam. It is then lost to the sight behind a bold piece of rock, and again rushes forward compressed into one sidelong mass of foam: a small stream just trickling over from above on the left hand gives a variety. After this it has another descent of about 2 foot the width of the river, running round the peak which rises from the bed of the river and which is higher on the East than on the W. side. The fall is perhaps altogether about 16 or 17 feet. The trees are chiefly ash and birch, some little alder grows at the edge of the water in the foreground. Viewed from the top it is a scene of boiling commotion awfully grand.

We crossed the hills by the road, if such it might be called, towards Borrowdale. My friend left me to ascend the tops of the hills on the right, but as it was a chance whether the view was good and I knew my friend to be adventurous I did not accompany him. Rain came on, and I sheltered under a wall, till I found the wet drop upon me and then proceeded. I had a fine view from the hill into Borrowdale and of the villages of Rosthwait and Seathwait, the clouds and rain hid the tops of the mountains. Descending into the dale the waters were greatly out and the meadows quite a swamp. Before I reached Bowdar Stone my friend overtook me: he had not found his excursion answer.

Mr Pocklington has built a house by Bowdar Stone and has cleared the wall and loose stone away and I think considerably spoiled the effect. I suppose he will next paint it white and scarlet.

Passing the village of Grange and Lowdore stopped to see Barrow Cascade behind Mr Pocklington's house. The perpendicular height is 125 feet the breadth perhaps 9 or 10. It falls in sprinkling torrents of white foam and almost covers the rock. It is never much broken into spouts nor falls in the same direction for any way together, but is an irregular thin sheet of white foam. In great rains I am told it is very tremendous. But its effect depends less upon a quantity of water than Lowdore. The whole of it is well wooded and seen to advantage from several places. Two trees grow amid the fall at the very top; and near the top on the left hand side, but happily not seen from the station below, is a building, the outside of which is white and the inside scarlet.

Ascent of Skiddaw

[6 August] Being fatigued with my former days walk I was not up so early as usual, and when I came down to breakfast I found that the party intended ascending Skiddaw as the morning promised fair. Horses were engaged for such as chose to ride and Stephen Graves attended as our Guide. At half past 10 we all set off on foot and crossed the Greeta at the Alpine bridge, passed Monk's Hall and met the horses at spooler green. We ascended on the W. side of Latrig, and saw a party before us of 4 ladies and a guide, on their way to the top of Skiddaw, labouring up the steep ascent of Greengate.

We first rested at Luckenhow and thence had a fine view of the Lake and mountains of Derwent water, and of the Vale of Keswick and Lake of Bassenthwait, much the same as from the top and side of Latrig on Sunday.

Passed over Gale, a green hill, and likewise Green Hawse, on the right of which is Latrig Intake, then lately purchased by the Bishop of Llandaff of Mr Hassel.

We next climbed Green Gate, a steep ascent on the S.E. edge of the mountain whence we had a fine view of Catchdecam and Helvellyn to Dunmail raise and into Naddale, separated from S^t. John's Vale by a rock, called Ridge, or S^t. John's Crag, beyond which, Great How, another rock, covered with wood, rises out of the middle of the dale. Wanthwaite on the N. of S^t. John's Vale stretches towards the foot of Saddleback. Large pieces of marble are scattered over this part of the ascent of Skiddaw. A little higher we again rested, previous to climbing the steepest part of the Journey: on the E. was Whitbeck and beyond it Lonscale hill, the property of the Bp. of Llandaff. Arriving at Clough we began to have an extensive view, as far as the Solway firth. Next to the head of Steels, then Broad end, whence we again saw the Lake of Derwent water after having lost it for some time: our guide got us some water, but it tasted very mossy.

We left the two pikes of Little Man and Carle's head on our left and ascended toward the third and highest point called Skiddaw great man, the way laying on a ridge of the mountain covered with loose slate. We here passed a gentleman with two Ladies & a guide returning homeward. They spoke with great pleasure of the view we were about to meet. We looked down on Ullock a large hill on the E. side of Bassenthwait. We reached in 2 hours and 45 minutes the great man where there are the remains of a Beacon formerly connected with Caermot and Castle Crag. Cap^{tn}. Budworth in his Ramble[119] imagines that there have been beacons likewise on the Top of Helvellyn and on the top of Old man at the head of Coniston

Lake. From this I took the idea of having a building erected on this spot to accommodate gentlemen, who might wish to remain any time on the mountain to see the sun rise or set, as the air is generally so cold, even on the hottest day as to make it scarcely possible to remain any time. I mentioned my idea to the Guide and advised him and his comrades to put it into execution. A small room, with a fire place and a long seat on each side to sleep upon, is all that would be required. The very spot itself affords materials sufficient for the purpose; lime only need be brought up, which might be done by the poneys. Care must be taken to make the building very strong.

To contemplate from this height the stupendous world of wonders below amid the golden blaze of noon, or the crimson resplendence of Evening, to mark its various changes of colour, light & shade till the whole melted from the faint twilight into the dark gloom of night or the solemn illumination of moonlight; and then again to observe the first faint dawning of morning, its cool and sober mists and colours, till it again awakened into all the glory of day; must be a feast of the most delightful kind to every admirer of the works of nature and the great author of them all; and I hope that some day or another I may yet experience so sublime a gratification.

Shivering now with cold we looked down on the vast mass of mountains

Coniston Water, apparently sketched in 1799

149

called Skiddaw Forest, among which the river Caldew takes it rise. Saddle-back is the principal object here, and the Ullswater, Windermere and Coniston mountains stretch round to those of Borrowdale on the S. Thro these we had a distant view of Windermere like two silver streaks among the hills. The Buttermere mountains more on the W. a most tremendous troubled sea of rock and crag; and on the N.W., N & N.E. an extensive stare over flat country, bounded by the Solway Firth, the mountains of Scotland and the Cheviot hills beyond.

In this flat tract I thought I discovered with the guide's assistance the Isle of man, the towns of Cockermouth and Carlisle, Ireby and villages in-numerable. Ingleborough is seen on the S.E. on a clear day, but it was now becoming very hazy. This highest point is not to be seen from Keswick or Lowdore, but from Dunmail raise, Ouse bridge or the road over the fells to Gowbarrow Park and Patterdale.

We proceeded to *Far mount*, a spot beyond great man, and looked down on a hill with a very steep side, called Gibralter, and beyond that to Over water, a pretty Tarn on the north of the Carlisle road. Returned back and from the Western side of Carle's Head looked down the precipitous side covered with loose shale or slate into the ravine below: this is the steepest part, but even this to a person on a pair of steady legs is not sufficiently so to inspire any fearful ideas. Those who have ascended Ingleborough, Ben Lomond and Ben-y-glo, will find the ascent of Skiddaw comparatively easy and pleasant. I got on to one of the horses for a few paces to see what it was [sic]: I was as well pleased when I found myself on my legs again.

In our descent we had abundant opportunity for attending to the views, and we produced some new effects with our glasses.[120] Tho the objects were distant yet they were so large as to be seen with effect in the Gray. The Claude Lorrain gave it a most pleasing moonlight but seen thro the dark red or rather orange glass it was tremendous, and with its burning glow called to mind that day, "in the which the Heavens shall pass away with a great noise, and being on fire shall be dissolved, and the elements shall melt with fervent heat, the earth also, and the works that are therein shall be burnt up". 2 Peter 3. 10 & 12.

About 10,000 sheep pasture Skiddaw which is a common; one man alone, who lives beyond Gibralter, has 2,000, another has 1,000.

We put up some dotrell[121] about half way. Towards the bottom we changed our road and returned by Ormathwait and the Vicarage[122], taking those two delightful views of the Lake.

Improvements were making in the land at the foot of Skiddaw, by drain-ing, paring and burning, and lime, and a piece of ground of about 4 acres, which a short time since let at about 30^s. now had a crop of oats worth 5 or 6£. We returned to the Inn just about 4 and after dinner I went with M^{rs}. D. to Huttons. His collection is not so good as Crosthwaits but is worth seeing. He has a good collection of minerals & plants of the country and several other curiosities, particularly a fine Indian gong. There are besides coins, shells and stuffed birds.

Derwentwater and Borrowdale

[7 *August*] We again landed at Lowdore and had the cannon[123] fired twice at 1^s & 6^d. each time. Half a pound of gunpowder is put in. The piece is pointed against Blea crag. The first explosion was uncommonly grand, resounding from the rock and dying away, again resounding from Ashness and Lowdore crags, dying away and a third time reverberated from Manesty banks. At the second return it reechoed against Lowdore crags, swelled into Borrowdale, was lost and swelled again and finely lost among the mountains of Buttermere. We walked on to Bowdar Stone where I left the party and proceeded onwards in search of a waterfall at the highest end of Borrowdale beyond Seathwait my friend not having enterprize enough for the undertaking. I stopped at the public house at Rosthwait, but the people were all out at hay; so I sent a boy to them to say I should be back in 2 hours and should want to eat, and pursued my way thro Seatoller to Seathwait. Quite at the top of the mountain on the right stands a house 1 story high, thro the parlour of which is the entrance into the black wad mines.[124] About half way down a level is now driving to take off the water and between these is another house of one floor thro which is another entrance to the wad mines. Sourmilk gill falls from the topmost point of rocks a little beyond, and runs in various directions foaming down the side: after rain it must be very fine. Seathwait is almost at the head of the western branch of Borrowdale and consists of about 6 or 7 houses with a few trees, a largish yew tree stands behind and the rocks rise very fine on all sides. Farther on a little to the left stands a single house surrounded by fir and other trees.

Several streams run thro this dale, the meadows were all wet and the road a perfect stream. The marks of winter's deluges were tremendous. In Cumberland they do not use forks for making hay in these parts but the Haymakers shake it and spread it with their hands. In Borrowdale it is brought to the stack upon horses. Keeping along the river side I soon had a good distant view of the fall above the trees. I followed the stony bed of the beck, keeping it on my left, thro a thick grove of small oaks and other wood till the path ended and I got opposite the fall. The rocks on each side open wide and are thinly scattered over with trees. The rock in front is nearly perpendicular and the water falls in 2 streams. That on the right is broad, nearly perpendicular and sprinkling; the left hand one runs first obliquely from right to left and then falls more perpendicular. It may be about 20 or at most 25 feet high. A clump of old ash trees stand by themselves on the shelving bank on the right. The descent of the bed of the water from the fall is very steep and stony and ash and birch trees grow in it. With this fall I was much pleased tho my expectations were disappointed, for Stephen had told me it was 40 or 50 yards high and finer than Lowdore or Scale force and fell into a very fine bason. When I got home I told him this, he seemed much surprized, and said, "then I had not seen the right one, that it was higher up, and really such as he had represented. Did I not take his son to shew me?" The fact I believe was that I had said the day before in going up Skiddaw, that I thought a guide of no use, except in case of a mist coming on, or to tell the names of the mountains; and as this struck at "the Guide business", Stephen had a mind to punish me, for he never mentioned that there were *two* falls (which would have been an additional inducement for me to go) so when I saw one, I concluded it was the right and only thought that Stephen had magnified its merits. He however persisted in its being 40 or 50 yards and that there were two falls; so some other traveller must settle the matter. The best way of seeing it would be to take it in the road from Keswick thro Borrowdale and by Sparkling Tarn, & over Styhead to Wast Water. It is on the stream that runs out of Sparkling Tarn. Should I ever again visit the Lakes I shall take this route to visit my friend Thomas Tysen at Wast dale head.

It is a wonder that no persons of confined circumstances but of liberal manners and information have undertaken the office of Guides of the Lakes. Such is the case in several parts of the continent. And in England, the Masters of the ceremonies at Bath,[125] &c, are of that description. And then, if travellers did pay dear, it would be at least for pleasing manners and information. To young Artists it would be peculiarly eligible; while they were studying landscape among the most delightful scenes in nature, it might be the means of making them known and bringing them forward to public notice and patronage. A series of drawings of the adjacent country (sold at moderate prices) might form an exhibition at their lodgings which might repay their trouble both by travellers coming to see and to purchase.

Returning homeward, near Seatoller, I heard someone in a field on the right calling, and looking over the wall, a woman asked me If I was going to Keswick?—yes—Would I take a letter?—Certainly—Then pray come in at those rails—I went thro and when the woman saw as she expressed herself I was a gentleman (for so she said she did) she made a great many apologies for calling me, but which I desired her to spare. Her son I learned was going to Guinea as a surgeon and had written a letter from Liverpool to which he desired an immediate answer. His brother was in the house writing, and they were *so thronged* with hay, it would save them a great deal of trouble if I would take it. Happy in an opportunity of shewing any mark of kindness to the hospitable people of this Country I accompanied her to the house, where the young man was writing the letter. I was desired to sit down and offered some ale, which I declined, at the same time desiring milk if they had it. It was immediately set before me together with bread and butter, and a couple of eggs were boiled, upon which I made a most excellent meal. Whilst I was eating it, the good lady looked earnestly at me and paid me the compliment of saying she thought me like her son Johnathan, for whom I was to take the letter—"Just such a thin spare young man—and then he was all for milk—and when he's his black coat on!—" He had been brought up at Keswick School, and then put Apprentice to a surgeon at Whitehaven. The brother was a civil sensible man. He had raised some firs from seed, which he had planted at the back of the house and were in a flourishing condition. I took leave of them promising if I ever again came that way to call. This was the third visit I had made at a *statesman's* house during my present journey to the Lakes, and I must say that every statesman seems to deserve the character given of Will Hearty[126] in the song in the opera of the Lakers.

I called at the public house at Rosthwait, and as I have [sic] given them the trouble of coming out of the field, and did not want to eat, I gave them a small gratuity, and pursued the path up Castle Crag by a steep, and in some places, particularly the slate road, difficult climb. The slate quarry is very curious. A Castle formerly stood on the summit of this hill, but there are no remains of it unless a rude seat formed out of the solid rock, part of the ditch which surrounded it, and a well about 4 or 5 foot square and as many deep: it is not a spring and the water of course not very good. Hence Skiddaw and Saddleback are seen in a new point of view. This is Wests IVth. station and his account of it, as all his indeed are, very just.[127] I descended by the slate road on the W. side, the views of the dale and Lake continuing very fine. The road led thro a pleasant grove of birch and oak to Grange, from whence I continued on the western side of the Lake, to me a new road. The views from hence are very good, but the road is too high up the side of the mountain, which takes off from the effect of foregrounds. Tho a good deal fatigued, the Evening was so inviting that I determined to ascend Swinside, an evening view, and Wests Vth. station.[128] The sun had just sunk behind Whinlatter when I reached the summit, and gilded with a rich golden purple nearly all the eastern shore of Bassenthwait, the tops of Skiddaw and Saddleback, Cross fell far in the E., Catchdecam and Helvellyn, and Gowdar Crag &c on the eastern side of Derwent water. The rest was all in shade, a solemn and delightful contrast to the richness of the other. The Vale of Newlands, the Lake of Derwent water, the country towards Penrith, the vale of Keswick and Bassenthwait water all lay spread out before me. There was a silvery effect in the bays under the dark green wood upon the E^n. bank of Derwent water which was truly enchanting. What was silver there was of a golden hue on Bassenthwait, and the glow from the sun itself when sunk behind the dark green of the mountains was divine. The golden hue at length became a regal purple, till growing darker and darker it at length subsided into shade. The Moon in nearly the first quarter seen in the S.W. was an excellent addition to this delightful scene. Tho far above it, I was scarcely too high. It is one of the most glorious prospects I ever beheld, and I must rank this view in my list of Wonders, with that from the Calton hill at Edinburgh, Moncrief hill above Perth, and the view from Stirling Castle in Scotland. All are different but each is glorious in its way . . .

From Swinside I descended towards Foe Park; but whoever sees the view from Swinside in perfection will be detained till it is too late to enjoy that from Foe Park on the same evening, if it is now to be seen at all; for (whether I went to the right place or not, I know not) when I reached the top of the hill, it was so grown up that I could not see the prospect at all. The owners might be persuaded I hope to clear these stations. Crosthwait proposed putting up white boards to point out the stations, but as this would have interfered with the "Guide business" he feared the guides would pull them down. The spots of white I certainly should object to, but some mark might be contrived which should not be offensive to the eye.

Lost among the mountains

[*8 August*] We breakfasted before 7 and at half past took leave of Mrs D. and M^r K, who were to return in a chaise to Ambleside, and set off with my friend on foot for Ullswater. A mile and half from Keswick we turned into a field on the right to see the Druid's Temple,[129] and sat there some little time comparing past times with those present, and the comparison was in favour of our own. Pursuing our course to Naddale bridge as soon as we were over it we turned off to Shundraw and by the Mill and hill top, over the fells to Matterdale, having Mell fell on our right,[130] and to Gowbarrow Park. Turning into the Park we descended to Airay force, a very fine Cascade. Crosthwait calls it 80 feet, but they told us at the Tower it was about 45 which I think must be much nearer the mark. In measuring the height of waterfalls it is often customary to take in the depth of the bason into which it falls and which is frequently very deep. But a cascade should only be measured, I think, at the highest part which is visible at one time, and then only from the top of the fall to the surface of the bason. It was in this manner that I measured the cascades at Rydal. I would however allow both *parts* of the fall at Airey, and also at Scale force to be taken into the *height of the fall*. We next went to to Lyulph's tower to see the views from thence, and refreshing ourselves with a draft of milk proceeded. As soon as you are thro the gate nearest to Patterdale there is a very fine view down the Lake. The winding shore on the left, edged with wood all the way to the end with yew crag, a fine rock, rising above. On the left the rocks rise immediately, and almost perpendicularly from the water's edge. Soft enclosures steal up the sides of the fells at the end softening off to the distance which is terminated by a part of cross fell. This view is seen again from Styborough crag with Lyulph's tower and more of the park on the left and the Island in a good point of view. The wood here had been cut and only one or two staring trees left here and there. The wood up the rocks on the right was very fine. As we approached the *Palace*[131] I was sorry to observe that it had been new fronted since I saw it last and the tall fir tree cut down; and whitewash, red stone and blue slate made it a very flaring object. *If* it is improved as a dwelling, it certainly is not so in picturesque appearance. We reached the Kings arms at Patterdale to dinner at 2. Here my friend and I were to part. He was to cross the mountains to rejoin his party at Ambleside and proceed to Black Pool where they were going for a short time for the benefit of sea bathing; and I intended going down Ullswater to Pooley Bridge and thence to Haws water, to see Mr Holme of Mardale, which lies at the head of that lake, and from whence I had received a very hospitable invitation 3 years before. Talking however with the Landlord he told me I could easily get over the fells to Mardale, that I must get a guide at low Hartsop to shew me the way and it was not above 3 miles. As this would save me a whole day and take me a new route, I determined to try it, and we according [*sic*] set off up Patterdale. About a mile and half from the Kings Arms a cascade falls down the mountains on the right from a spring in the rock: it is a pretty good one. At Hartsop my friend and I shook hands and parted, and I soon called at a house to inquire for a guide to shew me to Hawes water. "To Ayes water? said an old man—yes—Follow the beck and its behind this mountain. Theres no need of a guide—How far is it?—A mile and a half".—I then followed the beck up the mountain. Towards the top are some very pleasing cascades. The first descent that deserves that name is nearly 20 feet in height and 6 or 7 broad. After this I saw several others, and at length reached a largish Tarn, the mountains rising very steep and in an amphitheatrical circle round it and not a single tree. I now began to find I was in a mistake, and that Ayes (or as I understood it Hayes water, which I thought was the way of their pronouncing Hawes) water was not the object of my search. The map to Wests Guide to the Lakes mentions no such place, nor did the landlord at Patterdale. Knowing however from my map, and my experience of the course of the country, that I could not be far out of my direction, and the tops of the mountains being clear and plenty of daylight before me, I resolved to try to find it ...

I crossed a stone wall to some sheep shearing folds at the lower end of the Tarn, and ascending the fells on the N. side I made towards a descent and saw into a valley, having a few houses and inclosures and a small river running through. At a distance beyond I caught a sight of Ullswater. The valley, I concluded, therefore must be Martindale, and that Hawe's water was more to the E. Unfortunately I had not my compass in my pocket. I climbed to the top of some mountains on the E. higher than the former, and thence had a very extensive view over the tops of mountains of Skiddaw and Saddleback, Fairfield, Helvellyn and other stupendous mountains, a scene truly wild and awful, and heightened by the state of mind I was in from my uncertainty respecting my way. I walked on a few paces towards an opening into a valley below, and discovered a house and inclosures. This I concluded must be my destination; or at least a place where I should meet with kindness and hospitality. I resolved therefore to make towards it, and there, at all event, to pass my night. I descended a steep all but perpendicular. The road was very bad and stony, and I soon reached a stream caused by the wet draining from the mountains. Reaching a sort of level, and after walking some little way, I found I had another descent as far or farther than the former. I soon discovered horses and cows and fell into a sort of path; these circumstances gave me spirits. Following the brook (called Rigindale beck) till I came to the inclosures, where seeing a farm house with a rock above it, I thought I remembered the situation of Mr Holme's house, and presently getting a glimpse of the Lake, I felt assured I was right, and about 6 o'clock found myself absolutely at Mr Holmes door. I knocked and was desired to walk in, and entering saw Mrs H. She remembered me, and received me with a hearty welcome, prepared tea, and the family soon coming in from the hayfield, I found myself by a hospitable fire side, with friends about me, drinking tea and well repaid for all my anxieties. We passed the Evening in conversation and between eight and nine supped on bread and butter and new milk, and soon after I retired to rest, where I should have done very well had not my kind hostess, willing to make much of me, in addition to the cloaths I desired to have on the bed, laid a sattin quilt lined with flannel, which I feared to put off lest I should hurt it.[132]

Rover's last journey

[*12 August, Wigan*] I rose at 5 intending to reach Warrington to breakfast, to get to Northwich to dinner, and see the salt mines after.

My companion, who generally kept playing about me whilst I was dressing, impatient to be moving, still lay on the carpet by the bed side, and when I left my room followed me with great reluctance; the cause of it I could not tell, and when we got out of the town of Wigan, he would fain have laid down, but I led him on. I stopped short at Ashton to rest him and get my breakfast. I offered him his usual crusts, which he refused, and would scarcely eat some scraps of meat. No coach, or conveyance was going that day to Warrington so after resting an hour we again set forward with greater reluctance than before.

At Newton was a great fair for Beasts this day, for Horses the next.

Passed by the way on the left Haddock Hall Col. Leigh's, having a very handsome entrance from the road, a grand arch with collonades and lodges at each end.

Farther on, on the right passed two very neat pretty cottages, as Lodges to the Rectory House of Winwick about 3 miles from Warrington.

Two miles short of Warrington I overtook a coalcart, and got leave for Rover to ride upon some hay at the top, whilst I attended by the side. When we reached the town, I took him out and led him to the George Inn, where the landlady, upon my asking for a room, viewed me with a very suspicious eye, and said all were full. Then said I shew me and my dog into the Kitchin. She called the waiter, who shewed me into a sort of servants hall, and presently afterwards into the Bar. Finding mine Hostess of the George not much inclined to be civil, I briefly stated my case, and told her that she was obliged by law to take me in[133] and provide me with food if I required it, after some farther words both she and the waiter became civil.

My honest companion seemed to grow worse. Upon touching his right shoulder he cried out and supposing it to be bruised I bathed it first with brandy and then with hot vinegar, and gave him some crusts soaked in ale, which seemed to do him good. I would willingly have employed a *doctor* had I not feared his making a job of it and doing him no good after all. The cause of his disorder I was equally at a loss to ascertain. The only conjecture I could form was, that he had got bruised in the mail[134] Saturday Evening. I took him up to ride between my legs on the footboard to the box, from whence he slipt into the boot, but seemed to be easy in that situation. Unless he was hurt then, I know not when he could be, yet he ran as well as ever the next day. Being only 28 miles from my friends house, I determined to go directly thither, giving up the salt mines at Northwich, and made inquiries for a conveyance for that purpose. I had been informed at Preston, that when I got to Wigan there was a boat all the way thro Warrington to Northwich, and with this idea pursued my journey to Wigan, where I was disappointed, and again at Warrington. My pocket unfortunately began to grow low, for expecting to meet a reinforcement at my friends, I had so oeconomised my money as to hold out only till I got there. I could not therefore afford chaises at 15^d. a mile. All the one horse chaises were engaged to go to the fair at Newton, and no stage was going my way. I resolved therefore to remain this day at War^n. hoping an amendment in my companion, and that we should be able to proceed some how or another the next day. Meeting with a civil hostler in the yard I got a bed of clean straw made up for him in the stable, and there I left him to rest.

No other room being vacant I dined with a Traveller, who being *sociably* inclined, after dinner fell asleep, and as I was myself much fatigued with the cares of the day, there being a couch in the room, I took possession of it and fell asleep likewise. Another Traveller and his customer came in and had rum and water. The customer had a blue coat, brown wig with small curls and a cocked hat: Quick[135] would have acted him incomparably. Their first toast was success to the iron trade.[136]

I took a turn or two about the town but did not observe anything greatly worth notice. It is a largish town with the river Mersey washing one side of it. It is dirty and noisy with stage coaches moving at all hours. There are many very old houses in it, and very few good ones that I observed. The streets are narrow and ill paved ...

[*13 August*] My first business as soon as I was dressed was to visit Rover and bathe his limbs with hot vinegar, he seemed better, but unable to walk. I breakfasted with a Traveller from Chester, a very civil gentlemanly young man, and who seemed to enter into all my solicitudes. The waiter had found out a man going with a cart to Dunham, within 6 miles of Chester, who would take Rover; I agreed with him, and making a bed of straw for him, put him into the cart, following myself on foot. The morning was hot, but the roads were cool and not dusty.

About 2 miles we passed under the Duke of Bridgwater's canal. 4 miles saw on the right Haulton Castle on the top of a hill. The country is flat but rich, commanding a fine view over the Mersey with small vessels plying upon it.

We stopped at Dersbury stone delf [*sic*] to take in flag stone going to Frodsham bridge.

At Frodsham Bridge, where the cart was to stop some time to rest the horses, I found a waggon going to set off immediately as the driver told me to Trafford, and I shifted my companion to that. It stopped, however, at Frodsham, where I found a return chaise going to Chester. I availed myself of this, and we set off by this third conveyance.[137] Just beyond Frodsham two remarkable hills rise with their perpendicular fronts facing the west. These constitute Helsby point, a remarkable feature for many miles round.

Before we entered Chester there was a wake[138] and a vast croud of people gathered together expecting a bearbaiting. When I got out of the chaise, unwilling to trust my companion to less careful arms than my own, I carried him myself thro the streets, which excited not a few remarks on him and myself: "That Dog has been hurt by the bear—A pretty lap-dog— How pleasant that Dog looks—Is that your child?—&c &c". When I reached the Feathers Inn the chambermaid said the house was full, it being Assize time. Fortunately for me the gentleman with whom I had break-fasted had apprized me of this difficulty, and said, that if I would make use of his name to *Mister* Teigan the waiter, he would be certain to get me a bed. I desired therefore to see him, and he promised me a bed either in or out of the house. I stowed my sick friend in the stable, and having got tea, went in search of a conveyance for him the next day to my friend's at Gresford[139] 8 miles distant. For a one horse chaise I was asked 10ˢ..6ᵈ. To so exorbitant a charge of course I did not agree. At length, however, I en-gaged a Poney with a boy to take him in a basket before him, and at 10 o'clock, completely fatigued, I went to my bed at Mʳ Teigan's own house ...

[*14 August*] I rose at 6, but it was half past 7 before I could get the *steed* ready. It belonged to a milk woman, and he [*sic*] was to bring the milk from the field previous to carrying my sick friend. At length however we set off, the boy on the poney carrying Rover in a basket before him, whilst I walked by the side, gave directions for carrying him with ease, and tried to cheer him with endearing words. The day before he could still wag his tail if I spoke, today he only answered it by turning his eyes towards me.

The Reader may perhaps smile at all this regard shewn to a dog. But, if he does, he is a stranger to the feelings which arise from shewing kindness to an animal, who looks up to his master as his greatest and kindest friend, and than whom he knows none greater nor kinder. He had served me faithfully above two years. He had preferred me to another master. He had followed me one journey of above [blank space] miles: he had now followed me nearly 1700 miles. He had been my companion, my guardian and my friend; he had cheered the gloom of the hut at Kinlock, and alleviated the horrors of Glen Fallach. Would you then have done less for him than I did? If you would—I had rather be myself than you.

We at length reached Gresford about 10, where the arrival of myself and friend, in so unusual a manner excited some little mirth, and not a little anxiety; for Rover had been here before, and wherever he was known, there was he beloved. When I took him out of the basket he was quite stiff and unable to stand. I laid him upon a bed of straw and he seemed ill— very ill indeed.

The family had breakfasted, but a meal was soon prepared for me, and the greater part of our conversation turned upon a consultation on my friend's case. We gave him castor oil, but without effect; he seemed in great pain, not able to eat, and barking, or rather yelling. He continued getting worse and worse, till, about 3 o'clock, word was brought in that he was *Dead*. I felt real sorrow for his loss, tho none I trust that was either weak or affected. It was a matter of consolation to me that I had brought him so far, rather than left him on the road, where he might have died thro neglect or unkindness, and his skin been sold without remorse to a currier. "Thou hast one comfort at least in the loss of thy poor dog said my friends, thou hast been a merciful master to him—Alas! said I, I thought so when he was alive—but now that he is dead I think otherwise".[140]—Anger and caprice have often uttered harsh words and dealt unkind blows for trifles, which I would now willingly forego, could I again have him as my companion.

Had I lost my Dog in Scotland, I really know not what I should have done; but now in a good house, surrounded by excellent and cheerful friends, no time could I have missed him so little, and notwithstanding my loss, the day was passed amid the delightful society of pleasant relations.

I here met with two letters waiting my arrival. The one was from my friend, who had undertaken the care of my church,[141] saying that, on account of ill health, he was obliged to give it up, that he had provided for it one Sunday more, and I must be back by the Sunday following, which was the very next. Unable to reach home by that time otherwise than by travelling for two days and nights by a coach, which I knew would unfit me for my duty, if its effects were not worse, I wrote back to another friend[142] to do the best he could for me, and give me an immediate answer.

The other letter was from the worthy head of my village,[143] giving me the very pleasing intelligence of his having a Son and heir to his estates and virtues.

[*15 August*] I had often said to my companion, now deceased, in imitation of Cowper's Tame Hare, but little expecting I should so soon be called upon to fulfill my promise,

If I survive thee, I will dig thy grave;
And, when I place thee in it, sighing say,
Here lies the faithful Rover—Here my friend.

Task Book 3.[144]

Accordingly, this morning after breakfast, I performed this last act of attention to him, making his grave under a fine spreading Laurel on the grass plot behind the Vicarage House at Gresford, and some time after I wrote the following

Epitaph.
Life's Journey o'er, to his long peaceful home
A wearied Traveller at length is come,
On earth's cold lap his gentle head to lay
And dust to dust restore his kindred clay.
    To Guilt a terror, Virtue's steadfast friend,
Each action spoke benevolence its end;
Another's kindness with affection view'd
Had large return,—an honest *Gratitude*.
    But if unkindness, or caprice severe
Inflicted aught, he'd patiently forbear:
His noble heart still generously brave,
Benignly, when oppression ceas'd,—*forgave*.
    Still be his Virtues in remembrance dear,—
One sigh he claims, one sympathetic tear:—
Nor, Reader, thou with indignation turn,
Nor blush man's duty from A Dog to learn.

The following was sent me by a friend well acquainted with the object of his encomiums:

Epitaph.
Alas! poor Rover! whither shall I rove?
Depriv'd of thee, my safeguard and my Love—

How without thee shall I the road beguile,
Up hill and down hill many a tedious mile?
How without thee shall I endure the storm,
When low'ring skies fair Nature's face deform;
When gath'ring rains around in torrents pour,
And rattling winds incorrigibly roar?
But with thee over Northern Tracts I roam,
Far from old Camus[145] and my native home,
Content with Christian fortitude to bear
The Stinks of Scotland and her sorry fare
Exemplified in thee, sweet town of *Blair*.
So when at night I laid me down to rest
I found thee by my side my constant guest.
Alas! Poor Rover! 'twill be long I fear,
(Pardon thy Master's sympathetic tear)
Before Pedestrian plans he shall renew,
Robb'd of their chief delight and charm in you.
Thanks to indulgent fate that fix'd thy lot
To breathe thy last upon a friendly spot.
At Gresford thy remains a shelter have
With this Inscription mark'd upon thy grave:
> Travel who will the world's wide circuit over,
> The Nonpareil of Dogs was *Honest Rover*.

The Vale of Llangollen

[*23 August*] The Dee is seen winding in different channels among trees—corn fields and rich woods beyond, with a few cottages almost hid among them, the hills rising boldly on the left, and a fine hill, with thick wood on its side inclosing a gentleman's house, above which the naked rock rears his irregular head. A few steps farther on Dinas Bran, crowned with the ruins of Crow Castle, opens upon you, and continues a distinguished feature in the landscape all the way to Llangollen forming a fine termination to this charming vale, thro which the "Deva winds his Wizard stream".[146] A row of kilns smoked above on the left at the edge of a limestone rock.

Whilst I was walking on in admiration of these charming scenes, I met 3 travellers in a post chaise—*all fast asleep*. The Young Princes in Cymbeline, in complaining of their abstraction from the world, compare it to *travelling a bed*.[147] I pity the man who can shut his eyes to such scenes as these. His mind or his body must be sadly indisposed.

The view of the vale nearer to Llangollen is different in its character to anything I had seen before in my Tour. Were I at all to bring it into comparison, it would be with the scenery about the Pass of Killicranky in

Scotland, and I should give the preference to Llangollen Vale.

The situation of the town, which gives name to the vale, in approaching it is very good. It stands in a valley surrounded by mountains, upon whose sides the woods and corn fields rise to the top, and the church and houses, partially hid by the trees, is truly picturesque. The smoak from the burning fern on the sides of the hills added to the effect.

At the entrance of the town I met a fellow Collegian[148] on horseback, with saddlebag, who having imbibed some of our *high* ideas at College, seemed rather ashamed both of his own bags and mine. I had however "so often blushed to acknowledge it, that now I was brazed to it",[149] and began a laugh upon the subject. He turned back with me, and we dined together at the Hand inn, after which he proceeded on his journey.

A note to the Ladies at the Cottage,[150] soon brought me an obliging invitation to tea, which I immediately accepted, and met there Lady Stanley[151] and her daughter and M[r] Chapellow,[152] formerly of Trinity College Cambridge. The Evening was passed in pleasing and literary conversation, and we all returned to the Inn at 10 o'clock.

[24 August] Being engaged to breakfast at the Cottage at 11, for the Ladies tho early risers themselves, yet having very many friends & Tourists to see them in the course of the summer, generally fix that hour, that they may previously secure a part of the day to themselves for study and business,—I had time to look about me, and see some things which I had not seen on two former visits to Llangollen. The Church was the first of these. The inside is but indifferent. The E. window however is an ornament to it. It is bordered with stained glass, and in a circular compartment towards the top, about 2 feet in diameter, is a half length of our Saviour during the Agony in the Garden, by Eggington of Birmingham:[153] I do not however think it to be in his best style.

I next walked by the road at the back of the town to a gate nearly opposite the cottage where I took a sketch of this "Fairy Palace of the Vale",[154] situated at the edge of a beautiful pasture field, surrounded by plantations and backed by the mountain Dinas Bran and the Elwyseg rocks. The bridge next demanded my attention and my pencil, and the hour of breakfast being then arrived I directed my steps to the cottage. The Ladies having got an addition to their domain since my last visit, I had a new and a very delightful scene to behold. It is a pasture which lies on the side of a hill sloping down to a clear mountain rivulet. By the side of this is a walk amid trees from one end of which is a view into a wooded glen, with the streams of two overshot mills sprinkling their waters amid the dark foliage. In another spot by the waterside is a rustic shed, with a seat and table, which commands a fine view of Crow Castle.

An addition to the party being expected we waited till half ½ p. 12 when we sat down, a party of 12, to a most elegant & social meal.

The party being augmented by the arrival of 4 more visitors I took my leave and Mr C. desired I would accompany him to Valle Crucis Abbey on my way to Corwen. In our walk he intimated to me, that being obliged to be back at Llangollen in the course of a few days, he thought of making an excursion to Bala, Dolgelly and Barmouth, and if I would accompany him in his chaise, so far as our routes could be made to coincide, he should be obliged to me (as he politely and kindly expressed it) for my Company. I accepted the proposal, and it was agreed that he should overtake me the next day at Corwen.

We soon reached the Abbey situated in a sequestered spot by the side of a stream surrounded by mountains. The West end is very fine, over a (Saxon) doorway are 3 small windows in a line with a circular one of rich work above them. Over this window is the following inscription in Saxon characters:

Adam Abbas fecit hoc opus, in Pace quiescat. Amen.
This Abbey was one of the last built and the first destroyed.

The Abbots apartments are now converted into a farm house, which, with its various accompaniments, is very picturesque. The Dwelling itself is part of the old chapel. On the outside are three different kinds of architecture: Saxon and two kinds of gothic, the arch in one being being formed by convex lines, in the other by concave. The apartments within are in a very interesting style, the roofs consisting of gothic arches meeting in a center. In a chamber above is part of an old tomb stone put up as a chimney piece. It is curiously carved and the words *Hic Jacet* are very plain. We passed thro the house into an orchard where there is a good view of the E side. This end of the church contains 3 windows in a line below and two above. At the side of a square pond, surrounded by close cut hedges, is a summer house, which in this romantic situation among ruins has a very unpleasing effect. The inside of the church, which is filled with Ash trees of large growth, contains some beautiful specimens of architecture.

I here took leave of Mr C. and returning to the W. end found two artists taking sketches, Mr Arnauld and Mr Varley[155] who were on a Pedestrian Tour, and some of whose views taken in Wales have since appeared in the Exhibition. I conversed with them some little time and then proceeded on my way towards Corwen keeping on the N. side of the river. After a short way, on looking back, I saw Dinas Bran in a new point of view, rising beyond a hill in the middle distance cloathed with wood and sloping gradually to the Dee. A house or two at the edge of the water on the left is most picturesquely situated under a hanging wood. The foreground afforded some birch trees, which soon encreasing in number formed a grove. Looking thro the trunks and boughs of these, the stony bed of the Dee lying in inclined strata with the water rushing over had a very fine effect.

Dolgellau and Barmouth

[*27 August*] Being up before my companion[156] I walked out to see the place and according to my usual custom first directed my steps towards the churchyard. The church is of a tolerable size and neat within, having no pews, but seats with backs throughout. This manner of accommodating the congregation, I must own, I prefer to pews. Immediately in the presence of Him, in whose eyes often the least are greatest and the greatest least, I do not like to see that ostentatious distinction of seats which is too often made, and the high partition of a seat is frequently only a screen to ill behaviour or sleepy inattention. The living is in the gift of the Prince of Wales.

I was here accosted by an old man, who put the following paper into my hand.

M[r] Watt[157] from the Soho Birmingham
M[r] Tuffen from London
Recommend all Travellers to go over the Bridge above the second of the two last falls, about a quarter of a mile. — They will be amply repaid by a view of the finest scene in North Wales.

Robert Edwards
General Guide.

This was Rob[t]. Edwards who offered his service as our Guide to the Waterfalls, and I ordered him to wait on my companion.

The streets are not straight, very narrow and ill built. The Town Hall which is in general used as a School is a mean building. The Gaol looks like a common dwelling. Altho Harlech is the county Town, the Assizes for Merionethshire are held here and at Bala. The Bridge, from the date on a stone on the West side, was built A.D. 1638. It was originally of only 5 arches, but on account of its overflowing its banks and flooding the town, two others were built in 1794. The name of the river is the Onion, tho it is generally called the Dolgelly river. Below its conflux with the Mawdach it is generally called Mawdach or Avon Vour[158] the great river. Dolgelly is famous for its manufactory of gloves and leather breeches — as also for its woolen manufactory of broadcloth and stockings. We bought good stockings at 3[s]..6[d]. per pair and gloves at 1[s].

After breakfast M[r] C. and myself set off on two ponies, his servant and the guide on foot, along the Barmouth road, soon passing on the right Hungwrt, M[r] Vaughns, reckoned the most elevated situation of any gentleman's house in Britain. At Laneltyd, a small village consisting of a few houses and a church, 2 miles on the road, we crossed a bridge of 5 arches over the Mawdach, when we turned off to the right at the turnpike along the new Carnarvon road, and being tired of my poney I delivered it up to the servant and betook myself to my legs.

The road extends along the edge of a precipice above the dark waters of the river Mawdach, which being sometimes stopped by the stones in its rugged bed yielded a white foam. The mountains rise in the most picturesque forms and are not deficient in wood. Groves of tall trees, rather than thick brush wood prevail in this part. Other mountains either blush with the purple heath or brighten with the green of the thick fern. Cottages are thinly scattered & extend almost to even near the tops of the mountains. At about 5 miles we passed a public house kept by —— Bartlet, who, to a traveller not yet provided with a conductor, will take upon him the office of a guide. Beyond is Dol-y-mellynlyn, or the meadow of the mill-pool, the seat of Mr John Madox, lately purchased by him; where he has built, or rather added to an old house, in the style of the houses in Switzerland, with a long projecting roof, and a portico extending all round above the windows of the ground floor, which open to the bottom. The rustic pillars of this portico are twined round with honeysuckles and other creeping plants. On one side an out building, with a gothic glass door, and a cross on its pointed top, with ivy crawling over the walls, and its lines well broken by trees and shrubs, has a very good effect and appears like a chapel. It is however a wash house, which the open door too plainly shewed us, and I could not help feeling a sentiment something like contempt. The mind does not like to be imposed upon in that manner, and when it expects a place set apart to the duties of public worship, it does not like to see it applied to the servile offices of the family. This building is connected with the house by a wall with battlements, and the scene being well wooded, and the plantations made with taste, I was altogether greatly pleased.

We proceeded thro the woods at the back of the house to Rayder Dee, or *black*, or, as it is sometimes called from the place, Dolymellynlyn. It is divided into two falls, the upper being in three streams nearly parallel, falling in an oblique direction, but of different widths and characters. The stream at the top has a slight tinge of tawney, but is immediately converted into white foam. It is received into a very narrow bason, with a piece of rock rising perpendicularly from it and hiding part of the fall, and then tumbles again in one broad mass of white foam into a dark bason. A rocky bed conducts the stream away. The rocks are craggy and black and marked with the gray spots of the lichen; the sides are well cloathed, on the right with brush wood, on the left with timber, some oaks reaching aloft their withered tops. We viewed it in various directions, from the bed of the river at the top, and again from the opposite side of the alpine bridge thrown over the stream below. Here, a little way up the rise of the walk, an oak upon a crag to the left breaks the sameness of the lower fall, and another on the right hangs over in the true style for a foreground. The higher fall is

165

about 15 yards, the lower 10, measured to the bottom of their basons; but I think the falls themselves are not above 10 and 6 [*blank space*]. The name of the river is the Camline. A gentleman on horseback joined us as we were ascending to the fall. He had come from the Devil's bridge. He snatched a look at it, said it was nothing and went off.

We returned to the stable where we had left the ponies and proceeded. The scenery about the new bridge soon after we again got upon the road is good. A small cascade falls above the bridge on the left, and a mill below it on the right. Here a cottage with a cross on the top, on a hill beyond on the left, and a small building on a hill on the right, as they are not *native*, but the productions of a foreign country, seem placed there only as objects, and do not therefore please. A little farther is the junction of the Eden and Mawdach, where there is a pretty tumble for a few feet of the latter. We now left the new road to Carnarvon for the old one, crossing the Eden at a bridge just above the junction. The bridge is picturesque and a cottage stands just above it. The road now lay over barren mountains. On the opposite side quantities of fern were burning to make soap lees to send to Ireland. Leaving the road we followed a tract thro a narrow pass, in the rocks sloping abruptly on each side. We wound over the hill, and descended by a quick descent to fertile fields, above wooded glens of fine tall timber. We left the horses at a cottage, and descending to the river and crossing an alpine bridge, came in sight of the grand waterfall of Pistil-y-Cain, approaching it by a path cut from the side of the rock.

The river cain falls thro a space of about 40 yards, in an oblique direction, from the top of a rock crowned with wood on both sides, having an opening to the clouds just above the top of the stream. The rock in front rises almost perpendicular, shelf above shelf. The bottom is spread with immense loose stones from which a few trees rise on the left, as also from the perpendicular crags on each side. Ferns and moss grow in bright verdure on the rock. The water which runs from it is tawny tho the foam of the fall itself is white. In floods the water rises so as to dash against the footbridge below, a rise of at least 8 yards.

Barkers painting[159] of this fall, which I saw at Acton, has too little wood. In the real scene birch trees grow in the very spot where wood is wanted in ye picture.

A very short walk over a part of a wooded hill brought us to Rayder Mawdach, a still finer cataract. Standing amid a spacious amphitheatre of rock, with woods of fine timber rising from the very bottom, this stupendous fall tumbles in immense masses of tawny foam before you, and stuns with its deafning roar. The whole fall is only 30 feet, but the rock at top compressing it into a narrow compass makes it spread with the greater violence to another fall, when it is shattered against a craggy peak, and starts up afresh, to fall in smaller foam into the large bason below. The rocks are black and covered with dark green moss and fern. The spray spreads to many yards distance. Yet in this scene of violence and perturbation we saw a salmon struggle thro the waters, and attempt to surmount the fall. It was however a vain effort. The Mawdach and the Cain join just below this. The Mawdach then swallowing up every stream that falls into it, flows on to Ab*ber Mouth*ac, or *Bar-mouth*. Pistil Cain is the property of Sʳ. Roger Mostyn, Rayder Mawdach of Mʳ Lloyd of Plas Power near Wrexham.

We ascended to the bridge above, and thence to the station mentioned in the paper which the guide had shewn me in the morning. It is marked by a tree bearing the initials of the gentlemen's names who had discovered it about 3 weeks before: J.F.T. & G.W. From hence is to be seen a part of the great fall of Cain and a smaller fall above it, not seen when viewed from below. The highest appears to be about 6 yards, the latter about 12 and each about 8 yards wide. These are surrounded by wood forming two circular side scenes and a flat on the side of a green hill with barren rocks between. In front of these a wooded hill rises with a fine slope, on the front side of which a picturesque hovel is seen amid the wood. The hoary top of Rayder Mawdach is seen thro the trees immediately below. It is indeed a very noble scene.

The Guide told us he had often seen this before, but till the gentlemen told him, he did not see any *curiosity* in it. I find however that it was not entirely unknown before. Mʳ Pennant (in his Snowdonia p.100)[160] says "In the nakedness of winter there is a spot, far above, from whence these two cataracts may be seen at once, exhibiting thro the trees a piece of scenery, as uncommon as it is grand". From the cutting away of wood most probably, what was then only to be seen in winter, is now visible in summer.

We next walked to the top of the rock down which the cain falls, and I descended to almost the very edge of the precipice. The Guide said he never saw any one there before, and it was too tremendous to contemplate long. We returned to the cottage where we had left our horses, called Tudden-y-gladys, or the Lady's farm, and which often lends its name to pistil cain. Here we found bread and cheese and butter and milk prepared for us, of which we partook, and Mʳ C. and his servant mounting their horses, the Guide and myself were to meet them by a shorter cut at Eden bridge. The rain however came on faster (for it had been raining at intervals the whole day—a circumstance truly *favourable* for seeing the waterfalls) and when we got to the bridge, and the *cavalliers* overtook us, I was too wet to think of riding, so desired them to make the best of their way home, which I likewise reached soon after 6, when dry cloaths and a good dinner refreshed us after the fatigues of the day. In the Evening we were amused by a Harper who played Morver Rudland,[161] Handel's waterpiece, and a variety of other pleasing tunes.

[*28 August*] The morning being showery we set off at 10 o'clock in a chaise for Barmouth. It was low water the whole way, so that we did not see the views to advantage. The scenery is certainly grand, but not what I expected from the accounts I had heard of it, that it was one of the finest scenes in Great Britain. The mountains are more alpine than what I had elsewhere seen, but more barren and covered with shattered fragments.

Before the 4th. mile stone from Dolgelly on the right is a pretty view of a mill & waterfall with a bridge. Near the 5th. m. stone is pont Dee, or the black bridge with a small cascade just above it. The road runs for the most part at the edge of a precipice hanging over the water with rocks beetling above. With such materials and for so great an extent it would be much if there were no fine views. I expected however to have seen more *pictures*. The approach to Barmouth is grand. The road is blasted out of the solid rock, a precipice above the bay, while the rocks towering on the right, often cast large fragments into the road below. The town of Barmouth is situated on the side of these, the foundation of one house often rising above the roof of another and rocks rising amid the houses themselves. The town is small. It has a tolerable inn and is the resort of much company in the bathing season. The church stands a mile and half from the town on the Harlech road. The harbour contained several vessels of considerable size. A hut stands on a low Island in the middle of the harbour.

The views as we returned and fronted the mountains are much finer. The bay forms a fine Lake, and the alpine ridges wanted only more wood to complete the scene.—Surely Larch and pine would flourish here and with profit to the planter.—Above all Cader Idris reared his precipitous front and *the chair* formed a most curious feature in the scene, looking like the hollow of a crater. About 3 miles short of Dolgelly we caught a glimpse of the town up the vale. A building on the top of a hill above Mr Vaughan's is more conspicuous than picturesque.

The roads here are mended with shells, cockle and muscle, of which we saw large heaps lying by the road side.

We returned to Dolgelly by 4 and at 5, Mr C. and his servant set off for Bala, on their return into the vale of Clwyd, and I was myself to proceed southwards the next morning. By way of filling up the time, I resolved to visit a waterfall, which is a little to the right of the road going from Dolgelly to Bala, and which the Guide told me was well worth seeing. I therefore accompanied Mr C. so far in the chaise, the Guide going before. We got out near a bridge over the river about 3m & ¼ from Dolgelly, when I took leave of my kind companion, and proceeded over the bridge with the guide, a mile and half, or more, to Halylog. The Guide had informed me it was only ¼ of a mile from the road; but I found him not to be trusted in this instance as well as others.[162] Indeed he was unacquainted with the way and was obliged to inquire himself, and at a farm house we were directed to it. It lies in a deep wooded glen, and falls with impetuous force, perhaps about 35 feet, from a very narrow cleft in the rock above, shooting a little diagonally from right to left against the rock, and thence repelled in an opposite direction, and is almost lost behind a huge piece of rock standing up from the bed of the river, consisting for the most part of large loose stones, among which the water dashes in various wild and fine streams. A large oak at the top of the fall bends forward, extending its arms and trembling as if fearful of the gulph below. This waterfall is in the style of Airey force in Cumberland. We climbed to the top and saw several less falls above, but had no good view of them, and it was growing late and too wet to think of exploring.

We returned by the farm, called Halylog house, where a lady desired me to walk in and take refreshment, and I gladly accepted a glass of excellent wine. She shewed me a drawing of the fall by her son, a young gentleman of Jesus College Oxford, who had the last autumn opened the path to the bottom of the fall. It had been discovered only about 5 years before, by a gentleman staying at the house.

As night was coming on apace, I again set forward with the guide, who lost the way, and we wandered some time among ferns and briars, bogs and crags; at length however we regained our road and making the best of the way reached Dolgelly again about 9. I found two gentlemen in my room who were travelling for pleasure on Horseback. One of them had been at Oxford and sketched very well.

The accommodations at Dolgelly are but indifferent[163] and the charges high. Besides the usual bill we were charged 2^s..6^d. for candles and fire, tho the fire was only peat. 15^d. a mile was demanded for the chaise to Barmouth, but on M^r C's objecting the charge was relinquished.

The guide business at Cadair Idris

[*29 August, Minffordd*] While I sat at breakfast Edward Jones entertained me with his conversation. He mentioned, with some acrimony, Mr Warners having spoken ill of him in his walk thro Wales p.94.[164] But I make no doubt that what Mr W. said was perfectly just. I fancy he suspected me to be Mr W. for he did not know his person. I gave him some good advice respecting civility of behaviour to his customers and making reasonable charges. Mr Warner's remarks however I believe had had their effect, for he behaved with great civility to me, and charged me only 10^d. for my breakfast. When I asked him what he had as Guide up Cader Idris, his answer smacked somewhat of the character given by Mr W. He said he made no charge, people gave him from 2^s..6^d. to a guinea: he never grumbled. He is clever, and knows more than men usually do in his situation. He is a schoolmaster, and likewise cuts gravestones.

At 12 o'clock I set forward from Ninforth, when Edward Jones insisted upon setting me on my way. The road soon turns left through an opening in the mountains; and, as we began to ascend, on looking back, I had a good view of Raider Caû, tho not of the best part of it, and I could see other falls above, which I had not seen before. From hence, likewise, is a good view of the Lake, and through the mountains to Torwyn and the sea. The Lake is about a mile long and 8 yards deep in the deepest part. Its fish are trout; and sometimes young Salmon.

At the end of a mile, Edward Jones took leave of me, and still seemed to think that I was Mr Warner. He desired, if I saw him, I would tell him he "he wanted to speak with him. Would he say to his face, What he had said in his book?" I told him, I did not know Mr W. He said he lived at Bath, and perhaps I might see him there.

The day having been clearing for some time, the summit of Cader at length unveiled, and I almost wished to return and ascend, but my business was to proceed.

A Quaker meeting

[1 September, Rhayader] Whilst I was sitting at Tea, 3 Quakers, 2 males and a female rode up to the door. The landlord begged leave for them to be in my room, to which I immediately assented. They had tea at another table, and we conversed a little on common topics. The landlord soon came in and *half aside* told me they wished to have a Sermon there, if I had no objection. As it was Sunday Evening, and I supposed Quakers to be good sort of people and not particularly knowing their ways, I concluded they wished to read a sermon among themselves, or perhaps with the addition of the people of the house, and therefore I said that so far from having any objection I should like to hear it myself. But I found it was to be a *meeting*. Never having been at a quakers meeting, now that one was come to me, I resolved not to lose the opportunity, and walking out for a short time, I returned at 7, the appointed hour, when I found the room filled with chairs set round and in rows. Two farthing candles were set upon the chimneypiece with black teaboards[165] as reflectors, another was set on top of a cupboard in the corner and a fourth was stuck up against the wall with a fork.

The Lady, who I found was to preach, was seated on a chair on one side, her head leaning on her hand and shaded by her bonnet. The men sat on each side of her. The room soon filled, and after waiting about a quarter of an hour, the lady arose. She began by only half sentences, in apology for her calling the meeting and for a weak woman preaching; at the same time instancing the woman of Samaria who was sent by Christ to her country-men. She then recommended *silent* devotion, after which she sat down again, and in a few minutes more began praying. That lasted about 10 minutes, another pause ensued and she then concluded with an address to the congregation for not being more moved by her discourse, which I did not much wonder at, for there was neither method, matter nor elocution

neither wit, nor words, nor worth,
Action nor Utt'rance, nor the power of speech
To stir men's blood.

Julius Caesar A.3. S. [*blank space*][166]

As to silent devotion or meditation I believe it is the intent of our church, that we should practise it, by meeting together in the church, some time before service begins, properly to recall our thoughts from worldly concerns; but, like many other excellent institutions of our church, is shamefully neglected and few people come before, many not till long after the service is begun.

With regard to a female preacher, I know not how the Quakers and some other sects may explain those two verses in 1 Cor.14. 34, 35. To me they seem as positively to prohibit it as words can: "Let your women keep silence in the churches: for it is not permitted unto them to speak; but they are commanded to be under obedience, as also saith the law. And if they will learn any thing, let them ask their husbands at home: for it is a shame for women to speak in the church".

I walked out while the room was clearing and then supped with the quakers. They were simple and kind in their manners, and sensible.

The Picturesque

[*3 September, Yazor*] The Public house at which I had slept was kept by an old woman and her daughter. There being no parlour, I breakfasted in the *house* or Kitchin at a table on one side of the fire while they sat at the other, and by way of making myself agreeable by talking, I mentioned my object here, and made some inquiries about Mr Price[167] and his seat. They told me that he never suffered his house and grounds to be seen while he was at home, that he was a very odd man, and never suffered any person to come near him, and there was no use in my applying. A passage in M^r P's Essay on the Picturesque (Vol.1. p.378) which I well recollected, seemed so directly to contradict this, that I was not greatly discouraged . . .[168] The recollection of this gave me confidence, and I thought moreover, that even if it was M^r Ps *general rule* not to admit strangers when he was at home, yet, as I considered mine a particular case, I thought he might make it an exception, and therefore determined I would not lose the sight of what I so greatly wished to see, and for which I had come so many miles, merely for want of an application. At last I found on farther conversation that the old lady of the house was a tenant of M^r P's. and she was angry with him for not granting her a *lease*, a circumstance, which, while it sufficiently explained all she had before said, gave me an additional good opinion of Mr P. For however desirable a lease may be for a tenant in most cases, yet every lover of good order must rejoice when a public house is so much under the control of an excellent landlord, that the keeper of it may be turned out at any time for misbehaviour.

I therefore wrote a note, signifying I had come many miles for the express purpose of seeing the residence of the author of the Essay on the Picturesque, and begged permission to see the house and grounds. With this in my pocket, and my bag at my back, I set off from the Red Lion at Ayzer at about ½ past 9.

I soon entered Mr Price's domain by a gate on the left hand side of the road, and passing thro a corn field, came to another gate, on the other side of which stands a neat cottage with an honeysuckle overhanging the door and windows. Passing this I struck up by a path thro the wood on the left, and followed a road to the back door of the house, where I entered and seeing the servant desired him to deliver my note to Mr P. He returned immediately with M^r P's. compliments and I was welcome to see anything I wished; he was going out with company, or he would have attended me himself round the grounds. The gardener was not in the way, but the undergroom, an intelligent lad, was sent with me.

We entered a small flower garden at the back of the house surrounded by lofty trees where there is a conservatory, filled with fine plants, and creeping & trailing plants trained up the small pillars and the framework. A small alcove at the back had seats round made of straw work in the same manner as beehives. Before the house is a grass plot, with borders of flowers in irregular and picturesque situations.

We next walked thro the grounds or woods towards *Lady's Lift*. The woods are a rich treat to the lovers of Forest Scenery. The trees are the largest and of the greatest variety growing in groups with underwood of holly, thorns, brambles, and under these ferns, gorse, and luxuriant growing plants. Sometimes there is a look down into glades, at others thro the trees into the extensive country round. Broken roads and mouldering banks, dells and mounds vary this picturesque spot. As Scenery this is very fine, as a landholder I think I should at least clear my premises of weeds.

From *Lady's Lift*, a hill crowned with a small grove of firs, and commanding an extensive prospect over the country below, about 20 miles every way:

> its broad eye
> Catches the sudden charms of laughing vales,
> Rude rocks and headlong streams, and antique oaks
> Lost in the wild horizon.
>
> Masons Engl. Garden[169] B.2. l.312

To the North the eye stretches over Herefordshire to the Clee hills in Shropshire and the Malvern hills in Worcestershire; to the S.E. to Hereford, its tower and spire appearing from behind a wooded hill; to the S.W.

to S^t. Michael's Mount in Monmouthshire rising alone from the surrounding hills, and more to the West the seat of S^r. G. Cornwallis.[170] The Hatteral hills and the Brecnockshire and Radnorshire mountains bound the prospect from the S. to the W. The country below is a rich mixture of woods, corn, meadow and fallowfields, cots, houses and villages.

Proceeded along the top of the hill, and over a common to Burton hill, whence we had another extensive prospect to the N.W. bounded by the Welch Mountains. The handsome tower and spire of Weobley church below, and the town seen among wood. Again entered M^r P's. grounds and thro the woods on the declivity of a hill. The walks lie upon two ridges of wooded hills inclosing a valley. This valley is finely cultivated and here Lady Caroline Price has her farm: here are meadows, cornfields and hop-grounds. One end of the valley is enclosed by the hills sweeping together, the other opens into a rich and extensive country with the Shropshire and Worcestershire hills in the distance. The house is situated on the side of a hill embosomed in wood.

Descended and crossing the valley towards the house, to a pond surrounded by trees and crowned with an Island planted with Arbutus, alder, honeysuckle &c &c according to the principles laid down in the Essay on the Picturesque; the whole place indeed is a practical illustration of that work. By the side of the Pond is a delightfully cool grotto,

>   a rustic fabric, shelving deep
> Within the thicket —————————————[171]
> The surer to expel the noontide glare,
> Yet yielding liberal inlet to the scene;
> Woodbine with jasmine carelessly entwin'd
> Conceal'd the needful masonry, and hung
> In free festoons, and vested all the Cell.
> Hence did the Lake, the island, and the rock,
> A living landscape spread; the feather'd fleet,
> Led by two mantling swans, at ev'ry creek
> Now touch'd and now unmoor'd; now on full sail,
> With pennons spread and oary feet they ply'd
> Their vagrant voyage; and now, as if becalm'd,
> Tween shore and shore at anchor seem'd to sleep.
>   Mason's Engl. Garden B.4. l.335

I was next taken to the Managerie where there was a collection of choice birds. It is enclosed with a wall and planted with different kinds of trees whose branches overhang the grass plot, on which was seen the golden pheasant, the ringnecked and the common pheasant running across or peeping from beneath the shrubs. On one side of the grass plot is a root house. In the Managerie I saw a pair of birds called Damasels of so tender a nature that the house where they are kept is lined with carpeting.

The Powltry yard contains silver Pheasants in network yards. The common, pied and Japan Peafowls, Guinea fowls, Bantams and some curious breeds of fowls.

The House is fitted up in a style of simple elegance. The rooms are not very large, but good. The hall is the best room, opening by a flight of steps to the ground before the house. Here are some excellent prints and paintings, particularly one of old Par,[172] died at the age of 150, by Rubens. The ground before the house is laid out in the *neat picturesque*[173] style, or as M[r] Gilpin would perhaps express it, in a style of *picturesque beauty*, being a sloping grass plot with flower borders. The house is of red brick and is overgrown with creeping plants.

M[r] P. had obligingly desired that I should be offered refreshment before I left the house.

Having thus gratified my curiosity, I had only to regret the superior pleasure it would have been had M[r] P. been disengaged, and conducted me over his grounds himself, pointed out the various beauties, which a stranger eye, passing over in a hurry, does not perhaps notice, and illustrating the principles of his own works ...

[*4 September*] ... Crossing the bridge I ascended the hill into the Turnpike to Wigmore and in about 3 miles turned off, just at the beginning of the declivity of a hill to Downton Castle. The road is then for some way pleasantly shaded by overhanging trees. From the top of a hill is a good view of the Castle the seat of M[r] Knight,[174] author of the Poem of the Landscape, and the surrounding country. Here, as at Foxley, the trees and groups are fine, but weeds are suffered to encumber the soil. At an opening near the farm house about the river I stopped to take a sketch. Whilst I was thus employed a Gentleman and lady on horseback came up the road from the house, when the gentleman seeing me, rode up and addressed me as an Artist, and when I said that I only wished to see the Castle, he said he made no doubt M[r] Knight would give me leave and he was a great patron of Artists. He then rode on and I finished my sketch.

Having read M[r] Knights Poem of the Landscape with great pleasure, and knowing him to be the intimate friend of M[r] Price, and having heard much of the magnificence of Downton, I had certainly raised my expectations very high, and therefore saw the place to disadvantage, and my ideas were not answered. Yet had I seen the place without so much preparation, I should have been highly pleased, for it is infinitely above the run of modern built mansions. The plan upon which it is built is that of an ancient Castle, built round a Court, but in which all the irregularities of those edifices are imitated. No two parts of it correspond, and the towers are varied, circular, octagonal and square. The windows, being only thrown out where wanted to light the apartments, are distributed without strict attention to regularity, and in two of the towers there is only one window towards the bottom, yet from the building being covered with vines, virginia creeper and other creeping plants, the building is far from having a naked appearance. The great defect that struck me was the *flat* appearance of the whole, for tho it is somewhat relieved by the towers, yet they are not carried to any great height above the other parts and are themselves too much of the same size. The battlements moreover being of a plain single stone, without any copeing, have a very meagre appearance. The situation above the river and backed by hills is very fine.

I descended to the river and crossing a handsome stone bridge with Iron gates at the end and a neat stone house for the Porter's lodge, kept under a sunk fence in front of the house which led me round to the back entrance, where I inquired for the housekeeper who appeared to attend me round.

I was first shewn into the Hall a large handsome room which opens into the Portico. Next to this on the right hand side entering from the Portico is the Dining room, which occupies the large square tower nearly in the center of the South front. It is a circle within this square, having again circular, or rather semi-oval recesses into the corners, where there are plaister figures bronzed, in front of which are two pillars to each recess supporting a dome. The room is lighted by a Skylight and by a single window on the S. side: opposite to it stands an organ; the door is on the west and the fireplace to the E.

The Drawing room is on the opposite side of the Hall, and is of an oblong form, having a circular recess into the octagon tower at the S.W. corner of the castle. In this is a glass door into the garden, with a handsome door way of white marble supported by red porphyry pillars. The pillars at the entrance of the recess are a composition in imitation of it. At the side of this is The Library having a good collection of books and some paintings. Next to this is a bedroom and beyond that a dressing room, with a smaller dressing room at the corner in a circular tower. A handsome staircase leads to the first floor, where, over the drawing room, and of the same size, is the best bedchamber, having the bed in the recess. The rooms on this floor are not only neat but handsome. The Castle was built about the year 1775 and was first inhabited about 10 years after. It cost nearly £60,000.

Having viewed the apartments I waited at the Hall door while the housekeeper sent the gardener round to me, where I surveyed at more leisure the form of the building, the prospect it commands and the various beauties of the grounds. It is difficult to judge of the full effect of a place while the trees are as yet immature, but from what I could perceive, what now appears little and spotty, will, in a few years, be very fine indeed. The ground in front is in the style of the *neat Picturesque*, the grass is kept mowed, the trees are planted in groups, and large stones are left with trees and trailing plants and large flowers growing about them which break the ground in a pleasing manner.

The Gardener arriving, we descended to the bridge, and crossing it, entered the grounds on the right hand, and took our way along paths leading among trees and under rocks by the side of the river Teme. This Picturesque scene M[r] K. has celebrated in his Poem of the Landscape B.1. l.315[175] in the following lines. Bewailing the ravages which modern taste makes among woods and thickets he exclaims:

> Dear peaceful Scenes, that now prevail no more,
> Your loss shall every weeping muse deplore!
> Your Poet too, in one dear favour'd spot,
> Shall shew your beauties are not quite forgot;
> Protect from all the sacrilegious waste,
> Of false improvements and pretended taste,
> One tranquil vale, where oft, from care retir'd,
> He courts the muse and thinks himself inspir'd;
> Lulls busy thought and rising hope to rest,
> And checks each wish that dares his peace molest.

After some time the walk leads thro a *cavern* in the rock lighted by a small aperture above, and beyond this is an island of which there are several in the river and all well wooded.

Thro a *grotto* is an ascent by steps to an upper walk which soon descending again leads to the gamekeepers house, a most picturesque place, overgrown with virginia creeper and clematis.

> Nor yet unenvied, to whose humbler lot
> Falls the retir'd and antiquated cot,—
> Its roof with weeds and mosses covered o'er,
> And honeysuckles climbing round the door;
> While mantling vines along its walls are spread,
> And clustering ivy decks the chimneys head.
>
> Landscape B.2. l.288

Behind the Keepers Lodge is a corn mill with a dam on the river, and a fine alpine bridge with a railing of chains. We crossed this and kept along the walks above to the cold bath, which has a dome of spar and shells and is lighted from the top. In a nitch at one end is a nymph lying and looking into the water. By the side is a dressing room with a fire place and also a grotto overhung with creeping plants.

To Birmingham and the theatre

[*11 September, Stone*] As the time began to approach with a very hasty step when it was necessary for me to be at home, I fixed this as the last day to which it was possible for me to prolong my stay, and in compliance with the wishes of M[r] P.[176] who being no Pedestrian himself, thought it must be very bad for others, I assented to take the coach from Kidderminster to Birmingham, and having taken my leave of my brother and sister over night, the little ones were up to wish me good bye in the morning, and I took leave of them all, one only excepted who accompanied me to Kidderminster to breakfast, and set off at 7, the servant carrying my portmanteau. We breakfasted at the Black Horse at Kidderminster to which the coach was to come, as the Landlord had told me and according to a printed card at half past 8. 9 o'clock arrived and no coach came and my Nephew set off home with the servant. At 10 no coach being arrived I talked with the landlord and he then told me that on Wednesdays the coach waited at Bewdley for the Ludlow Coach, and he did not think it would be in before 1. I therefore set off on foot leaving my portmanteau to come by the coach determining to take my chance as it happened. Going out of Kidderminster I saw a mob collected round a house to see a virago with a soldiers helmet in her hand scolding her servant. It was dreadful to hear her.

Short of Hagley is a full view of the House[177] backed by wood and the grounds. The obelisk stands staring on the top of a hill without any wood about it. A seat backed by dark firs is another conspicuous object and a white building rising up among the wood below, above which rises a hill spotted with clumps of trees. The appearance of the obelisk improves when more under it, as there are then trees in the foreground to break its lines.

Short of Hales Owen is a good view of the Leasoes, a place I had often passed and as often wished to see without having a convenient opportunity. It was my intention to have seen it this time, but being put off my original walking plan, and being now in expectation of the coach, I was obliged still to defer it. The House is pretty, consisting of a small centre of 3 windows in front and 2 stories high, with small wings of one window wide and two high, joined by corridors or passages of two windows wide, and only one floor. It stands on the side of a hill well environed by wood and hills rising behind. I am informed the grounds are greatly hurt by a canal running thro them.

At Hales Owen is a good Church & spire. I stopped here at the New Inn for an hour at one o'clock to dine and had an excellent dinner for 1[s].

The Country towards Birmingham gets flatter but is still very rich. This overgrown town extends its suburbs to a great distance. It is enveloped in smoak, and presents an unpleasant assemblage of dirty brick houses, and all is noise and confusion.

I reached the George Inn Digbeth at ½ past 4 without the coach having overtaken me, and went to the Office to make a complaint and threatened to put a paragraph into the paper to caution travellers against an imposition which might frequently be attended with great inconvenience. The bookkeeper however "Hoped I would not be so great an enemy to the concern", thinking only of his master's profits and paying no attention to the accommodation of travellers. Fearing I might involve myself in trouble which I could not stay to carry thro, I desisted from performing so great a piece of public benefit and justice. I would willingly have incurred the *odium*, of an *Informer*;[178] the clamour which is excited against them is the artful cry of villainy to screen itself; and blind prejudice having adopted it, only mercenary knaves will now take it up. Would honest men do their duty, the Informer would be the upright benefactor of mankind.

I took a place in the Leicester & Cambridge Coach for the next day and finding the *astonishing* Play of Pizarro[179] was to be performed, I got tea, and at ½ past 6 went to the Theatre, which is very large and I suppose the handsomest out of London.

The Play of Pizarro, which has excited more attention than any play for some years past, can only have owed its success to the corrupted taste and morals of the times. In a production of the German school and from the pen of Kotzebue and altered by Sheridan, we are not to wonder at seeing Christians held up to detestation, and what is intended to be exemplary virtue attributed to pagans. It is however merely a little glittering tinsel not the sterling bullion of Christianity. The principal character Cora, has broken her vow as a virgin of the sun, and borne a child to Alonzo before the sanction of marriage. Elvira too has broken hers at the convent and followed the fortunes of the infamous Pizarro. Yet she thinks herself guided by *divine* impulse in seeking the *death* of Pizarro, tho she herself acknowledges that she is guided by *revenge*. The piece too is badly constructed, and the alteration it has undergone in many instances for the worse. Such is I think the case with the scene of the battle in the 2nd. act between the old man and Ataliba. The play however is not entirely without interest and stage effect: but it is too pantomimical.

From the character I had heard of Mr Elliston[180] and from his having received a good education, so indispensible to make a perfect actor, tho so often dispensed with in attempts at theatric excellence, I had formed great expectations of his performance of the part of Rolla. But he sadly "oerstepped the modesty of nature. He strutted and bellowed and outheroded Herod". The speech to the soldiers was "torn to tatters, to very rags", and a great deal of it I could not understand; yet the "groundlings" and the "*higher*lings" too, who seemed to be "incapable of any thing but inexplicable dumb shew and noise",[181] applauded him to the very cieling, while Mr Powel,[182] in Alonzo, always true to nature, scarcely seemed to share their favour. Mr Harley's Pizarro was indifferent, Mrs Johnson good in Elvira and Miss Biggs[183] very pleasing in Cora . . .

I did not stay the farce but walked to the Inn with Mr Powel, with whom I had been acquainted at Cambridge, while he was in the Norwich Company, and we passed the remainder of the evening together.

The coach journey home

[*12 September*] I was lucky in having secured an inside place in the coach for it rained in the morning and continued the whole day. I got breakfast before 8 at which time the coach set off with 3 others & myself.

A little way from Birmingham on the right is Spike Hall,[184] so called from the owner having gained a fortune in making spikes, (400,000 I was told) for government.

We dined at Coventry with the company of the coach from Leicester, and had a bottle of wine. One of the company proposed a second which I declined for myself. The others however had it, and it had its effect upon them, for when we again set off, two of the persons began cutting their jokes on each other, till at last they were downright abusive. They swore and talked indecent, and one of them taking a *ruffian* wig out of his pocket & putting it on, the other said that he had strange ways of *appearing*, meaning of disguising himself, and that he looked like a *presbyterian Jew*. As it rained hard we invited a decent looking woman on the outside to come in, which she accepted, and that put an end to to the worst of the conversation. The person in the wig who belonged to Leicester told us, he had lately lost his wife (who I afterwards found had been a rich widow) and his only child, and had been on a tour to divert his attention: it seemed completely to have answered the purpose.

We crossed several canals this day. In one place two ran abreast for some way, as the proprietors could not agree on the terms for having them united.

We drank tea at Hinckley, where we took in a gentleman with whom I was acquainted at College, and as we did not greatly like our company, when we got to Leicester we had a room to ourselves and passed the evening together.

[*13 September*] We set off again in the coach at 7 there being 6 of us, having got rid of the worst of our former days company and made an exchange for the better. Had I not been straightened for time I should have walked all the way from my brothers, and should have visited at so many friends houses, that I should not have had occasion to pass a night at an Inn the whole way.

One of the places was Humberston[185] within 3 miles of Leicester, the residence of the friend I met at the Lakes; and another Skeffington Hall,[186] 10 miles from Leicester, on the road we were now going. I was however obliged to pass these without even saying how do you do. The day was fine, and the country, all the way to Uppingham, very delightful, rising finely in hill and dale, well wooded and the inclosures chiefly pasture. We did not reach Uppingham to breakfast till 12. At Stamford while the coach stopped 2 hours I had an opportunity of paying a short visit to my brother,[187] with whom I had staid a day when I set out, and from staying longer with whom business now urged me and prevented my again visiting my friends, from whom I had received so much civility at Stukeley.[188] The Evening was fine and the setting of the sun and rising of the moon glorious.

We reached Cambridge at half past 10 having been 15 hours and a half coming 74 miles.

I found a fire in my rooms and tea things set out according to my usual custom and was happy to be thus safely returned.

[*14 September*] I breakfasted with one of my neighbours in College, after which I set off to attend to the duty which had called me back, namely the care of the Parish of Hinxton, 10 miles from Cambridge on the Epping road to London. I was greatly amused with my walk, for I had not seen *such* a Country of 5 months.

MEMORANDUMS TAKEN DURING
A FIVE WEEKS TOUR
IN THE SUMMER OF 1800

[*Editor's note*. Neither of the tours Plumptre made in 1800 rivalled the previous year's expedition. The first, in May and June, is recorded only in a private note-book of memorandums. It embraced visits to the Isle of Wight and the New Forest, where he stopped at Boldre to call on William Gilpin, whose writings had commended both these regions to Picturesque travellers. Yet Plumptre cuts a rather different figure from the cultivated traveller whom the 1799 Narrative portrayed admiring the view from Skiddaw or seeking out the waterfalls of Dolgellau. For most of the time, indeed, he is immersed in family and business matters: whisking about by coach to see relatives, inspect the little Hampshire property his father had left him, and finally to accompany his unmarried sister Lydia from Hackney back to Hinxton as his housekeeper. The preoccupations that emerge from this hurried round are those of the increasingly earnest, and Evangelical, clergyman. He is more interested in Gilpin the Vicar of Boldre than in Gilpin the arbiter of taste. In his cousin Frank Newcome he finds a striking and thought-provoking example of Evangelical conversion. And, significantly, after all the travelling he has done in the previous decade, it is a visit to a parishioner held in Chelmsford jail that he finally chooses to label 'The most important journey' of his life.]

To London and Salisbury

[*19 May*] Rose at 5, being called by Richard Scott,[1] and left Hinxton at ¼ bef. 6 on foot. The morning showery. Took the footway from Littlebury to Audley End. The grounds formal[2]—too many firs and Larch, and the Belt shocking. The Gamekeepers lodge, as a convent, a poor meagre card-house-looking place.—The Lawn and river too bare.

Breakfasted at the Fighting Cocks at Wenden, kept by Edward Moore, formerly my Parishoner, and who married one of my Clerke's sisters.

Reached Hockerhill[3] at 11. and in half an hour the Fly came. Inside full, 4 Johnians[4]—Boon, Romney, Smith and [*blank space*]—but they did not offer to take me in. Could only get a place behind with two men, but another man soon applying for a place, I was taken bodkin[5] on the box: we were 8 besides the coachman. Saw the Irish Giant[6] at Epping.

Reached London at ½ p. 5 and took a Hackney coach to N°. 14 Caroline Street, Bedford square,[7] where I saw Anne & Bell and got my tea. When I got into the coach again the coachman grumbled at my having kept him waiting: "Hay and oats were so dear and I'd kept him waiting earning 2ˢ. while he might have got 5ˢ."– I told not [*sic*] to be impertinent but drive on to the Bell & crown Holborn. When I got there I found there was no Salisbury Mail set out from thence, but from the swan with 2 necks Lud Lane. So went thither. There was no Salisbury mail, but the Exeter which went thro it was full for that Evening. There was a Post Coach going to Exeter next morning at ½ p. 3 but, I could only *secure* an outside place, 3 places being already secured within: I however took an outside.—Ordered a bed and went into the coffee room. There I took up a paper the observer which had an account of the attempt to Assassinate the King[8] at the Play the Thursday before, and the first of which I had heard from Anne just before, who was in the Pitt at the time. The place was so noisy, and I so much disconcerted that I went to bed at ½ past 8. without having had anything but giving the waiter 1[s]. for Candle and houseroom.

The house so noisy I could not sleep.

[*20 May*] I laid in a room with a skylight and heard the rain beating upon it all night. I heard the Clock strike 1. 2. & 3 at which I got up. At ¼ bef. 4 the Coach set off. There was a Russian officer[9] & a black (or rather Tawney) servant within side, and a Russian servant to the officer on the outside. I was jolted on the box as far as the Whitehorse cellar Piccadilly.

We there took up a woman, a Lady's maid, and no other place being secured I got within side.

We breakfasted at Bagshot and there the Lady discovered she had got into the wrong coach. But it was the fault of the coachman. The coach however by which her place was taken was behind, and when it came up she got into that.

This lady was very violent against Ministers, and M[r] Pitt in particular I believe on account of the powder tax.[10] As the Russian officer could not talk English & no one else french, I acted the Interpreter as well as I could. When the waiter wanted to know if his servant was to breakfast I asked him *Votre serviteur dejeune.*

As we were passing thro Brentford 3 Russian sailors, who were drinking in a public house, seeing the Russian servant on the roof (for he had an odd helmet cap on his head and whiskers) ran out and gave him some porter, they then offered it to the officer who refused it in rather an ungracious manner. I think an English officer meeting 3 sailors in a foreign country would have shaken hands and drank with them.

The day was so wet and I was so illdisposed that I did not see much of the country or make many inquiries. The road however was pleasant all the way. Even on Bagshot heath the ground lies well. So also it does on Salisbury plain tho it is but little inclosed: there are fine rising hills and sweeping vallies, the soil seems good and now and then you see a wood or some inclosures well disposed.

Our Tawney had come from the Island of Surinam about 11 months ago, was going with his master from Weymouth to Guernsey and thence to America, from whence he was to visit his own country.

Reached Salisbury, (well situated in a bottom, with fine sweeping hills rising on all sides) at ½ p. 6. As soon as I got out of the coach at the White Hart saw Robert, Jemima and Miss Taylor coming along the street, after our greetings, got my portmantua and went to the Antelope, where Mrs P.[11] was, and was happy to find them well and my coach journey at an end. Had tea and went to bed before 10.

William Gilpin[12]

[*27 May, Boldre*] Reached Mr Gilpins and delivered the letter which Mr Holden[13] of Sydney had favoured me with.

Found Mr G. but indifferent, with dropsy and astmah. He said at the age of 76. a man must not expect to be free from complaints. He received me with much complacency and was sorry he could not accompany me himself to the School and Poor House.

The room we sat in was hung with some good paintings, a portrait of Mr G. and a good cast of a Bull on the table. A fine view from the window thro an excellent foreground of wood to Lym^n. (and in a clear day to the Needles.) Walked up stairs with Mrs G. to see the view from the upper windows. This room hung with M^r G's drawings, the subjects compositions.

Had some conversation with Mrs G. about M^r. She said "she had known him from infancy and she believed he had never been guilty of an excess, they had been married 50 years and she thought him one of the best men that ever lived. He practised what he preached".

She told me he was the author of The Amusements of Clergymen.[14]

Mr G. gave me notes to the master of the school, Mr Servyer, and Mr Salter, the master of the Poor House ...

On an 8vo piece of paper is printed and hung in this and the Girl's school room:

THE

Interest of the Poor
and their Duty
is the Same
For
Sobriety brings Health
Industry yields Plenty
Neatness gives Comfort
Honesty makes Friends
Kind Parents have good
Children
and
The Fear of God draws down
his Holy Blessing.

This School was built and is supported by Mr G. out of the profits of his

Picturesque works. Thus, as he says, he has made his amusement subservient to utility, and he has expended money without diminishing his children's patrimony, and he hopes permanently to endow it by the sale of his drawings at his death. His own books are taught here. Mr G. told me none of the cheap Repository Tracts were his except the Life of W^m. Baker and his funeral sermon.[15]

Went to the Poor House, for an account of which see M^r G's printed account,[16] all which I myself saw most fully verified in the neat appearance of the place and happy looks of the inhabitants.

Mr Salter is now turned Quaker which is in some respects better, in others worse for the institution.

There has lately been a disturbance in the parish by some ill-disposed people who wished to turn him out. But they are now happily silenced. On this occasion there was the greatest distress in the house lest Mr S. should be turned out.

Returned to M^r G's where Chocolate was provided for me, and I had the pleasure of enjoying another hour of M^r G's conversation. I was sorry I had not an opportunity of talking with him upon the subject of his *tints* and the *liberties* he takes in his drawings.[17] Nor could I ask him his opinion of Mr Knight's and Mr Price's works.

Mr G. apologized for not being able to shew me more civility, or to ask me to dinner, but his health would not permit.

He shook me by the hand when I took my leave, and I hope my visit to Mr Gilpin will ever remain in my memory as a moral Lesson.

Visiting a cousin

[*31 May, Chiddingly, Sussex*] Looked out of my window at 5 and seeing it rain laid still, but continuing & not seeming likely to clear I got up at 6 and set off.

Passed thro Horsebridge & stopped to breakfast at the Woolpack at Gardner's-street, where I had a very good one by the Kitchin fire side, being wet below, tho my Umbrella kept my upper parts perfectly dry.

At 10, as it did not hold up I proceeded, and found my way thro Lady Webster's park at Battle Abbey (a very fine ruin, containing a mansion) to Battle. Inquired my way to Westfield, and was directed thro a dirty slippery Lane, thro a wood which was worse—but it was picturesque—got out of my way and was directed cross the fields to Westfield where on inquiry I was directed to the Vicarage House, at which place I arrived about ½ past 2 o'clock.

This house was inhabited by Richard Baker and [*blank space*] his wife, and 5 children (James, the Eldest apprentice to a shoemaker was out & I did not see him) Richard, Samuel, Hannah and George. R. Baker is a woodcutter, and a very honest industrious man. His wife formerly kept a school, and is a sensible industrious, & civil woman, the children are well brought up, and well-behaved. Here resides, and here I came to see, my cousin Francis Henry Newcome,[18] of the same age with myself. He studied Law at the Temple for [blank space] years, and had indifferent ideas of Revealed Religion; but reading the Bible to see how Moses acted as a *Lawgiver*, he soon found out the wisdom & divine inspiration of that book, became a convert to Christianity and found his chief delight in reading the bible. The Law of course was neglected, and as he found his chief delight and duty in studying the Bible, and the Law a hindrance to it, he resolved to go into the Church that nothing might interfere with his duty. His father, who hoped to see him a shining luminary in the Law, was disappointed at his changing his profession, and did all he could to thwart him in it. But, on his persevering, he "*Cursed* him, and attributed his change to the suggestion of the Devil". On this—and his making no concession— Frank renounced his father—got ordained to this Curacy (on a Title given him by Mr Coppard the Vicar) by the Bishop of Chichester, and came here resolved to live on his Curacy, and told R. Baker, he must consider him as his Eldest Son, and he now almost lives with the family.

When I arrived Frank was gone out for a walk—but on my announcing who I was, they told me I was expected. I pulled off my wet cloaths, and had an excellent dinner of bread and cheese & eggs, and butter, by an excellent wood fire. Towards 4, Frank returned, and gave me a hearty shake by the hand in welcome; after talking in the Kitchin some time, we retired into the Parlour, where a fire was lighted. At 6. we had tea (i.e. tea & supper both in one) when we had a common Cake, what they here call biskit—and *dinner Cake* made of flour, butter & milk & a few <plumbs or> currants—these R. Baker often takes with him into the wood to *dine* upon.

In the Evening we joined the family round their cheerfully blazing fire, and I enjoyed the chimney corner, and their plain, but sensible, conversation, much. Frank played a few tunes on the flute. At 9, being very tired, I went to bed & slept very soundly.

[*Sunday 1 June*] Rose at 6. Franks usual breakfast hour, breakfasted at ½ past. At 9 went up to the church where Frank married a couple. At ½ past, Mr Coppard, the Vicar, arrived, who came to administer the Sacrament it being Whitsunday. At ¼ past 10 went to church, where I read the prayers and went thro the duty, considering it was a strange place and I had much *new* duty, very well. I had The Athanasian Creed to read for the first time, a man to pray for, and the New Thanksgiving for the King's most happy Escape from Assassination.

Mr Coppard preached a very good Sermon, and he and Frank administered the Sacrament. There were 43 Communicants. The number of inhabitants are about [*blank space*].

The church is neat within, & without very strong and picturesque with vast massy butresses. It stands on a hill, much exposed to the wind. There are several yew trees round the ch.yard.

Dined at 1 on *chick pudding* (a chicken made into a pudding) and goosberry pudding.

At 3 again went to church, and Frank read prayers, very well, but too low.

Very good Psalm Singing.

After church Mr Coppard returned home and we went to drink tea with Mr Gutsell, a farmer, who teaches the singers at church. Met several of the neighbours, and after tea, Frank played on the flute, and some ofthem sung psalms.

Returned home at ½ p. 8. The boys were gone to bed. But I heard Hannah & Betty, the maid, read a chapter each in the Bible and Han^h. said her catechism very well.

Went to bed ½ p. 9.

The day was cold and rainy.

[*2 June*] Rose in time to breakfast at 6. Between 7 & 8 set off to Hastings (called here Harsting) called at the Butchers.—The rain coming on we were obliged to shelter at Master Cats—waited there about an hour and half, and the rain not subsiding set off homeward.

In our way called at the shop at the Moor (Cats) to get some sugarcandy for the children. Saw here a boy (Richard Cat) son to the woman who kept the shop, who had what his mother called The *Falling Sickness*: would fall down in fits and bruise himself, and throw himself into the fire or into the water. If he got hold of scizors or a knife he would cut his hair or his cloaths, or do himself any mischief. Yet when out of his fits he was pretty tractable. He was not able to read or learn much, he could repeat after another, but did not remember correct. He had no idea of God. Yet he was aware that falshood was wrong, and shewed much art in evading being detected in it. He was quick.

He was 11 years of age and was kept chained up round his body, under his arms, to prevent his falling and getting into mischief.

This seems like the Devil cured by Jesus Christ [*blank space*] Math. [*blank space*] Mark [*blank space*][19] only that this boy was neither deaf nor dumb.

Returned home and wrote a letter to Mr Green[20] & another to Speare[21] saying I should be home by Saturday the 14th. Wrote some of my Journal.

Master Brook, the Clerke, came in to desire of Frank to make out a petition for him, to make a subscription to replace the loss of his sheep (valued at about £10) which had been killed by a Dog. He killedthe Dog and so saved many sheep, for he had killed above 60 in a few days.

I am told that some Dogs are so cunning about killing sheep, that when they have sucked their blood they will vomit it up again lest they should be found out.

Had the Day been fine, as it was Whitsunday Monday and a holiday,

Frank was to have gone Pandling (that is catching *pandles*, *shrimps*) with the family.

Dined soon after 1, on mutton pudding and goosberry D°.

Talked after dinner, particularly about the Devil cured by Christ and the boy we had seen.

Before 5 walked out, thro the wood at the back of the house to a hop garden.

Hops are raised from offsets[22] and bear the 2nd. year. 3 or 4 poles are set to every mound and 2 plants are trained to every pole. They will last as many as 50 years. The longtailed fly had just taken the plants. They breed *lice*, which brings on the *black*, and spoils the crop.

On account of the high price hops were likely to bring many farmers had planted much of their wheat lands with hops. Thus are their avaricious & unpatriotic (for bread is more necessary than beer) views frustrated.

Returned & drank tea in the Kitchin. Afterwards walked up to the church, tho it mizzled and took a sketch.

Returned and passed our Evening round the fire side. One of their Chapters happened to be in course. Mark. The boys read and said their catechism, and spelled—Frank played on the flute, and at his desire I sung the song of the Auctioneer,[23] which greatly pleased the party. Master Baker sung a Psalm whilst Frank played. And so well did we like our Evening that we did not retire to rest till after 10.

[*3 June*] Rose little before 6. The morning seemed clearing. Breakfasted—resolved to set off and at 8 Frank accompanied me on my way. Went part of our former Evening's walk as far as the Hopgarden, and ascended the Hill towards *Beau Port*, Genl. Murray's. From the hill had a fine view of the country, the sun out and the day clear. Got into the Turnpike road from Hastings to Battle and had a fine view towards the sea. On the left the High Land of Fair Light (called here by the people *Far Li*) with Rye Harbour beyond and Dunge Ness in the distance. To the right Beachy head, and South Down stretching some way beyond. Somewhere here abouts W^m. the Conqueror landed and the Abbey of Battle was afterwards founded by him on the spot in commemoration of the event. The Abbey was formerly a mile in circumference. The Night before the Battle the Britons feasted, but the Normans passed it in prayer.

Near Battle are the Powder Mills, which blew up about 2 years ago. It was the day of appeal on the Assessed Taxes, & the people thought it was a judgement for the many false oaths taken on that occasion. It was felt as far as Gardners street & shook the house & furniture at the woolpack. 3 men were killed. They had not blown up of 20 years before.

Passed Genl. Murrays on the r^t. and soon after Crowhurst, Mr Pelhams, on the l^t.

Got to Battle, and called upon Mrs Geer (formerly Mary Venus, the School maid at Hackney) and shook hands with my old acquaintance.

187

Frank saw me out of the Town and then we took leave. I was much pleased with my visit to him. I think him improved and his religion mellowed, but there is yet some little *acidity* left. Christianity is "sweeter than Honey in the Honeycomb".[24]

Is he right in his mode of life?[25]

Back to Hinxton

[*14 June, Hackney*] Rose soon after 6 and at ¼ bef. 7 set off on foot. The morning was showery but my Umbrella protected me. Got to the Bald faced Stag on Epping forest at 10' to 9 and had an excellent breakfast with good cream. Set off again and enjoyed my walk thro the Forest. Some of the extensive views very good. The fault of the nearer are that there are few timber trees, being almost all pollarded; but some of the ponds and gladeways are very excellent.

I was only 2 miles from Epping when the Fly overtook me. The inside was full, so I got upon the box.

From Epping I walked on, as the inside company stopped to breakfast. And so did [*blank space*] Bayley, Mr Newcome's Gardiner, who was anoutside Passenger, going down to see his Father, who keeps a Garden & Nursery at Newport. We walked on 3 miles and he gave me an account of the Death of Mr Chiswell,[26] with whom he lived as under-gardener at the time he shot himself.

2 miles short of Harlow, a Lady, an inside Passenger, was set down, and I took her place. The Company inside were Mr Hopkins of Duxford and Miss Pugh and Mr Beauchamp[27] scholar of King's Coll. who had had 4 of his front teeth knocked out by an accident, in a school-boy quarrel about breaking windows. He wore an handkerchief about his mouth.

Walked on 2 miles from Hockerhill and again from Chesterford to my own Dear Home at Hinxton.

Dined on bread and cheese and went to tea at Mr Greens, who I had not had the pleasure of seeing of about 9 weeks. Found all well and Mrs Letty Jackson on a visit with them.

Called on George Moore,[28] and heard from him an account of his son in Chelmsford Jail whom he had twice been to see during my absense.

Looked over my duty for next day—recollected myself for the Sacrament—exhorted Dennis[29] to take it, but without success.

The most important journey

[*16 June, Hinxton*] Rose at ½ p. 6. did some jobs in the garden—in which a Hare and a mole had done me some damage—breakfasted at 8 and at 9 set off on The most important journey I ever undertook in my Life: to visit my erring Parishoner, Richard Moore, in Chelmsford Jail, to endeavour to convince him of his wickedness, to inspire him with penitence to make him "arise and go to his father and say unto him, Father I have sinned against Heaven and before thee and am no more worthy to be called thy son". Luke 16.[30]

The day was hot. I passed thro Walden to Thackstead, where I stopped for an hour to dine.

Here is a very fine church. Thence to Dunmow, where I stopped another hour to tea. I had intended to have slept that night at Great Waltham 26 miles but when I got there I found myself so fresh and had so much day light before me, that I walked on 5 miles farther to Chelmsford, where I arrived about ½ p. 8. and went to the Cross Keys Inn, opposite the new Jail. Mrs Beckwith did not receive me with that cordiality I would have wished; but, on my saying who I was and what was my errand, she changed her tone and I afterwards found her very civil. I was tired with my walk and went to bed at ½ past 10, first addressing myself in prayer to the Disposer of all Events to prosper the purpose I had in hand. I slept soundly and [*blank space*].

[*17 June*] Rose at ½ p. 6, dressed myself, had my breakfast and at 8 inquired what steps I must take to get admittance to the jail, when I was informed I could not be admitted before 10 o'clock. I walked therefore up the Town and to the Church, to see where it fell in in the course of the winter. Two men had been digging a vault and in doing that had undermined 2 of the pillars, they had not been long out before they gave way and in falling pulled great part of the roof with them. It happened between 9 & 10 at night and greatly alarmed the Neighbourhood.

At 10 I repaired to the Jail, where, on ringing, the Turnkey came to me.

I asked if he had not a Prisoner of the name of R^{d}. Moore, and if I could not see him? — Yes — How had he behaved? — Badly. He was then under confinement for bad behaviour, having been stealing provisions from his fellow prisoners. (Who were as badly off as himself.) The Turnkey went to the prison while I waited in the lodge and in a few minutes returned and carried me into the yard where R^{d}. M. was waiting. I asked him if he knew me. — Yes. I was Mr P. — I told him I was & was sorry to have to visit one of my parishoners in Prison, particularly the son of so respectable a man as G. Moore. But I wished to see if he could not be convinced of his errors, and resolve to lead a new life. He was hitherto without excuse. His father and mother respectable— indulgent—gave him a good education.—But he got into bad company, went on badly and broke his mother's heart. Got connected with Anne Bates.[31] Left the parish on having a child sworn to him.—After two years absense (in which his father had maintained the child and supplied him with money) he returned almost naked—his father took him in, cloathed him, and forgave him, on his promise of remaining with him, and leading a good life.—Had not been there 24 hours before he robbed his father's house, and ran away; subsisted by thieving and is now

189

in prison.—And there when he ought to have behaved well, and done all to atone for what was past, that the Gaoler might have spoken in his favour, when the Judge asked his character, he had not even that chance.—All this was registered before God and must be answered for. Is there no resource? In Repentance and amendment, & Trust in God thro the merits of Jesus Christ, who died for sinners.—Mentioned the Prodigal Son.—Lead a new life—begin with Industry and sobriety in the Prison and set an example to the Prisoners.—His situation difficult, whether transported or restored to his father, but God would assist him with his Grace if he asks it.

He cried much, but I could not get him to talk. I was with him near an hour, and when I took my leave told him, since I found he had been behaving so ill in Jail, I could neither shake hands with him nor leave a trifle with the Gaoler for him—but I would give him a Bible, which if he made a proper use of might turn to his eternal advantage.

I went and bought a Bible and some of the Repository Tracts (and having Gilpin's Expl[n]. of the Duties of Religion[32] with me) left them with the Gaoler for him—and prayed to God to prosper them, that they might make an impression and turn his heart.

Home again to Hinxton

[*21 June, Hackney*] Rose between 6 & 7. At 8 we Lydia[33] & self break-fasted and before 9 the chaise came we got in, bag and baggage, Lydia's boxes, bandboxes & baskets, 2 baskets with a doz bottles Arack & Rum, books, sandwiches &c &c. and basket of plants. The Fly went by as we were getting in. Took leave of M[rs] N. at the window. Between the Turn-pike and Lee Bridge overtook the Fly on the top of which Haggitt[34] had just got, having followed it in a Hackney Coach from Town. It overtook us again, and we again passed it while it was changing horses at Woodford. Got to Epping and while changing Chaises the Fly came in—John Kelty on the box. Introduced Haggitt to Lydia. Reached Hockerhill about ½ p. 12. Saw Sumpter[35] of Kings and his sister there. Took on our chaise to Hinxton which place we reached after a quick and pleasant journey at ½ p. 3. where I welcomed Lydia as the Mistress of my happy Mansion. May she be happy in it—may we all be happy, and when I pen my Fold for Heaven, may none of my Flock be wanting, and may the shepherd himself be found faithful. Amen!!

End of my Journey.

A JOURNAL
OF A TOUR
TO THE
SOURCE OF THE RIVER CAM
MADE IN JULY 1800
BY
WALTER BLACKETT TREVILYAN ESQ[R].
A.B. OF S[T]. JOHN'S COLLEGE,
AND
THE REV[D]. JAMES PLUMPTRE. A.M.
FELLOW OF CLARE HALL, CAMBRIDGE

[*Editor's note*. Though he recorded it in a carefully written-up journal, Plumptre's last tour was a mere four days' stroll from Hinxton to the source of the River Cam and back. At first blush, it forms a curious valediction to the career of a traveller who had earlier taken such pride in tallying the thousands of miles he had walked. Of course, there are perfectly good reasons why the well-travelled man should not neglect his own backyard. Plumptre's opening remarks make just this point in sententious language that does not completely remove the suspicion that he is slily engaged in a mock-heroic version of James Bruce's famous and still controversial expedition to the head of the Blue Nile, duly invoked for comparison when he arrives at the spring near Ashwell which marks his own modest goal.

At the same time, by taking him through scenes associated with his past, the journey was also a sentimental pilgrimage. He had known Wimpole Hall, the grandest landmark on his route, since the childhood days when Dr Robert Plumptre had been Rector of the church in its park. His interest in Philip, the third Earl of Hardwicke, and his family is natural in a man whose father had flourished through the patronage of the first and second Earls, and who had himself been ordained by another member of the family, James Yorke, Bishop of Ely. At Gamlingay, a little further along the route, he had gained his first, brief taste of clerical duties in 1794. And, as one of the better livings in his college's gift, Great Gransden held an obvious interest, though of course he had no means of knowing then that he would become its Vicar.

Leaving Clare College, Plumptre identifies with minute care the best points from which to view the scenery of the Backs. Shortly afterwards he regrets his own inability to do justice to the Picturesque possibilities of Harston church, and praises the view from James 'Athenian' Stuart's garden pavilion at Wimpole, while lamenting the decay into which the building had been allowed to fall. This is to be expected from a writer whose expertise in the language and criteria of the Picturesque had grown steadily during the 1790s. Yet in fact such touches play no larger a part in this journal than in the memorandums for his previous tour. Like its immediate predecessor, it shows the Picturesque tourist changing into the Evangelical tourist. He may still take his sketching equipment with him in July, but on his return visit to Wimpole in December he goes armed instead with Hannah More's Cheap

191

Repository Tracts. Travelling through a landscape marked more by recent inclosure and agricultural distress than by Picturesque 'improvement', he enquires if landlords like the Earl of Hardwicke are carrying out their duties and picks up ideas for encouraging the poor cottagers of his own parish in proper habits of industry.

Plumptre travelled with Walter Blackett Trevelyan, a recent graduate of St John's College whom he had first got to know when he stayed at Netherwitton Hall on his way through Northumberland in 1799. Trevelyan died in 1818: a 'sudden and singular' end, according to a circumspect obituary in *The Gentleman's Magazine* for April of that year. The anonymous writer stressed Trevelyan's eccentricity and his piety with equal force, summing up in this cautious tribute: 'He was truly a disciple of Jesus. With limited powers, perhaps, and narrow views, he was sincere, ardent, and indefatigable in the service of his divine master'. From this we may gather that Plumptre found a companion for his last tour as fitting to his earnestness as John Dudley had been to the rather different mood of earlier tours round Wales and the Peak District.]

It has often been a complaint against Travellers—and not without reason— that they explore distant regions, ascend their lofty mountains and trace their rivers to their sources; view their works of art and Antiquities; and make inquiries into their commerce and manufactures—while their own Country has been unnoticed, tho constantly spread out before their eyes and easy of access; and when they are questioned concerning its ingenuity and its riches, they are unable to give any satisfactory information.

That such an imputation might attach to myself I was fully conscious, and had often resolved to repair the affront therein offered to my neglected native county, and to take a journey thro Cambsh.

I had often fixed upon times for putting my plans into execution, but something as often intervened to oblige me to defer them. At length, on making mention of them to Mr Walter Trevillyan of S^t. John's College, he very flatteringly offered to accompany me, and the summer of 1800 was fixed upon as the time. Little interruptions however occurred, till on Saturday the 19th. of July he obligingly walked over to Hinxton to say he was at my service for the ensuing week. Having nothing particular to prevent me, I readily acquiesced, and the following evening walked over to Cambridge to be ready to start the next morning.

On considering our route, the cource [sic] of the Cam and its various branches seemed to offer as much amusement as any; as Villages generally are situated on the banks of a river for the convenience of the water; and as Villages, Churches, Mills, water and wood, promise the best materials for the *picturesque* in a country not abounding in lofty hills and rapid broken torrents. Accordingly

Monday July the 21st.
Mr T. did me the favour of breakfasting with me at 9 o'clock in my rooms at Clare Hall, and at 10 we set off with our gaters on our legs and our staffs in our hands, and a change of linen in our pockets, to which I added a few

implements for drawing, which, as my pockets were already full, I carried in an old shooting bag at my back. I am sorry to say it was still stained with the blood of some poor harmless feathered animal, which, in times now past, I had deprived of life out of wantonnness; but I was not displeased to reflect upon the change, when it was the companion of the pencil instead of the Gun. My companion had likewise provided himself with a small phial of Hartshorn[1] to apply a little to the tassel of our nightcaps at night, to keep off the gnats, in case we should be assailed by such "foes to our rest and our sweet sleep's disturbers".[2]

Within but a very few paces after we set out there are three stations exhibiting views which I have seldom seen equalled. The first is from our own bridge, where, having first contemplated the simple elegance of the College, you look up the river to Kings bridge and into the recesses of the trees which form Queen's grove. Turning round to the right you look thro the trees to a flattish country terminated by a rising hill. Before you, you look up an Avenue forming a delightful shade in all the magnificence of gothic and Cathedral solemnity; farther on thro the trees you get a pleasing view of Coton spire among the trees, backed by Madingley hill, and quite to the right, the trees of Clare Hall, and Trinity, and Trinity Hall walks, form a small amphitheatre with recesses, even superior to those of Queen's; while Garrat's Hostle and Trinity Bridges break the strait line of the water in a very pleasing and picturesque manner.

We pursued our way along the terrace thro the fine Avenue of Limes, and a few paces from the gate on Clare Hall piece, about the middle is the second station to which I alluded. You here have a fine view of the W. end of Kings College Chapel, with the N. side admirably foreshortened. The whole W. front of Kings new building, with Kings bridge and an irregular row of trees forming a good middle distance on the r^t. On the l^t. you have the S.W. corner of Clare Hall and the Lime-avenue, with the Iron gates between stone pillars, forming a very good foreground. The middle space is composed of King's Lawn, the river running at the end of it, and King's field, which is generally well filled with horses.

The 3^d. station is from the corner just above Erasmus spring (so called from its being at the end of the walk bearing his name & said to have been planted by him during his residence in Queen's College.) Here you have the S side & W end of K^{gs}. Chap. both in perspective, as well as the new building, and the S side of Clare Hall, with King's bridge in the middle, and a good foreground of wood from the trees in Kings and Queens grove and Erasmus walk, with the addition of the water of the river and the moat round Kings grove.

Turning to the r^t. along the foot road to Grandchester, we passed on the left Mr Wilkin's new-built house,[3] consisting of a center & 2 wings of white brick with a projecting roof in the Italian style. This does not seem to be generally admired. I must own, for my own part, that I prefer it to the high, square, citizen-like looking houses which one generally sees, and it would be unfair to form a decided opinion against it, till one sees the house and garden completed.

Crossing the new turnpike road from Camb. into the great north road we got into [*blank space*] Lane which leads into *Paradise*. But wherefore it has acquired that name I know not, as it consists only of gravel-pit-pools overgrown with willow herbs & coltsfoot &c and surrounded by trees: the place contains good studies for broken ground, but is not *paradisaical*.

The next object which attracted our notice was a very neat Barn situated very picturesquely under some overbranching ash trees. Thence we crossed the meadow towards Grandchester, keeping as near the water as we could, and in our way had a good look back towards Camb. Kings Coll. Chap. looking remarkably well over the trees. The chief defect in our views was the littleness and sameness of the pollard willows which marked the course of the river. Had they been suffered to grow, or had they, still better, been changed to Alders, it would have added much richness to the Scenery. But the windings of the river were, generally, very pleasing, and its banks well edged with thorns, rushes, willow-herb, water-dock, coltsfoot, butter-burs and meadow sweet. The extensive savannahs on each side seemed very rich, and Trumpington wood on one side, with Grandchester on the other, were certainly fine.

We passed thro the willow-walk, and from a field on the other side, where Gr. Church, rising on the hill above the trees, looked very picturesque I took a sketch.

The Mill was the next place we stopped at where I again took a sketch. We here saw the flowering rush in bloom.

From Gr. Mill we crossed the meadow to [*blank space*] where the board erected by the late Rev^d. Jeremiah Pemberton,[4] still gives its friendly warning to bathers and records the melancholy event, which I well remember, of two young men being Drowned there. The Inscription is as follows:

Cavendo Tutus

A caution to all Persons who may be inclined to bathe in or near this
deep Hole
If you can not swim you must not venture to go in between the two
posts above and below
The Hole on each side of the river the ground sloping very steep into the
depth of the Hole.
For want of which Caution two Exemplary young gentlemen of the
University were drowned
Here in each other's arms in the Evening of the 10th. of June 1791
If you can swim you must not venture to jump into the deep part of the
Hole
A large Tree being at the bottom there, which might be of fatal
consequence to you.

From near this spot we had a good view of Grandchester church and Mill, and also cross the Meadows to Cambridge. The Meadow upward was finely surrounded by trees. Got to the sluice, where the two streams part—and where formerly, as it is said, Trumpington Mill stood, where the Miller lived, celebrated by Chaucer in his Tale. From which Mr Colman has borrowed the idea of the gallery scene in the 3^d. Act of Ways and Means.[5] Passed Mr Pemberton's stewponds,[6] and going at a little distance from the river for some way, met it again, & saw some men laying the dirt from out the river upon the land, which seemed to bear but very coarse grass chiefly rushes, and stood much in need of such improvement. As we intended seeing the Mill at Hauxton on our return up this branch of the river, we only stopped at the Turnpike to inquire whether there was a way by the waterside to Harlston (commonly called Harson) and being answered in the negative, we passed on over the bridge, and followed the road to the village, having new inclosures on each side of us. In the village we saw some of the good effects of the new inclosure, for almost every cottage had a piece of ground allotted to it, which being layed near the house and turned into a garden, gave an idea of comfort which a garden always conveys. Being the first year, they were not yet got into the order, nor had they the picturesque appearance which time will give them.

Taking [sic] into the footway under the cottages we saw men, women and children busily employed about the stream, which ran, or perhaps stood still, on our left hand; and, upon inquiry, found it was the time of the Muscle Fishery. We joined the fishers, and were shewn some of immense size, one in particular which my companion bought of a little girl and gave a penny for, so great is the price the shells bring, tho the fish itself is not held in estimation. I bought another of a Cobler, who had taken it the preceeding Evening. The manner of catching them is, when they come up from the mud and open their shells, to put in a long stick, upon which they close upon it, and are taken out hanging fast to the stick.

The church was the next place which attracted our notice, and which formed a good subject for the pencil, too difficult a one for so indifferent a one as mine. It had a handsome Tower and body, with a good side aisle, butresses, a portico and many fine windows. In these there seemed to be some good old painted glass, but much worn—we did not however go in to inspect it farther.

The Vicarage and its garden seemed to form a neat and comfortable residence, for the present minister Mr Leworthy.

Near the Church stands a good old house [blank space] and another at the entrance of the town, the property of Mr Bridge Little.

Crossed the river at the Mill, and from a little way beyond it had a good view with Foxton on the left, with hills rising pleasantly at some distance. On the right the woods of Haslingfield at the bottom of a hill, and Barrington in front, embosomed in trees. We followed the cart road to the village, which we entered at a pleasant lane, and crossing the green with the church on our right, left Mr Bendyshes on that side likewise and keeping up the village inquired the public house. The *Wheel* presented itself to our view, which we thought seemed to promise good *Fortune*, but being informed that the *Boot and Shoe* was a better, we would not tempt fortune, as I told my companion it *boots* us to go to the other. *Psha*! did he *not* exclaim, tho, being a *Johnian*, it would not have been unbecoming him to have said so.

We here got bread and cheese and butter and eggs and some very small ale, all indifferent in their kind, but the civility of our Host [*blank space*] Empson made ample amends for any deficiencies of fare. While we were eating our repast, the Overseer's[7] son, and another man, came in to collect the *poor* rates, and I heartily recommended the ale to their notice, being, from its *poverty*, an object of concern.

The companion opened his story to us, being but lately come to the village. He had lived in Wiltshire or Devonshire (I forget which) and dealt in sheep. He bought a number of a man and sold them again. They proved rotten, and the purchaser came upon him, when the man from whom he bought them made off. He offered to divide the loss, but the other would not consent. A lawsuit ensued, which was tried at Exeter, and he got it; it was tried again by the other at Salisbury, and went against him. He paid the money for the sheep and the costs of the suit came to £160. For this he had fled, making over his small effects to his wife, not having the money to pay, and not chusing to work there for his daily bread.

This I told him I thought was wrong. He had incurred the expence. He must pay it and beware of *law* for the future. With his wife was the proper place for him to live at—and the worst his neighbours could then say of him would be: "That man was ruined by the roguery of others, and now he works contentedly, as an honest poor man should do, for his daily bread".

His name was Ind. Related to Mr Ind of Cambridge.

He did not acquiesce, but said "I did not understand it", and went away with the collector.

We inquired our way to Malton, (Walton it is called in the map)[8] and as Master Empson was going into the field with his gun, he said he would shew us the way. We crossed the lane in which the house stood to a field, where we saw the meeting house lately rebuilt. Empson returned for the Key, as it was kept at his house, tho he himself was a churchman, and let us in. It was built for Presbyterians, and the pulpit stood in the proper place for the altar, a table in one of the seats serving for that purpose. It was pleasantly situated among trees; a church in the same spot, with a tower or spire, would have been a very good object.

Talking about the inclosure, Master E. inquired if we were come about that. We told him no. He seemed to wonder what could be our object, and, after several inquiries and hints, said "He hoped we were come after *some good*?" I told him I hoped we were not come after any harm.—He did not know that.—"Were we come to lay the farms together?"—"What, he was a friend to small farms, was he?"—"Yes".—We had much conversation in this way.—He showed us a place at some distance on the top of a hill to the right, two small hillocks, which seemed to form a Dean, or the sides of a ditch. There he told us was an old quarry, from whence the stone for Kings chapel was taken. This I believe is not true; and no stone is to be found there now.

On the left was Artser bridge which is partly in Barrington and partly in Sheperheath parish. The road to Royston lies over it.

We took our leave of him, and I told him, laughing, "when Barrington belonged to me, as he was fond of small farms, he should have the smallest".

We soon reached Malton, a single farm House, with the remains of an old chapel. We had now a view of Orwell on the right at the bottom of the hill. The woods of Wimple beyond, but more in front, with the Pavilion, a very conspicuous object. The avenue was right before us. Crossing the open field, we made to the river and crossed it at a Horse bridge. We had now a full view of Whaddon church about a mile on the left.

Came to a field where there was a crop, but what it was we could not tell. Inquired of a boy keeping sheep, and were told it was wild parsnips, they cut them and give them to the cows in winter. Got to Wimple hedges and crossing over a style, came into the Avenue, just by what *was* the great bason, but now no longer so, being dry. I now walked, where formerly we had fished. From the Bridge we had a good view of the House, and admired the Avenue as a specimen of the grandeur of the old taste. Kept on the r^t. hand side of the river to Arrington bridge, where there is a new bridge lately built. Formerly it was only a narrow one at the side of a ford for foot and horse passengers. The present is more convenient, but less picturesque. From hence we turned aside from the River to go to the Hardwick Arms, formerly the Tiger, at Arrington to take up our abode for the night. Got there soon after seven and had our tea. There happened to be a meeting held there that day on account of the Gilden Morden Inclosure, and some farmers who were smoking at the door asked if we were not *surveyors*.

After tea I took my companion up to Arrington church to shew him the view from thence, which I had often contemplated with pleasure, while young, and still continue to do, though I have since seen some of the finest parts of this Island. The Evening was not very clear, and was rather too far advanced to see it to the best advantage, still however it was fine: a rich tract of Wood and pasture ground, farms, cottages and churches, and bounded by gently rising hills at a distance.

A paper on the Church Door attracted my notice. I read it, and having read it, copied it:

Arrington May 16. 1800.

Notice is hereby given to the Cottagers and labourers in the Parish of Arrington, that Premiums of one guinea and a half, one guinea, and half a guinea, will be given by the Earl of Hardwick to the three persons of that description, who appear to have taken the greatest care of their gardens, and to have raised and brought to perfection in the course of the following summer the greatest quantities of Peas, Beans, Carrots, Turnips, cabbages, onions, or potatoes, in proportion to the extent of the ground which they occupy. The gardens will be inspected by Mr Stephens, Gardiner to the Earl of Hardwick, Mr Pigott, Mr Mayes, Mr Patterson, or any three of them, as often, and at such times as they think proper; and the Premiums will be adjusted and distributed on the 20th. day of October next.

Such Persons as wish to be considered as Candidates for the said Premiums are desired to signify their intentions to Mr Stephens, Mr Pigott, Mr Mayes, or Mr Patterson.

So excellent a plan for encouraging the industry and promoting the comfort of the poor, pleased us both, and we thought our labour in the walk well paid, had we no other benefit or amusement from it but this. I resolved to put it into execution in my own Parish, and I think my companion will do something of the same kind at Netherwitton.

We returned to the Inn, had bread and cheese put upon the table. I wrote my Journal, and soon after ten, we retired to our respective rooms.

Tuesday July 22.

We rose soon after 6 and at 7 went out to walk in L^d. Hardwick's park before breakfast.

The entrance into the park is thro a triumphal arch,[9] having a lodge on each side. The building itself is handsome, but the straight line on the top seemed to want some relief; Horses, cows, deer or sheep, would be more appropriate than Lions or Unicorns, which are usually seen in such places. Deer, of some kind, are the supporters of the Hardwick Arms.

We proceeded up to the Pavilion[10] on the hill and were much pleased with the rich and extended prospect before us. It was not sufficiently clear to see the distance to advantage, but we had now a morning, and a better view, of nearly the same tract that we saw from Arrington Church the former Evening. The Church itself was a good object on the left, and the fine trees on the slope of the hill upon which we stood formed a good foreground.

But the Pavilion itself was a scene of desolation and ruin. It has been built about 25 years and cost about £1500 building. When finished it was one of the most elegant buildings I ever remember. The Tea room was simple and elegant; the little room on the side was a rare specimen of paintings of Etruscan figures in colours. It was done by Stewart and cost £700. What the inside is now, we did not see, but we could discern from the outside, that the blinds were falling to pieces. The pillars which supported the center, were rotting away, and the building supported by rough props. A railing of posts & wire, which formerly extended all round it, and kept off the cattle, was removed and the pavement and steps torn up, and the place made a shelter for deer & sheep, whose dung sadly soiled the place. The stucco which covered the outside, and gave it the appearance of stone, was every where falling off. I brought away a piece of it. It is almost as hard as stone, and seems to have been made in pieces about 12 inches by 8 and ⅜ of an inch thick, and stuck on with some kind of cement.

There is a large print of this, which I believe is only a private plate in the family. From this a small one was done for the Westminster Magazine for Feb. [*blank space*].

We took our way along the fir walk to the Ice-house which is likewise beginning to fall to decay. It is sheltered by a small grove of chesnuts which are excellent trees for forming a thick shade.

We were soon stopped by the sunk fence which bounds the Park this way, we walked along by the side of it and had a good view of the Gothic tower[11] on the opposite hill, with the water running between, and the whole well wooded. The tint of this building is much mellowed by time, and the ruin has a very good and natural effect. I have no where seen so good an imitation.

Walked within sight of the back of the house, and keeping at a little distance from it, came to the front. Many were the alterations made since I first remember it, some for the better, some for the worse. I missed in particular a chesnut walk the bows of which hanging down touched the ground and formed a most delightful retreat from the heat of a summers sun. This formerly stood in the garden; that is now laid into the Park, and I suppose it was necessary to strip the trees some way up to prevent the deer from spoiling them.

We had a fine view up the avenue, one of the few remains of these specimens of ancient magnificence; and we then turned our steps towards our inn, and I troubled my companion in my way with many remarks upon the alterations, of trees I missed, and pointed out many spots, scenes of my former haunts, and of days and pleasures never to be forgotten.

At ½ p. 8. we got our breakfast at the Inn, and at 10 again set forward on our Journey, taking the footway thro the fields to Wendye.

In our way Croydon church in one or two points of view exhibited a good picture and only wanted one of the trees from Lord Hardwick's Park, which Mr Gilpin[12] would have removed in a moment, to give it a foreground.

199

We joined the river again a little below Wendye, where several smaller streams ran in different directions and windings. On the edge of one of these Currant trees grew almost in the water.

At Wendye we crossed the river and made towards the Church, a small oblong stone building and neat on the outside. The arms of Lord Sands are over the W. door. He had a house here formerly which is now the property of Captn. Windsor.

In the church yard I observed the following very curious lines on a grave stone; which do not instruct "the rustic moralist to die",[13] but contain a very extraordinary *hope*.

Sore affliction brought me here,
Which was great loss to my wife dear,
For here I lie, and here must be
In hope her body will be brought to me.

On the N.E. corner of the churchyard stands a hut very much resembling a highland hut. With the chimney made of wattle work and daubed over with clay.

Proceeding towards Shengay we crossed a branch of the river which comes from Bassingbourn, which with another stream from Abington join the Cam at Shengay Mill.

Keeping along a rough lane, and by a fine old oak tree, after some time, we had Shengay church (or rather what was once a church) on our right, but a moat lay between us. We crossed it by a narrow thin plank, almost as "unsteady footing" as "a spear" Henry 4th. P^t.1. A.1. S. [*blank space*].[14] And found the church in ruins and horses sheltering in it, and treading down the pews. It is a very small place, but has been neat. Now it is often a harbour for Gypsies and Trampers, and "the house of prayer is turned into a den of thieves".[15]

We called at a neat white house, with an avenue of limes in front, to inquire our way, and continuing thro the fields till we came to a wood called Clobber's grove, we met a man on horseback, with whom we had some conversation. He was the Miller of Shengay Mill and expressed concern that he was not at home to "treat us with a bottle of wine". We told him we might come to taste his *Ale* at some future time in a *voyage* up the river. At the corner of this grove stands a cottage delightfully situated.

At Gilden Morden we stopped to see the church, a large and handsome building, and contains two pews on each side of the entrance into the chancel with very curious carved work.

Wide of this on the right stands Hook's Mill, between which and a place called *Labour in vain* is a spot, where a man may tread in three counties at the same time, viz. Cambsh. Herts and Bedfordsh.

Our way now lay cross the open field to Ashwell, as the windings of the

river are very intricate and there is no footpath by them. We reached Ashwell about [blank space] and went to the [blank space] Inn to get dinner.

The house was out of order as it was undergoing a repair, and we dined
in the kitchin on pigs fry. Whilst dinner was preparing a man came in who
was walking from Newport to Biggleswade. He had stopped by the way
and got some beer, which had turned sour on his stomach and disordered
him. My companion being both a chemist and Physician, prescribed some
Hartshorn and water, an alkali to correct the acid, which did him good.

After dinner we inquired out the Clerk to shew us the church. From the
top is a very extensive view. On the N.E. we could see the Pavilion at
Wimple—Cambridge and the Gogmagog hills, and almost to Ampthill and
Wooburn on the S.W. The tower of the church is very lofty and handsome,
the inside is decent. The chancel belongs to Mr Whitbread who has covered
the top with [blank space].

On account of the clergyman having been insulted in his duty an extract
from

Stat. 1. M. C. 3
1 W. & M.[16]

was hung up in the church.

The clerk next conducted us to the spot from whence the Cam takes it's
rise. From the bottom of a chalk rock innumerable springs, not less than
between 30 and 40, issue out, and in the distance of about between 2 and
300 yards turn a Mill. This place is very much overrun with weeds. Were it
kept clear and a little pains taken to keep it in order, and its banks planted
with a few trees and shrubs, the source of the Cam would be a very curious
and pleasing spot. Even now it may rival Mr Fuzellis source of the Nile.[17]

Near this spot formerly stood an ancient house belonging to the Bald-
wyn family, which has been only pulled down within the last 30 years. The
site of it is now to be seen, and a spring rose up under the kitchin floor.

From Ashwell we crossed the stream at a tree which hung over the water
and passed the new farm and thro a newly inclosed Country to Dunton,
thence to Sutton, and leaving Potton on our left got to the Cock at Gamlingay about 8 o'clock.

As this was the very first Parish of which I ever had the care, tho it was
only for a short time, I found myself particularly interested in thus visiting
it after an interval of 6 years. I called on Mr William Parsons who lived in a
farm close by the Public House, where I used to sleep on my journies
(frequently pedestrian) from Cambridge hither to do duty. He regaled us
with a glass of his (or rather his Sister's) currant wine, which had not
degenerated in its flavour since I tasted it last, and then Mr P. came to eat
his bread and cheese with us at the public house, while I drank my tea.
Soon after 10 we went to rest. Mr T. slept at the pub. H. and I resumed my

ancient station in the blue checked bed at M^r Ps.

Wednesday July 23.

At 7 o'clock I called upon my companion by agreement and we went to see the great Wonder of Gamlingay, The Weeping Ash Tree. It is a curiosity singular in its kind, as it is the only *natural* one known in the Kingdom, perhaps in the World. All efforts to propagate it have proved ineffectual, as plants raised from the keys or succours when they thrive do not weep. The plants we have are all graftings from this tree, and never grow in height above the stock grafted upon, the shoots bend down immediately unless trained up against a stake, as is done in the Botanic garden at Cambridge. This is older than the memory of the oldest man in the Parish. It grows in the vicarage garden. It is 31 foot high and 40 across. One of the shoots this year was 3f 5i another 4f 1i.

We walked round the Church yard, where on the S. side, over a vault, a little garden is railed in.

This is the first Church I ever did duty in. I was ordained by the Bishop of Ely, at Ely, on Palm Sunday, April the 13th. 1794 to my Fellowship as a Title. The Bp. had at that time undertaken to provide a Curate for Mr Turno[18] (who was in a very unhappy state and unable to take care of it himself) and desired me to take it for a short time. I accordingly accepted it, and on the Friday following, being Good Friday, I did duty for the first time. I went over on the Thursday and staid over Sunday at the Pub. House. I kept the curacy a quarter of a year, and had the pay been better and the distance less, I should have liked much to have continued it.

Mr T. returned to the Inn and I went to call upon old Mr Parsons, whom I found much aged since I had seen him last. Returned to Mr T. and we breakfasted in the room with the folding doors open to the street.

Having traced the Cam from Cambridge to its source at Ashwell, we now intended to find the source of that branch[19] of it which runs from Bourn to my Lord's bridge and joins the Cam above Grandchester. But Mr T. having heard of Cucumbers being cultivated on a very large scale at Sandy in Bedfordshire we resolved to make a digression this morning and see them.

I went first to call upon Mrs Say, widow of The Rev^d. Mr Say,[20] who lived at Brook End while I was curate here, and from whom I had received great civilities. But it was only to leave my name as Mrs S. was absent.

We set off soon after 10 and took our way towards Sandy by the S.E. side of Gamlingay Park, formerly the residence of Sir [*blank space*] Downing, who left the money to found Downing College[21] in Cambridge. The Park is now, tho inclosed, little more than an unsightly common and let out to a man who takes in cattle to joice.[22]

The House formerly stood on the S.E. side and some of the foundations are yet to be seen and some of the walls of the stable. It stood upon a rising ground above a valley in which is a pond or two. An avenue of fruit trees on the S.W. still rear their stunted heads.

On the opposite side of the valley stands a gateway and two side towers, built of brick, which I suppose was meant to represent the remains of an old Castle, but as it is ill executed and bare of accompaniments either of walls, trees or ground it is an unmeaning eyesore. On the edge of the Park to the N. is another strange fabric of brick, a high piece of wall with an oval opening thro it: a strange frame to a strange picture.

Walking on over the heath and leaving the village of Everton on the right, we came to the paling of the park at Hazles, Mr Pym's, where just within the gate which leads to the house we observed, by way of a lodge, one of the neatest cottages I ever saw. Built of a reddish yellow stone and thatched. Only a ground floor and with a rustic portico to the door. It consists of an outer (or sitting) room. A back wash house with an oven &c behind it, and a bedroom at the side, making a wing to it. I went to the house and borrowed a chair to sit down to take a sketch of it, while my friend entered into conversation with the goodwoman of the house. She spoke in the highest terms of her master, and seemed very happy in her neat mansion, but complained heavily of the new inclosure.

We followed the road towards the house, but as it would only lead us up to the very door, we turned off to the left, and made a round, joining it again in a glen on the other side the house. The Park is very pretty and contains a great quantity of fine Spanish chesnuts.

When we got again into the high road, after a little time, we descended a high hill having a rich view over Bedfordshire, and turning on the left came to an extensive garden where we saw a man and two women gathering peas. We entered the garden and fell into conversation with them, and saw the Cucumbers, but then not in a very forward state. Being sowed in the open ground, they sow them in drills every 8 or 9 days that some seed may always be in the ground to come up and succeed in case that which is up should be cut off by frost. In this state perhaps half or a whole acre of ground is to be seen. So much are they cultivated here that 2, 000 bushels have been sold out of the parish of Sandy in one week. They are carried to London, Cambridge, S^t. Neots, &c &c and sold all round the country at the low price of 3 large or 5 smaller for a penny.

This extensive manner of growing cucumbers and the cottages situated in the gardens brought to my mind a passage in the first chapter of Isaiah v.8. "The Daughter of Zion is left as a cottage in a vineyard, as a Lodge in a garden of Cucumbers".

The method of preserving the seed is when the fruit is ripe to cut the seeds out into a tub and let it remain till it begins to ferment, then put it into water and wash it from the mucus and lay it out upon cloths to dry.

The heat of a burning meridian sun, reflected from the sand, was very oppressive indeed. We however walked on to the Village of Sandy and observed some extensive plantations of larch, fir &c on the hills, both on the right and left, belonging to Sir Philip Munnocks.

The Village afforded nothing that demanded our attention and we returned to Gamlingay by a different and more round about road, and at half past two set down to an excellent dinner of Pork and Goosberry pudding at the Cock. After dinner I called on M^r R^d. Guy, a farmer, and one of my old acquaintance, and towards 5 we again set off. We kept along the Turnpike road till we came to Waresley and then turned in at a gate on the left, thro Mr Marshes grounds, the road laying at a sufficient distance from the house. Took the road to Gransden. Great Gransden[23] is a Vicarage in the gift of Clare Hall, who hold the great tythes. This was the living of Barnabas Oley,[24] who left his money (an Estate in this Parish) in the hands of trustees for various charitable purposes. Here is a school founded by him. The alternate Presentation to the vicarage of Heath (or Warmfield or Kirkthorp) near Wakefield in Yorkshire is in their gift. Mr O. was a very excellent man. He republished Herbert's Country Parson. He was one of those who took the College plate to King Charles in the rebellion.

From Gransden we crossed the fields to Caxton where we arrived at the Crown Inn about ½ p. 7. This place is remarkable only as the birth place of William Caxton[25] the first printer.

It was so hot and I was so tired I could not stir out any more.

We slept in a large two bedded room with green stuff damask furniture.

Thursday July 24.

We left Caxton soon after 6 hoping to find the morning less sultry than the middle of the day. The brook which runs thro this town, and in winter is very considerable was now dry. It is not supplied by springs but rain. This however runs to the Cam and we followed the course of its channel some way towards Bourn. Notwithstanding it was yet early it was so hot that we did not wish to go needlessly out of our way, and did not therefore go up to the Church and Mr Lisle's house, but kept thro the town where we observed the first *spring* in this branch of the Cam.

From Bourn we made our way to Kingston and thence to Eversden, where we intended breakfasting with Mr Hewett, fellow of Queens, who was then fitting up a farm House that formerly was my Fathers.[26] But not finding him at home we went to the public house where a fire was made, water fetched from the brook, for they have no wells here, and a kettle was boiled and we had breakfast.

So greatly did the heat of the day encrease that we determined not to go out of our way by following the course of the river to *my Lords bridge* (so called from having been built by Lord Oxford who formerly owned the Wimple estate) that we made to Harlton and Haslingfield, where we crossed the river there making a sort of Island, and passed thro the new inclosures of Harlston.

A little to the right of the road which leads from Hauxton Mills to Harlston is a very good view of Hauxton church with the Gogmagog hills in the distance.

At some distance on the right see a hill with an obelisk on the top called Maggot Mount.

Thro the village of Hauxton to Shelford, where we had a good view of Mr Finche's house, and saw in a field men at work thrashing Coleseed.[27] This is always done on the ground where it is grown as it would scatter in being carried. It is taken up in a large coarse cloth on a sledge and carried to another large cloth laid on the ground and then thrashed. We took our way thro the village of little Shelford to the George Inn at Great S. where we got some boiled beef and potatoes for dinner. After which I refreshed myself by taking a little sleep.

When we set off again we crossed the water at the mill and kept along the meadows to Stapleford Mill where we saw the process of grinding rags for making paper. Thence to Sawston Mill—Pampisford Mill, Wittlesford Bridge and home to Hinxton and so put an end to one of the *hottest* Journeys I ever took, but the fatigues of which were greatly alleviated by the rational and pleasing conversation of my companion.

We wished to have traced this branch of the Cam, the Granta, up to its source beyond Newport, the next day and then the other branch which comes from Linton, but on account of the heat of the weather we determined to defer it.

Appendix.

Having heard the result of the Premiums given by Lord Hardwick (mentioned p.23)[28] for industry in gardening, I much wished to see the respective gardens (a circumstance I was very negligent, in not doing when at Arrington in the summer) particularly as Mr Green[29] and myself intended to do the same at Hinxton for the ensuing year. As the cross roads were so bad I determined to wait for a frost; but Mr Thackeray[30] intending to go over to Wimple in a chaise to visit Lady Anne York[31] who was indisposed, and offering me a place, I accepted it with pleasure and on Thursday

Decr. 18.

I breakfasted with him at 9 o'clock and at half past we set off in a chaise. It was a thick fog or rather a scotch mist. Between Cambridge and Barton we were amused with the various parties of ditchers, dispersed on each side at work at the inclosure at Grandchester and Coton. In a few years when the country is drained and the fences get up the improvement will be wonderful.

The New Turnpike road continues tolerably good for about half a mile or rather better beyond Lord Oxfords bridge when it becomes very bad and in many places dangerous. Mr Thackerays chaise and horses stuck in a hole a few days before where it remained, till a waggon coming by the man lent his horses and assistance and dragged them out.

Just before we began to ascend Orwell hill, we overtook a gentleman in a sort of taxed cart driven by a lad. As we went up the hill side by side Mr T. fell into conversation with him and finding he was going to Wimple and intended to dismiss the cart at the top of the hill, he offered to take him in which the Gent. accepted. It proved to be Mr West, Engineer, of Wisbeach, who was inspecting a mill &c erecting there. As soon as we entered the inclosures at Wimple we turned to the left to The Mill, built near the Farm house, formerly Mr Challands, now Mr Goodcheap's. A stream of water is brought by a new cut from the ponds at the back of the house, & turns an undershot mill, which is to turn all the machinery within. The stones were not then put up, but we saw a thrashing machine at work. The corn in the straw was put in at top. The straw was discharged again on the other side, thrashed, and the corn winnowed and dressed, came out at bottom, the prime at one place, the tail at another. Here we left Mr W. and again getting into the chaise went on to L^d. H^s. and got out in the stable yard. Mr T. would have me go into the Kitchin to see the improvements made on Count Rumford's plan.[32] But here unfortunately we met with L^y. H. I stepped back at first, but recollecting myself, and Mr T. saying he had taken the liberty of bringing me to see the kitchin, I made my bow and inquired after Lord H. L^y. H. spoke with civility and leaving Mr T. to shew me the Kitchin took no farther notice. Surely civility & hospitality required something more!!

The Kitchin was fitted up with fireplaces, stoves and roasters according to the plans given in the first part of Count Rumfords 10th. Essay.

I then called on Mr Sheepshanks at the Rectory but he was gone out and was not expected home till Monday. I begged the key of the chapel to see the New Monuments[33] erected since I was last there. One to the late L^d. H. and to Lord Dover. Both neat and the Inscriptions good, but not equal to the former monuments, nor yet very handsome in themselves. Here are likewise small monuments to The Rev^d. C. Yorke and Miss Mary Y. son and daughter of the Bp. of Ely.

I went back to L^d. H^s. to inquire for Mr T. to introduce me to Mr Stephen's, his L^{d}ships Gardener. I was shewn into the housekeepers room and Mr S. came before Mr T. and wishing to make the most of what daylight remained, I set off with him to see the Gardens.

Those of the 3 Prize men lay all together at the new built cottages in the Avenue leading to Cambridge. There are about 6 gardens laying together with a strong fence round, and separated by young quick hedges in a very thriving condition. Each garden may be about 16 poles.[34] All were in very excellent order and well stocked with cabbages, Kale, &c as winter gardens. Mr Patterson his Ldships Bailiff had joined us, and we went into the house of the prize men and saw some of their potatoes, which were I think the finest I have seen this year. The sorts were the champion, the Ox noble, the Wimple kidney, and the red kidney or painted Lady. I made each of these sons (or rather daughter's, for only the women were at home) of Industry a present of the Information for Cottagers[35] which I had brought for that purpose and with which they seemed highly pleased. The 12 golden rules accompanied each.

We then proceeded by Mr Patterson's house, which was formerly the shop kept by John Radford, and down the Lane to some new built cottages, with chimneys on Count Rumfords plan. Then to the school. A very neat cottage standing in the shrubbery with a vine growing against it. Here is a parlour with a glass door looking into the shrubbery. This is a new way lately made for Lady H. or Lady Anne to come and hear the children and look after the school. L^y. H. pays for the schooling of 12 and likewise cloaths them. She puts the same number to school at Arrington & Whaddon. Just by here is a fence of sweet briar.

We next saw the garden of John Rogers, which he only began to make in June and had got into excellent order. It is not above 3 poles. Mr Patterson now left us, and I proceeded with Mr S. to the Gardens. The chief thing which I observed here were forcing frames upon Macfell's construction.[36] (See his Treatise on forcing). The hot house was in excellent order. We got again into the shrubbery where I recognized a hawthorn tree, which was once in our field, and under which, in haytime, we have often drank tea.

Tempora Mutantur et nos (et vos) mutamur in illis.[37]

We passed thro the churchyard where I observed the graves of two old servants to our family James & Elizabeth Smith. James died [*blank space*] Elizabeth had been buried only two days before. Mr S. went in to his dinner and I walked on thro the Park to Arrington, went & ordered a Beef Steak at the Hardwick Arms against 4 and then proceeded to visit the gardens here.

The first I saw was Samuel Story's on the hill near the church who got the first prize. His piece of ground was about 20 poles out of which he got 50 bushels of potatoes besides other vegetables. Potatoes at that time sold at 4^s. per bushel. He is a very hardworking man and has 7 children, the eldest about 15. He used to be up at 3 & 4 o'clock to work in his garden.

The next garden to his is W^m. Collin's which was about the same size and in good order. But he grows old and cannot work as he would. As I only had enough Inform^n. for Cottagers for the successful candidates, I gave The Cottage Cook[38] here.

As I was going away the wife of W^m. Wilton desired me to look at their garden. It was well stocked and tolerably neat. I gave her the Cottage Cook.

Descending the hill again I met Mr Stephens and we proceeded some way on the London road to the cottages of Richard Hunt and Charles Theverley (or Thurley) and I was as well pleased with theirs as the others.

We reached the Hardwick Arms again soon after 4 and I had my dinner, after which Mr S. sat and drank a glass with me.

He gave me much and pleasing information respecting L^d. H. and his family and the villages.

Lord H. always reads prayers himself to the family when he is at home. But when he is not L^y. H. never has them, tho her brother Mr Lindsay, a clergyman, is in the house. He goes constantly to church twice every Sunday.

When the Premiums were given away, all the successful candidates, and those likewise recommended to his Lordships bounty, attended at church on the Sunday, after which Mr Stephens conducted them into the great Hall, where L^d. gave each their respective rewards with some excellent advice on the occasion, recommending industry and promising his friendship so long as they were industrious.

Those recommended to his generosity had 5^s. each given them.

Besides the gardens L^d. H. lets the cottagers sow potatoes on the fallows, for their dunging the ground for them. One man from 6 load of dung had got 70 bushels of potatoes. He lets them sow them likewise in his new plantations, and enclosed some waste ground likewise by the road side for them which was sown in what is called Lazy Bed. A space 8 foot wide is marked out for the bed and then another 2 foot wide for the path. The potatoes (or eyes) are laid on the sward in alternate rows, the sward is then cut up from the space marked out for the path and laid over the potatoes, and as they grow they are earthed up by the earth out of the path, and if the season is wet the water drains into it.

Soup is given away twice a week to the poor, and L^y. had some time ago had a parcel of Digesters[39] from London which she gave among the poor.

Mr Stephens sat with me till 7. He then left me. I had tea. Read the Repos^y. Tract. Thoughts on the Scarcity in 95 and Tom White[40] and at ½ p. 9. went to bed.

Friday Decr. 19.

I rose at 8. Breakfasted. Read the Cottage Cook. Left the Hardwick Arms at 5' p. 9. Mr Myer the Landlord was just dead and had left his widow with 3 small children and expecting daily to be brought to bed of a 4th.

Passing the cottages on the left hand side seeing a woman at the door of one I asked to see the garden. It belonged to —— Onion. She said "they had the prizes whose gardens were not so good". I however doubted it, but gave her a Cottage Cook which I said was better than giving her a guinea & which she in her turn did not assent to. At Kneesworth I bought a pair of Gardening gloves.

Between Kn^h. & Royston wishing to ask a question about the country, I waited till a man overtook me, I saw behind. He was the blacksmith of Kneesworth and had likewise a shop at Royston. After he had answered my questions he asked me if I was not a minister. I said yes. He said it was a nice easy way of life and he was thinking the other day of bringing his son up to it. I represented to him that his son must in that case be sent to a large and expensive School and then to College, where he could not possibly live under £100 per ann^m. But if he was not well disposed and frugal (and neither a public school nor College were likely to teach it him) he might run some hundreds in debt, and then perhaps after all only get a £50 curacy.[41] That the same money would set him up in any trade. Why not in his? It was too laborious and there was no pleasing people. That was the same in all stations.—Then a Carpenter.—That was such a *low* way.—But the Virgin Mary's husband was a Carpenter.—Or a Gardener.—That was a poor way.—Then a farmer. That was so expensive, it cost so much to set him up. Not so much as the church and his morals had a much better chance than at School or College among fashionable and profligate young men. He might try him in a small farm first. And above all make him begin to do the work himself: plowing, thrashing, &c. A man who cannot *do* work, does not know how to *overlook* it. The man seemed struck with my arguments and I believe when we parted had resolved to give up his new formed scheme of ease and wealth for his son. I hope he has.

I skirted the town of Royston and followed the turnpike road almost to Duxford, when I turned over the fields to my right and thro the village & to Hinxton, which I reached just after two, just as Lydia had begun to cut up a hot roast fowl.

Hinxton church, sketched by Plumptre in 1802

APPENDIX 1:
GLOSSARY OF PLACE NAMES

Though precise in his directions, Plumptre treated place names with the customary freedom of his age, and occasionally he misheard what a local guide told him; the notes comment on the few occasions where he is seriously at fault. The right-hand column of the list below gives the accepted modern spellings, taken from the Ordnance Survey wherever possible, in those cases where the difference is more than a matter of omitting a hyphen, contracting two words into one or splitting one word into two. A handful of vanished places and vanished place names are left out.

Abergeley	Abergele
Abington	Abington Piggotts
Air	Aire
Airay force, Airey force	Aira force
Alveston	Alvaston
Angelsea, Anglesea	Anglesey
Angling stone, Angling crag	Angler's crag
Ard Garton	Ardgartan
Arroquhar	Arrochar
Artser bridge	Archer Bridge
Arx	Arks
Ashbourn	Ashbourne
Ashton	Ashton-in-Makerfield
Ayes water	Hayeswater
Ayzer	Yazor
Barslow	Baslow
Bassenthwait	Bassenthwaite
Ben-y-glo	Beinn a' Ghlo
Bettus y Coed	Betws-y-Coed
Bildwas Abby	Buildwas Abbey
Blair in Athol	Blair Atholl
Boater Crag	Boathow Crag
Bowdar Stone	Bowder Stone
Bowness knot	Bowness Knott
Bran	Braan
Bridgenorth	Bridgnorth
Buarchliah	Buachaille Etive Beag (or Mór?)
Burrow Hill	Burrough Hill
Cader Idris	Cadair Idris

Caermot	Caer Mote
Camline	Gamlan
Capel Cerig	Capel Curig
Carle's head	Carl Side
Carnarvon	Caernarfon
Carn Dhu	Cairndow
Carrie	Carie
Cashaville	Coshieville
Castell Dolbadern	Dolbadarn Castle
Castle Dinas Bran	Castell Dinas Bran
Castle Rig	Castlerigg
Catchdecam	Catstycam
Catum's wife's hole	Tatham Wife Hole
Chapel in Dale	Chapel-le-Dale
Chester in the Street	Chester-le-Street
Coitmoss	Goyt's Moss
Colebrook Dale	Coalbrookdale
Coltersworth	Colsterworth
Conway	Conwy
Corryhabar	Corrieyairack?
Craig	Crag Farm House
Critch	Crich
crooked Devon	Crook of Devon
Dereham	East Dereham
Dersbury	Daresbury
Dinas Bran	Castell Dinas Bran
Dolgelly	Dolgellau
Dol-y-mellynlyn	Dolmelynllyn
Drumhastle	Drumchastle
Dunderaw	Dunderave?
Dunham	Dunham-on-the-Hill
E Dale	Edale
Elden Hole	Eldon Hole
Elwyseg	Eglwyseg
Esthwait	Esthwaite
Ewer	Ure
Finkle street hause	Newlands Hause?
Flutering Tarn	Floutern Tarn
Foe Park	Fowe Park
Fold's Foot	Falls Foot
Garrat's Hostle Bridge	Garret Hostel Lane Bridge

Gennet's Cave, Jenny's hole	Janet's Cave
Gibralter	Gibraltar Crag
Gilden Morden	Guilden Morden
Ginglepot	Jingle Pot
Glen Crow	Glen Croe
Glen Kinglass	Glen Kinglas
Glostershire	Gloucestershire
Gowdar Crag	Gowder Crag
Grandchester	Grantchester
Great Gavel	Great Gable
Great Stukely	Great Stukeley
Greenford	Greenfield
Greeta	Greta
Gunnersby hill	Gonerby Hill
Haddock Hall	Haydock Lodge
Haltnie	Keltney Burn
Halylog	Helygog
Harbro'	Market Harborough
Hardknot	Hardknott
Harlston	Harston
Hatteral	Hatterrall
Haulton Castle	Halton Castle
Hazles	Hasells
Herdhouse	Herdus
Hockerhill	Hockerill
Hoilick	Hoylake
Hullan Ward	Hulland Ward
Humberston	Humberstone
Hungwrt	Hengwrt
Inglebro	Ingleborough
Keddleston	Kedleston
Kelds head	Keld Head
Killicranky	Killiecrankie
Kilwick	Kildwick
Kinloch Rannock	Kinloch Rannoch
Kirby	Kirkby Malham
Kirby Lonsdale	Kirkby Lonsdale
Knock Morton	Knock Murton
Laneltyd	Llanelltyd
Latrig	Latrigg

Latterborough	Latterbarrow
Leasoes	Leasowes
Lee Bridge	Lea Bridge
Lingmel	Lingmell
Lingmel Beck	Lingmell Gill?
Little Stukely	Little Stukeley
Llanberris	Llanberis
Llandulas	Llanddulas
Llangunnog	Llangynog
Llanrhayder	Llanrhaeadr-ym-Mochnant
Llansannon	Llansannan
Loch Ketterin	Loch Katrine
Loch Rannock	Loch Rannoch
Loch Tumel	Loch Tummel
Lonscale hill	Lonscale Fell
Lord Oxford's Bridge	Lord's Bridge
Lowdore	Lodore
Lynn	King's Lynn
Machynleth	Machynlleth
Maggot Mount	St Margaret's Mount
Mawdach	Mawddach
Meir (or Mare) Gill	Meregill
Melross	Melrose
Menay Straits	Menai Straits
Middleton	Stoney Middleton
Moncrief hill	Moncreiffe Hill
Morgin Tarn	Mockerkin Tarn
My Lord's bridge	Lord's Bridge
Naddale	Naddle
Neine	Nene
Nesson	Neston
Nether Wastdale	Nether Wasdale
New Byre Castle	Newbyres Castle
Newton	Newton-le-Willows
Ninforth	Minffordd
Norton	King's Norton
Oakover Hall	Okeover Hall
Onion	Wnion
Ormathwait	Ormathwaite
Oxenford Castle	Oxenfoord Castle
Pardsha	Pardshaw

213

Peak Cave	Peak Cavern
Peak in the Forest	Peak Forest
Penmanmaur	Penmaenmawr
Penman Ross	Penmaen Rhos
Pennygant	Pen-y-ghent
Pentridge	Pentrich
Pistil Rhayder, Pistill rayder	Pistyll Rhaeadr
Pistil-y-Cain, Pistil Cain	Pistyll Cain
Plumpton	Plompton
Pomfret	Pontefract
Pontysylty	Pont-y-Cysylltau
Pool's Hole	Poole's Cavern
Raiadir y Wenol	Swallow Falls
Ratcliff crag	Ratcheugh Crag
Ravlig	Revelin Crag
Rayder Dee	Rhaeadr Dhu
Rayder Mawdach	Rhaeadr Mawddach
Rhayder-y-Wenol	Swallow Falls
Ridge	Rigg
Rigindale beck	Riggindale beck
Robin Tiptoes Hill	Robin-a-Tiptoe Hill
Rosthwait	Rosthwaite
Router Rocks	Rowtor Rocks
Row beck	Lingmell Beck?
Rudland Castle	Rhuddlan Castle
Rumbling Brig	Rumbling Bridge
Rythin	Ruthin
Salter's kill fell	Souther Scales Fell?
Schehallion	Schiehallion
Seathwait	Seathwaite
Shengay	Shingay
Sheperheath	Shepreth
Side fell	The Side
Skiddaw great man	Skiddaw Man
Sparkling Tarn	Sprinkling Tarn
spooler green	Spoonygreen Lane
Styborough crag	Stybarrow Crag
Styehead	Sty Head
Tally bull	Tullibole
Thackstead	Thaxted
Thornton	Thornton Lonsdale

Thorp Cloud	Thorpe Cloud
Tilton	Tilton on the Hill
Torwyn	Tywyn
Tudden-y-gladys	Tyddyn-Gwladys
Ullock	Ullock Pike
Valle Crwcis	Valle Crucis
Walden	Saffron Walden
Walsal	Walsall
Wastdale Head	Wasdale Head
Watinleth	Watendlath
Weatherby	Wetherby
Wenden	Wendens Ambo
Wendye	Wendy
Wimple	Wimpole
Wisbeach	Wisbech
Wittlesford	Whittlesford
Wooburn	Woburn
Wyburn	Wythburn
Yeaborough	Yewbarrow
Yordas	Yordas Cave

APPENDIX 2:
PLUMPTRE'S WRITINGS

Published works

This list is confined to bound books and pamphlets published separately. It omits items from magazines and broadsheets, notably those in 'The Vocal Repository', the series derived from Plumptre's *Collection of Songs* which appeared from 1809 onwards. Where it is not possible to determine the chronological order of works published in the same year, they are given alphabetically.

The Coventry Act: A Comedy in Three Acts. Norwich, 1793.

Osway: A Tragedy. Norwich, 1795.

Observations on Hamlet; and on the Motives which Most Probably Induced Shakspeare to Fix upon the Story of Amleth, from the Danish Chronicle of Saxo Grammaticus, for the Plot of that Tragedy: Being an Attempt to Prove that he Designed it as an Indirect Censure upon Mary Queen of Scots. Cambridge, 1796.

An Appendix to Observations on Hamlet; Being an Attempt to Prove that Shakespeare Designed that Tragedy as an Indirect Censure on Mary Queen of Scots. Containing I. Some Observations on Dramas, which Professedly Allude to the Occurrences and Characters of the Times in which they Were Written, and an Answer to Objections Brought against the Hypothesis. II. Some Farther Arguments in Support of it. And III. An Answer to the Objections Brought against Dr. Warburton's Hypothesis Respecting an Allusion to Mary Queen of Scots in the Celebrated Passage in the Midsummer Night's Dream. Cambridge, 1797.

The Lakers: A Comic Opera, in Three Acts. London, 1798.

The House of Mourning and the House of Feasting: A Sermon Preached before the Hinxton Friendly Society, in the Parish Church of Hinxton, Cambridgeshire, on Sunday, September the 30th, 1804. Being the Anniversary. To which Are Added, Psalm cxxxiii. and Hymns to Be Sung at the Funerals of Deceased Members. Cambridge [1804].

A Collection of Songs, Moral, Sentimental, Instructive, and Amusing. The Words Selected and Revised by the Rev. J. Plumptre. The Music Adapted and Composed by Charles Hague. Cambridge, 1805.

The Plague Stayed: A Scriptural View of Pestilence, Particularly of that Dreadful Pestilence the Small-Pox, with Considerations on the Newly-Discovered Remedy by Inoculation with the Vaccine or Cow-Pock; in a Sermon, Preached before the University of Cambridge, on Sunday, February the 24th, 1805. With Copious Notes and Illustrations. Cambridge, 1805.

The Water of Bethesda: A Sermon, preached in the Parish Church of St. John, Margate, in the Isle of Thanet, on Sunday, August the 30th, 1807; for the General Sea-Bathing Infirmary at Margate. Ramsgate, 1807.

Joseph's Consideration: A Sermon on Genesis xxxix.9., preached in Clare-Hall Chapel, on Monday, Feb. the 29th, 1808, Being the day of Administering the Holy Sacrament of the Lord's Supper at the Division of the Term. Cambridge, 1808.

Four Discourses on Subjects Relating to the Amusement of the Stage: Preached at Great St. Mary's Church, Cambridge, on Sunday September 25, and Sunday October 2, 1808; with Copious Supplementary Notes. Cambridge, 1809.

The Way in Which We Should Go: A Sermon, Preached in the Parish Church of St. Botolph, Cambridge; on Sunday December 11, 1808; for the Benefit of the New School, Established on Dr. Bell's and Mr. Lancaster's Plan of Education. Cambridge, 1809.

The Case of the Jews and the Samaritans: A Sermon, Preached before the University of Cambridge, at Great Saint Mary's Church, on Sunday, January 27, 1811. Cambridge, 1811.

Letters to John Aikin, M.D. on his Volume of Vocal Poetry: and on his 'Essays on Song-Writing; with a Collection of Such English Songs as Are Most Eminent for Poetical Merit'. Published Originally by himself in the Year 1772; and Re-published by R.H. Evans, in the Year 1810. By James Plumptre, B.D. Fellow of Clare-Hall, Cambridge. To which Are Added a Collection of Songs Revised and Altered by the Editor; with Some Original Songs. Cambridge, 1811.

An Inquiry into the Lawfulness of the Stage. Taken Principally from Four Discourses on Subjects Relating to the Amusement of the Stage, Preached at Great St. Mary's Church, Cambridge, on Sunday September 25 and Sunday October 2, 1808; and from the Preface to The English Drama Purified: Published in 1812. Cambridge, 1812.

The English Drama Purified: Being a Specimen of Select Plays, in which All the Passages that Have Appeared to the Editor to Be Objectionable in Point of Morality, Are Omitted and Altered. With Prefaces and Notes. 3 volumes. Cambridge, 1812.

Forbidding to Marry, A Departure from the Faith: A Sermon, Preached before the University of Cambridge, at Great St. Mary's Church, on Sunday, Nov. 8. 1812. Cambridge, 1812.

The Experienced Butcher: Shewing the Respectability and Usefulness of his Calling, the Religious Considerations Arising from it, the Laws Relating to it, and Various Profitable Suggestions for the Rightly Carrying it on: Designed not only for the Use of Butchers but also for Families and Readers in General. London, 1816.

Three Discourses on the Case of the Animal Creation, and the Duties of Man to them. London, 1816.

Original Dramas: Containing Royal Beneficence, or The Emperor Alexander; Winter; Kendrew, or The Coal Mine; The Force of Conscience; Mrs. Jordan and the Methodist; and The Salutary Reproof: with Prefaces and Notes. Cambridge, 1818.

Three Discourses on Tithes: No. I. On Trust in God. No. II. On the Origin of Tithes, and Tithes under the Law. No. III. On Tithes under the Gospel. Preached in the Parish Church of Great Gransden, Huntingdonshire, in the Years 1814 and 1817. Cambridge, 1818.

The Truth of the Popular Notion of Apparitions, or Ghosts, Considered by the Light of Scripture: A Sermon. Cambridge, 1818.

A Letter to the Author of a Tract Entitled The Stage: Three Dialogues between Mr. Clement and Mr. Mortimer. Published by the Religious Tract Society. Cambridge, 1819.

The Sinner Made a Terror to Himself and his Friends: A Sermon, Preached in the Parish Church of Great Gransden, Huntingdonshire, on Sunday, November 21, 1819, and Repeated the Following Sunday, at the Desire of Some of the Parishioners. Cambridge, 1819.

A Letter to the Most Noble The Marquis of Hertford, Lord Chamberlain of His Majesty's Household and Master of the Revels, on the Subject of a Dramatic Institution. Cambridge, 1820.

A Selection from Fables by John Gay. In Two Parts. Selected and Revised by James Plumptre, B.D. Huntingdon, 1823.

Fables in Verse for the Female Sex. By Edward Moore, Henry Brooke, and Others. Selected and Revised by James Plumptre, B.D. London, 1825.

One Hundred Fables in Verse; by Various Authors. Selected and Revised by James Plumptre, B.D. London, 1825.

A Popular Commentary on the Bible, in a Series of Sermons, Following, in the Old Testament, the Course of the First Lessons at Morning and Evening Service on Sundays. Designed for Parish Churches, or Reading in Private Families. 2 volumes. London, 1827.

The Resurrection of Our Friends, Who Are the Friends of Jesus. A Sermon, Preached in the Parish Church of Great Gransden, in the County of Huntingdon, on Sunday, April 6, 1828, Being Easter Sunday, and the First Anniversary of the United Friendly Society, after the Death of Thomas Lantaffe, Butcher. Huntingdon, 1828.

Wimpole Hall: Extracted from A Journal of a Tour to the Source of the River Cam, made in July 1800 By W.B. Trevilyan & J. Plumtre [sic]. Cambridge: privately printed at the University Library, 1976.

Descent into a Coal-Pit: Extracted from the Journal of James Plumptre, 1799. Cambridge: privately printed at the University Library, 1985.

Blind Jack & Mother Shipton [extract from 1799 Narrative, 7 May]. Cambridge: privately printed at the University Library, 1986.

Manuscripts

All the items listed below are in the Cambridge University Library (Manuscripts Room), though the list does not exhaust the Plumptre papers deposited there by the widow of the Rev. A.J. Edmonds of Great Gransden in 1914. It includes manuscripts directly of use in preparing this edition, and omits: manuscripts of published works; notes for sermons; loose slips of paper; and several boxes of letters by and to Plumptre (Add. 5864–5867), written largely after 1800 and usually in connection with the publication of his books.

'The Olio: A Pantomine [*sic*] written in the Year 1788'. Add. 5785.

'Plot upon Plot: A Farce in Two Acts written in the year 1788'. Fair copy, not in Plumptre's hand: Add. 5786. Revised version (1789) in Plumptre's hand: Add. 5787. Fair copy of 1789 version, not in Plumptre's hand: Add. 5788.

'The Wars of York and Lancaster, An Historical-Play Alterd [*sic*] from The Second and Third Parts of Shakespeare's Henry VI'. 1789–1790? Add. 5790. Fair copy not in Plumptre's hand: Add. 5789.

'Richard III, An Historical Tragedy Altered from Shakespeare'. 1789–1790? Add. 5792–5793. Fair copy not in Plumptre's hand: Add. 5791.

'Journal'. 1790. Add. 5794.

'A Letter to a Friend on his going to reside in the University'. First version (1791): Add. 5799. Revised version (1792) with 'Advertizement': Add. 5800.

'An Epitome of Locke's Essay on Human Understanding'. Notebook dated 1791. Add. 5795.

'A List of Subscribers to The Coventry Act. April 1792'. Notebook also containing publication expenses for *The Coventry Act, Osway, Observations on Hamlet* and *Appendix to Observations on Hamlet*. Add. 5798.

'A journal: of a Tour through part of North Wales in the year 1792'. Two notebooks. Add. 5802.

'Notes, taken at Lectures in Modern History; given by D^r. Symonds. Began [*sic*] Feb. 18. 1793'. Notebook. Add. 5803.

'The Senior Wrangler, or the Wooden Spoon: upon the Plan of the Greek Drama'. 1793. Incomplete manuscript, 'Elucidations' (i.e. footnotes) and incomplete fair copy. Add. 5801.

'Journal of a Tour into Derbyshire in the year 1793'. Add. 5804.

'Poems, &c'. 1793–1798? Mutilated notebook of verses by Plumptre and others, not all in his hand. Add. 5805.

'An Abstract of Blair's Lectures on Rhetoric and Belles Lettres'. Two notebooks dated 1794. Add. 5806.

'Some Particulars relative to those Gentlemen who have performed Parts in the Plays acted at Mr Newcome's School at Hackney'. Notebook started 1795, resumed 1829. Add. 5807.

'Memorandums from Pennant's Tour into Scotland and Voyage to the Hebrides and from Johnson's and Boswell's Journals, with Additions from Gilpin, Knox and F. Newcome' and 'Memorandums, taken during a Tour into Scotland and to the Lakes of Cumberland and Westmorland in the summer of 1796'. One notebook. Add. 5810.

'A Journal of a Pedestrian Tour by the Caves in the West Riding of York-shire to the Lakes and Home thro Parts of North Wales in the Year 1797'. Add. 5811.

'Memorandums Taken during a Tour into Scotland'. 1799. Two notebooks. Add. 5812-5813.

Sketches and itinerary, on loose sheets, from 1779 tour. Add. 5817.

'A Narrative of a Pedestrian Journey through Some Parts of Yorkshire, Durham and Northumberland to the Highlands of Scotland and Home by the Lakes and Some Parts of Wales in the Summer of the Year 1799'. Three bound volumes. Add. 5814–5816.

'Memorandums taken during a Five weeks Tour in the summer of 1800'. Add. 5818.

'A Journal of a Tour to the Source of the River Cam made in July 1800 by Walter Blackett Trevilyan [sic] Esqr. A.B. of S^t. John's College, and the Rev^d. James Plumptre. A.M. Fellow of Clare Hall, Cambridge'. Add. 5819.

'Account Book begun A.D. 1801'. Add. 5820.

'An Account of the Parish of Hinxton and of its Inhabitants taken at the end of the year 1802. By the Rev^d. James Plumptre. A.M. Sequestrator of Hinxton Vicarage and member of the Societies for Promoting Christian Knowledge, and For the Suppression of Vice, and for Increasing the Comforts and Bettering the Condition of the Poor'. Add. 5821.

Diaries. 1804–09, 1811–24, 1829. Add. 5835–5855.

'Lectures on Poetry chiefly as it applies to Dramatic and Lyric Composi-tions with a view to its Improvement'. 1806. Notebook. Add. 5823.

'Charity'. 1807–13. Notebook. Add. 5861.

'Memorandums respecting the Vicarage of Great Gransden. Begun March 14, 1812'. Notebook. Add. 5826.

'A List of the Inhabitants of The Parish of Great Gransden taken 1812'. Notebook. Add. 5827.

Untitled, undated notebook about Great Gransden. Add. 5822.

'Memorandums'. 1812–26. Notebooks numbered 1–4, and one unlabelled notebook. Add. 5856-5860.

'An Account of the Parish of Great Gransden in The County of Hunting-don and of its Inhabitants began [sic] at the beginning of the year 1816 By James Plumptre, B.D. Vicar'. Add. 5830.

'A Statement of the case of the appointment of the Parish Clerk at Great

Gransden in the County of Huntingdon'. 1818. Add. 5833.

'A Memorial respecting the Small Tithes, Vicarage Glebe and Poor Rates at Great Gransden. In a Letter addressed to Thomas Quintin, Esq'. 1818. Add. 5829.

'An Account of Books Read Beginning with the year 1819'. Add. 5831.

'To the Provisional Committee for the Encouragement of Industry and Reduction of Poors' [sic] Rates'. 1821. Add. 5829.

'Notes and Extracts Relating to the Plumptre Family'. 1820s. Add. 5832.

'Pedestrianism'. 1820s. Loose notes, extracts, and outline of 'The Pedestrian's Pocket Companion'. Add. 5817.

NOTES

General Introduction

Passages quoted from the travel journals are footnoted only if they do not also appear in the text of this selection.

1. **three brief extracts**. They appear as the last items on the list of publications in Appendix 2, which also gives details of Plumptre's papers.
2. **World at large**. Plumptre's will, dated 5 September 1829 and proved 6 March 1832, is in the Huntingdon Branch of Cambridge County Archives.
3. **history of the parish**. A.J. Edmonds, *A History of Great Grandsen in the County of Huntingdon, from the Earliest Times to the Present Day* (St Neots: privately printed in monthly parts, 1892).
4. **to the public**. 1800 Memorandums, 20 June, which refers to 'the 4 weeks M.S. of my Tour'. No manuscript or tour fits the description, and 'weeks' is presumably a slip of the pen for 'months', Plumptre having the 1799 tour of four and a half months in mind.
5. **hold good livings**. *Correspondence of Thomas Gray*, edited by Paget Toynbee and Leonard Whibley (Oxford: Clarendon Press, 1935), 2: 646. John Twigg, *A History of Queens' College, Cambridge 1488–1986* (Woodbridge, Suffolk: Boydell Press, 1987) quotes Gray in his useful account of Robert Plumptre's Presidency (chapters 12, 13 and 15).
6. **other preferment**. Letter quoted by D.A. Winstanley, *Unreformed Cambridge: A Study of Certain Aspects of the University in the Eighteenth Century* (Cambridge: Cambridge University Press, 1935), 138.
7. **property in Hampshire**. Robert Plumptre's will, proved 20 November 1788, is in the Public Record Office (PROB11/1172).
8. **intended me**. *Four Discourses on Subjects Relating to the Amusement of the Stage*, Dedication, vi.
9. **smallpox vaccine**. For Plumptre's interest in Jenner, see his sermon of 1805, *The Plague Stayed*, and 'The Cow', a very odd poem included in his *Collection of Songs* the same year.
10. **ever experienced**. Diary for 5 March 1805.
11. **ruinous state**. *The Resurrection of Our Friends*, 8.
12. **disgraceful . . . national sin**. *Forbidding to Marry*, 12 and 11.
13. **know of her**. Plumptre noted her place and date of birth (26 September 1770) in his 'Account of the Parish of Great Grandsen', f. 13. His diary records the death of her mother, Mrs Jordan Robinson, on 11 May 1818.
14. **Wife too ill . . . quite out of tune**. See, for example, diary for 28 October to 13 November 1820.

15. **very unsettled ... important secret.** Diary for 7 and 9 August 1819.
16. **subject of W^m.** Diary for 21 November 1820.
17. **taking it off.** Diary for 21 October 1821.
18. **her Journal ... after dinner.** Diary for 12 and 14 March 1822.
19. **wire worm.** Diary for 16 March 1818.
20. **in the evening.** Diary for 9 October 1817.
21. **care a pin ... parson or bishop.** Diary for 21 February 1821.
22. **friends or interest.** From the passage in 'Letter to a Friend' noted below, note 24.
23. **Jacobins and infidels.** Quoted by Winstanley, *Unreformed Cambridge*, p.278.
24. **awful warning.** 'Letter to a Friend', first version, ff. 3–6. Plumptre cut the passage from the version made in the hope of publication.
25. **gloomy pilgrimage.** *The Coventry Act*, Dedication, unpaginated.
26. **classical education.** *Amusement of the Stage*, Dedication, iv.
27. **from that time.** *Amusement of the Stage*, Dedication, iv.
28. **actor and an author.** *Amusement of the Stage*, Dedication, v.
29. **object of my studies.** *Amusement of the Stage*, Dedication, vi.
30. **Adelaide.** See Sybil Rosenfeld, *Temples of Thespis: Some Private Theatres and Theatricals in England and Wales, 1700–1820* (London: Society for Theatre Research, 1978), 180.
31. **Anne Plumptre.** Some sources, though not her brother or her father, call her 'Anna'. Plumptre's draft obituary, quoted at the end of my account, is tucked in the manuscript of 'The Olio' in the Cambridge collection; I do not know if it appeared in print. Though brief, Robin Jarvis' entry in *A Dictionary of British and American Women Writers 1660–1800*, edited by Janet Todd (London: Methuen, 1984), helps rescue her from obscurity.
32. **intellectual Jacobinism.** The phrase is from Albert Goodwin's account of Norwich in *The Friends of Liberty: The English Democratic Movement in the Age of the French Revolution* (London: Hutchinson, 1979), 147–58.
33. **Voltaire and Tom Paine.** *The Sinner Made a Terror to Himself and his Friends*, 8–13.
34. **can be given.** *The Lakers*, Preface, xii.
35. **Wordsworth ... Turner.** Significantly, he mentioned both men before they had made their reputation, quoting Wordsworth's 'An Evening Walk' in the 1799 Narrative (27 July, passage not included in this selection) and praising the Lake District canvases Turner exhibited at the Royal Academy in 1798 (*The Lakers*, note to xiv).
36. **brightened atmosphere.** 1799 Narrative, 21 May, not included in this selection.
37. **instead of the Gun.** Plumptre's compassion for animal suffering stopped short of the vegetarianism advocated by Joseph Ritson and

others. He dealt with their arguments in *The Experienced Butcher*, a curious book, and *Three Discourses on the Case of the Animal Creation, and the Duties of Man to Them*, both published in 1816.

38. **Democrat**. 1799 Narrative, 13 June, not included in this selection.
39. **summer half year**. 1799 Narrative, 10 May, not included in this selection.
40. **French Cookery**. 1800 Memorandums, 25 May, not included in this selection.
41. **Palace of the Vale**. See note 154 to the 1799 Narrative.
42. **encountered them in 1797**. *Original Dramas*, 130, describes how the Bishop of Ely's wife introduced him to the tracts on the day he was licensed to the Sequestration of Hinxton.
43. **convivial Songs**. *Amusement of the Stage*, Dedication, viii.
44. **a Christian**. From the account of the 'principles which have guided the editor in his former works' in the Preface to *A Selection from Fables by John Gay*, ix–x.

1790 Journal

1. **Lectures . . . &c &c**. The first two items on this list refer to the satirical monologues on contemporary manners made popular by George Alexander Stevens' *Lectures on Heads*, which he first performed in the 1760s, and John Collins' *The Evening Brush*, enjoying a great success in the 1780s and 1790s. Attic entertainments mixed lectures and recitations with music and song. Olios were medleys: Plumptre himself had already written 'The Olio: A Pantomime' (1788), with a cast of magicians, harlequins and a zany.
2. **tales of the Genii**. James Ridley's *The Tales of the Genii* (1764), a popular exercise in Orientalism modelled on *The Arabian Nights* and presented as a translation from the Persian.
3. **My brothers house**. His oldest brother Joseph (1758–1810) then held the living of nearby Newton as well as that of Stretton in Rutland.
4. **Scraggs company**. William Scraggs joined forces with David Fisher from the rival Theatre Royal Company in 1792 to form the Norfolk and Suffolk Company of Comedians, which survived until the 1840s.
5. **Strong**. William Strong, a native of Peterborough and graduate of Queens', then held the livings of Billinghay and Hareby with Bolingbroke north of Boston. He was Canon of Peterborough when he died in 1842.
6. **Skeffington**. See the introduction to this journal.
7. **Zukero**. Federigo Zuccaro's name was often promiscuously attached to portraits of Elizabeth, as Holbein's was to portraits of Henry VIII.
8. **sheep**. Apparently Jacob sheep, a fashionable ornament to many gentlemen's parks.

9. **new church**. King's Norton church had been rebuilt in 1757–71 with a Gothick exterior and neo-classical furnishings. It was paid for by William Fortrey rather than his nephew Henry Green of Rolleston.

10. **Queen Mab**. From Mercutio's speech in *Romeo and Juliet* (I.iv.53 onwards). The phrase that follows is a slight misquotation from *The Merchant of Venice* (V.i.15).

11. **Mattocks**. Isabella Mattocks (1746–1826) enjoyed a long career on the boards at Covent Garden, where *The Widow of Malabar*, an insignificant tragedy adapted from the French, had been staged the previous May. She was chiefly admired as a singer and comic actress.

12. **Richard the third**. While at Queens', Plumptre adapted Shakespeare's *Richard III* and *Henry VI, Parts Two and Three* (retitled 'The Wars of York and Lancaster') but failed to interest a London management.

13. **the Agreeable Surprize**. A comic opera first performed in 1781, by the prolific John O'Keeffe, remembered for *Wild Oats* (1791).

14. **Wartnaby**. A fellow undergraduate at Queens', Thomas Wartnaby became Curate of Draughton, near Market Harborough, in 1790, the first of several appointments in or near his native Leicestershire.

15. **Andrew**. John Andrew, another fellow student at Queens', served as Curate of his native Daventry before his early death in 1801.

16. **Anne Bullen**. The Blue Boudoir displays a small late eighteenth-century portrait of Anne Boleyn.

17. **good Lady**. Presumably Mrs Home, housekeeper here for more than seventy years. When she died in 1834 at the age of ninety-three *The Annual Register* reported that she had saved more than £30,000 from showing the castle.

18. **The White Lyon**. The Henley Street hotel made famous in the Drury Lane pageant David Garrick had rescued from his abortive Jubilee celebrations at Stratford in 1769.

19. **olympus habet**. 'Earth covers, the people mourn and Olympus now has a Nestor in judgement, a Socrates in genius and a Virgil in art'. The misspelling of 'Terra' and 'maeret' would seem to bear out Plumptre's admission elsewhere that he neglected his classical studies.

20. **the worse for it**. Most visitors seem to have disliked the recolouring of Gheerart Janssen's bust financed by John Ward's benefit performance of *Othello* in 1746: 'Lady Caroline Petersham is not more vermilion', exclaimed Horace Walpole. It was whitewashed in 1793 at the insistence of Edmond Malone but coloured again in the next century.

21. **House where he was born**. Shakespeare's birthplace was still divided into the Swan and Maidenhead inn and a butcher's shop where Mrs Hart and her successors showed relics like the chair, which had mysteriously reappeared after being sold to a Polish princess the previous July. Visitors more favoured than Plumptre were allowed to cut pieces from it. The Shakespeare Birthplace Committee, forerunner of the present

Trust, bought the building in 1847 and heavily restored it.

22. **Sharp's.** The founding father of Stratford's souvenir trade, William Sharp used wood from the mulberry tree Shakespeare had supposedly planted at New Place to produce an implausible amount of knick-knacks ranging from toothpicks to small items of furniture. He died in 1799.

23. **my Brothers at Worcester.** John Plumptre (1753–1825), a first cousin who had married Plumptre's oldest sister Diana (1757–1825). A future Dean of Gloucester, he then held the livings of Stone and Wichenford, both near Worcester.

24. **seventy and eighty pounds.** Presumably the box-office takings.

25. **All the world's a stage.** A farce, first produced in 1777 and often revived, by the Irish playwright Isaac Jackman.

26. **Lion.** 'As we Cantabs call the curiosities of any place', Plumptre explained when he used the colloquialism again in his 1799 Narrative.

27. **scorbutic disorders.** Scurvy.

1792 Journal

1. **Pennant.** Thomas Pennant's *A Tour in Wales* (1778–81 edition, 1: 34), the obvious authority to consult for antiquarian detail.

2. **conscious peace.** Lightly adapted from James Thomson's *The Seasons* (*Autumn*, lines 1299–1302).

3. **smitten cliffs.** From Thomson's description of a thunderstorm in *The Seasons* (*Summer*, lines 1163–66). Though the Penmaenmawr road had been repaired, broadened and fenced some twenty years before, rock falls still happened often enough to give travellers a pleasurable shudder.

4. **1545 feet.** A detail from Pennant's *Tour in Wales* (2, Part 2: 306).

5. *Dim Saxenag.* Dim Saesneg: 'No English'.

6. **River S^t. Helens.** Usually called the Seiont.

7. *a Llanberris? . . . yea a.* Pa'r un am y ffordd i Lanberis? (literally, 'Which one is the way to Llanberis?'). 'Yea a' is either 'ie' (yes) or 'yw' (it is).

8. **years well spent.** Lightly adapted from Nicholas Rowe's *Jane Shore* (I.ii.20–23), a pathetic tragedy in pseudo-Shakespearean verse which remained popular for many years after its first production in 1714. Plumptre adapted it for his *English Drama Purified* (1812).

9. **pillow hard.** From Shakespeare's *Cymbeline* (III.vi.34).

10. **Banks . . . Shuckborough.** Sir Joseph Banks (1743–1830), the naturalist who had accompanied Captain Cook on his voyage to round the world, was then President of the Royal Society. The mathematician Sir George Shuckburgh-Evelyn (1751–1804) was author of *Observations Made in Savoy to Ascertain the Height of Mountains* (1777). In giving the height of Snowdon as 3568 feet, Pennant's *Tour in Wales* (2, Part 2: 165–6) noted that recent experiments using barometric pressure and the boiling

point of water produced lower estimates than earlier calculations using trigonometry. The Ordnance Survey gives 3559 feet.

11. **ever-dripping fogs.** From Thomson's *The Seasons* (*Autumn*, lines 807–812).

12. **shreds and patches.** Hamlet calls Claudius 'a king of shreds and patches' (III.iv.103).

13. **steep to steep.** From Thomson's *The Seasons* (*Autumn*, lines 611–12).

14. **9 feet perpendicular.** 'Must be much more, I think', Plumptre added in a pencilled note.

15. **thunders through.** From Thomson's *The Seasons* (*Autumn*, lines 97–105). Plumptre has altered part of the passage ('Then o'er the sanded valley floating spreads, / Calm, sluggish, silent . . . ') to suit better the more dramatic spectacle of the waterfall.

16. **ancient castle.** A slight misquotation from Shakespeare's *Richard II* (III.iii.31).

17. **Howard's Plan.** John Howard's *The State of the Prisons* (1777) did much to stimulate penal reform. He had died in 1790.

18. **Bwlch-y-Rhiw Velen.** The turnpike route over the Horseshoe Pass.

19. **female Hermits.** The Ladies of Llangollen, Lady Eleanor Butler (1739?–1829) and Sarah Ponsonby (1735?–1831), had begun their life of rural retirement and romantic friendship at Plas Newydd in 1780. Wordsworth, Burke and the Duke of Wellington were among their many famous visitors. Plumptre himself gets a closer look in the 1797 Journal (7–8 August) and the 1799 Narrative (23–24 August).

20. *black* **stream.** Plumptre added a note reminding the reader that '*Dee*, in welch, signifies *black*'.

21. **Exits and their Enterances.** From Jaques' speech about the seven ages of man in *As You Like It* (II.vii.140).

22. **Gwynedds.** The gwyniad is a white fish of the salmon species. Plumptre later added a note: 'I have since met with a Gentleman, who had travelled in Switzerland, and mentioned a circumstance of the same kind taking place in the Lake of Geneva, where the Ferrarr [i.e. the *féra* or *ferrat*], a fish peculiar to the Lake of Geneva, are never found in ye Rhone, which runs through it, nor are ye trout and pearch of ye river ever found in ye Lake'.

23. **Wynn.** Sir Watkin Williams Wynn (1748–96), the fourth baronet, represented the most powerful landowning family in Wales, whose estates included several beauty spots attracting tourists. Plumptre passes Llangedwyn Hall, one of the baronet's homes, later in his tour.

24. **many People.** Pennant noted that in summer the mount was 'usually covered in a picturesque manner with knitters, of both sexes, and all ages' (*Tour in Wales*, 2, Part 1: 68).

25. **horrid situation.** A famous episode in *The Seasons* (*Winter*, lines 275–321) which Plumptre acknowledged as a source for his own play called

Winter, written many years later and published in *Original Dramas* (1818). The fate of people stuck in snowdrifts seems to have fascinated him: see 1799 Narrative ('John McNab', 25 June).

26. **S^t. Chads.** An inventive building by George Steuart which the Hon. John Byng, another tourist who saw it when new, thought 'as ugly as improper'.

27. **House of Industry.** Opened in 1783. One of several early, much-discussed experiments in dealing with the growing poverty brought about by agricultural change, it pointed the way to the New Poor Law of 1834 by replacing the parish system of outdoor relief and maintenance with a workhouse administered by a union of several parishes.

28. *Colebrook dale*. Plumptre returned to the Iron Bridge, furnaces and mines at Coalbrookdale in his 1797 Journal (10 August), though still without managing to see the gorge by night—a scene painted by Philippe de Loutherbourg.

1793 Journal

1. **in draft.** In pulling or drawing vehicles.
2. **the ordinary.** Where meals at fixed prices were served.
3. **bloods.** The Hooray Henrys of the time.
4. **Boothby's grounds.** Sir Brooke Boothby (1744–1824), a member of the Lichfield circle centred on Erasmus Darwin and an admirer of Rousseau, whose work he holds in the delightful open-air portrait by Joseph Wright of Derby in the Tate Gallery.
5. **Holy Family by Raphael.** Apparently a copy of the Madrid *Madonna della Perla*, itself executed by Giulio Romano from Raphael's design.
6. **Morgan rattler.** A street ballad with highly suggestive words, not included in Plumptre's *Collection of Songs, Moral, Sentimental, Instructive, and Amusing* (1805) but printed as No. 123 in Roy Palmer's *Everyman Book of British Ballads* (London: J.M. Dent and Sons, 1980).
7. **O'Keef's farces.** Like *The Agreeable Surprise*, already noted in the 1790 Journal (at Kibworth).
8. *crescent*. Begun in 1779 as the centrepiece of the fifth Duke of Devonshire's campaign to give Buxton the fashionable appeal of Bath. Its architect, John Carr of York, also designed the massive stables, later converted into the Devonshire Royal Hospital.
9. **candlelight painting.** A genre developed from the Utrecht school by Joseph Wright of Derby (1734–97) in such works as *A Philosopher Giving a Lecture on the Orrery* (Derby Museum and Art Gallery) and *An Experiment on a Bird in the Air Pump* (Tate Gallery).
10. **inhabitants of earth.** The witches in *Macbeth* (I.iii.40–41), often invoked by travellers describing the guides in the Derbyshire caves.
11. **old Castle.** Peveril Castle, built in the eleventh and twelfth centuries

but ruined since the seventeenth.

12. **darkness visible**. The atmosphere of Hell in Milton's *Paradise Lost* (Book 1, 63).

13. **entrails tore**. From the war in Heaven in *Paradise Lost* (Book 6, 586–8). 'Contagious' should be 'outrageous'.

14. **chaos to retire**. From Satan's journey out of Hell in *Paradise Lost* (Book 1, 1034–8).

15. **Lonsdale**. James Lowther, Earl of Lonsdale (1736–1802), landowner and bulwark of the Tory interest in the Lake District, where Wordsworth's father was his attorney. Many contemporaries agreed with Horace Walpole in finding him 'equally unamiable in public and private'.

16. *Lead Mine*. The Speedwell Mine, no longer worked but still open to visitors.

17. **Rule Britannia**. England had been at war with France since February. Patriotic airs, both traditional and specially written in abuse of Tom Paine and the French Revolution, get generous space in Plumptre's *Collection of Songs* (1805), first planned this summer.

18. *Router Rocks*. Though 'improved' by the vicar of Birchover in the early 1700s, Rowtor Rocks seem to be natural formations. William Mason's *Caractacus* (1759), the source of Plumptre's quotations, encouraged the fashion for associating any conceivably prehistoric site with the Druids that Dr Stukeley had pioneered at Stonehenge.

19. **Arcwright**. Sir Richard Arkwright, who established the first of his water-powered cotton mills at Cromford in 1771, had died in 1792 without seeing the completion of Willersley Castle, intended to mark his elevation from industrialist to country gentleman.

20. **Midsummer night's dream**. In Titania's description of the chaos caused by her quarrel with Oberon (II.i.99).

1797 Journal

1. **account of Malham**. *A Concise Account of Some Natural Curiosities in the Environs of Malham in Craven, Yorkshire*, a brisk little guide published under Thomas Hurtley's name in 1786. Plumptre's own description of Craven owes more to *A Tour to the Caves, in the Environs of Ingleborough and Settle*, published anonymously in 1780 and reprinted among the addenda in later editions of Thomas West's *Guide to the Lakes*. (Subsequent references in the notes are to the first edition and accept Plumptre's assumption that West himself was the author.)

2. **Granby**. In Plumptre's handwriting this looks more like 'Gaulby', but he must surely be thinking of the soldier and politician John Manners, Marquis of Granby (1721–70), who resigned his public appointments after 'Junius' made him a target in his campaign against the Grafton ministry.

3. **maddled.** Crazed or bewildered.

4. **Flowers here.** The scientific names for the less obvious items on the list are: bird's eye, *Primula farinosa*; orchis, *Orchis mascula*; yellow hearts-ease, *Viola tricolor*. There is no native red *Ranunculus*, so perhaps 'red bell' is the water avens (*Geum rivale*), which looks a bit like a *Ranunculus*; 'lady cup' is unidentifiable. 'Stepmother' and 'bird's eye' are Yorkshire dialect names which Plumptre presumably got from his guide.

5. **on the Management of Landed Estates.** The reference, scribbled between lines, was added later: the agriculturist William Marshall did not publish his book in this form until 1806. The note on page 90 describes the Ebbing and Flowing Well behaving properly in 1801.

6. **Catcott on The Deluge, p.343.** Alexander Catcott's *Treatise on the Deluge* (second edition, 1768) cites Ingleborough as a 'natural proof' that mountains and caves were made when the biblical Flood destroyed the earth's original uniformity. Such speculation had been common since Thomas Burnet's *Sacred Theory of the Earth* in the seventeenth century.

7. **moss and plants.** The scientific names for the less obvious items on the list are: rose of the root (so called because of its smell), *Sedum rosa*; white stone crop, *Saxifraga hypnoides*; purple stone crop, *Saxifraga oppositifolia*; hurtle berries, *Vaccinum myrtillus*; grass upon grass, *Festuca vivipara*; stinking rhamp (with a smell like garlic), *Allium ursinum*.

8. **damps.** Here choke-damps, or suffocating vapours. For fire-damps, see the 1799 Narrative ('Descent into a coalpit', 24 May).

9. **Mr West's dining table and chair.** Features described in West's *Tour* as 'a natural seat and table in a corner, . . . well suited for a poet and philosopher' (20).

10. **Peak.** The Peak Cavern, which Plumptre had visited in 1793.

11. **Claud glass.** A convex tinted mirror, named after the painter, for enhancing Picturesque effects. See also 1799 Narrative ('Preparations for the journey' and 'Ascent of Skiddaw', 6 August).

12. **Rover.** His dog.

13. **Yorda, a Giant.** West's guide told him that Yordas Cave 'had alternately been the habitation of giants and fairies' (15).

14. **S^t. Winifred's well.** West's *Tour* (10) claimed that Keld Head was 'more fluent' than St Winefred's Well, which Plumptre had seen in 1792.

15. **Ladies at the Cottage.** Glimpsed in the 1792 Journal and visited again in the 1799 Narrative ('Vale of Llangollen', 23–24 August).

16. **Organist of Wrexham.** A Mr Randal, blind since birth and 'an exquisite Performer on the pedal Harp', according to Anna Seward, 'Swan of Lichfield' and friend of the Ladies, in a note to *Verses on Wrexham* (1796).

17. **Mr Butler and Mr Eyres of Trinity Coll.** Presumably Thomas Butler, a Fellow since 1791, and George Eyres, who received his BA in 1796.

18. **Miss Bowdlers transparencies.** Harriet Bowdler (1754–1830), religious

writer, sister of the Thomas Bowdler who expurgated Shakespeare, and close friend of the Ladies.

19. **glass of the gothic door**. A note by Anna Seward to her poem *Llangollen Vale* (1796) gives more details: 'In the elliptic arch of the door, there is a prismatic lantern of variously tinted glass, containing two large lamps with their reflectors. The light they shed resembles that of a Volcano, gloomily glaring'.

20. **lends his ray, &c.** Plumptre is apparently misremembering a line from *The Merchant of Venice* (V.i.90): 'How far that little candle throws his beams!'

21. **Ld. Berwicks**. Attingham Hall.

22. **New Iron Bridge**. Thomas Telford's first iron bridge (1795–96), no longer standing.

23. **work by great**. That is, are paid by the task, not by time.

24. **my sister**. Diana, John Plumptre's wife, whom Plumptre had visited at Stone in 1790.

1799 Narrative

1. **huge feeder**. Shylock's description of Launcelot Gobbo (*The Merchant of Venice*, II.v.45–6).

2. **Vicar of Wakefield**. Chapter 25 in one-volume editions of Goldsmith's novel.

3. **infinitely bound**. *Cymbeline* (I.vi.23): 'to whose kindnesses I am most infinitely tied'.

4. **fellow-traveller**. Dr Johnson 'wore boots, and a very wide brown cloth great coat, with pockets which might have almost held the two volumes of his folio dictionary; and he carried a large oak stick', according to the opening remarks in Boswell's *Journal of a Tour to the Hebrides* (1785).

5. **Grays glass and a Claude Lorrain**. Convex tinted mirrors, named after the poet and the painter, for enhancing Picturesque effects—as in Yordas Cave (1797 Journal, 'The West Riding', 12 June) and, during this tour, on Skiddaw (6 August).

6. **pocket pistol**. A note by Plumptre identifies this as a hip flask of the sort Falstaff carried at the Battle of Shrewsbury, adding: 'Mine however was seldom charged with anything stronger than tea'.

7. **maps of Scotland**. Thomas Kitchin's *Scotland Divided into its Counties, from the Latest Surveys* (circa 1770), at a scale of about 25 miles to the inch, and Thomas Brown's *A New and Accurate Travelling Map of Scotland* (circa 1790), at about 10 miles to the inch.

8. **Tours in Scotland**. Thomas Pennant's Scottish tours of 1769 and 1772 and Johnson's *Journey to the Western Islands of Scotland* (1775), the most influential works of their kind, were adapted for the first two volumes of William Mavor's six-volume *The British Tourists; or Travell-*

er's Pocket Companion (1798–1800). Thomas Newte's less important *Tour in England and Scotland* (1791) was abbreviated in the fourth volume.

9. **Bayley**. Then a second-year undergraduate. His relation at Little Stukeley is Mrs Sarah Bayley, descended from a Bishop and a Prebend of Peterborough.

10. **do likewise**. These three biblical quotations, all loosely adapted, come respectively from the Sermon on the Mount (Matthew 6:3–4 and 5:16) and the parable of the Good Samaritan (Luke 10:37).

11. **tomorrow**. To the future Henry VII the sunset on the eve of Bosworth Field 'gives token of a goodly day tomorrow' (*Richard III*, V.iii.21).

12. **slow-winding Trent**. Plumptre is presumably misremembering Hotspur's 'smug and silver Trent' (*Henry IV, Part One*, III.i.101).

13. *queaziness*. Morton's word for the faint-heartedness of Hotspur's troops in *Henry IV, Part Two* (I.i.196).

14. **Taste**. Samuel Foote's robust comedy, published in 1752, mentioned the Yorkshire schools only in passing and did not anticipate Dickens's *Nicholas Nickleby* in exposing their horrors.

15. **Byram**. Byram Hall, designed by John Carr of York with interior decoration by Robert Adam, about 1780.

16. **the Mansion**. Plumptre added a note: 'Should not the buildings in these cases be suited to the inhabitants, or vice versa?—I have often been struck at the ridiculousness of the idea of *a lame old woman tottering out from a triumphal arch*'.

17. **the Dramatist**. Or *Stop Him Who Can!*, first performed in 1789. The forgotten Frederick Reynolds also wrote tragedies, melodramas and *The Caravan* (1803), which owed its success to performing dogs. John Melvin was a leading member of the York Company and a 'comedian of spunk'.

18. **life of him published**. At York in 1795. Like Plumptre, it lays as much stress on Metcalf's colourful adventures as on his work building more than 180 miles of turnpike roads in the north of England. He died in 1810.

19. **Plot ... Stukeley ... Gale**. The antiquaries Robert Plot (1640–96), William Stukeley (1687–1785) and Roger Gale (1672–1744). Stukeley's theory that Stonehenge was Druidic made him the most influential authority of his period.

20. **Smiths and Hills at Knaresborough**. Custodians of St Robert's Chapel and a nearby tearoom, whom Plumptre had praised as 'a pleasing instance of what industry can do, and by what shifts and unexpected ways people may get on in the world' (7 May).

21. **Mr Mair**. Presumably one of the Maires of nearby Hardwick Hall, a family with a strong Catholic tradition.

22. **chaldron**. A measure of 53cwt.

23. **explosion of a mine**. The three-volume *History and Antiquities of the County Palatine of Durham* (1785–94) by the local antiquary William Hutchinson. Plumptre's interest in mining disasters finally led to *Kendrew: or, The Coal Mine* in *Original Dramas* (1818), based on a report of an accident at East Ardsley in 1809 but using his visit to Heaton for 'the foundation of his scenery' (91). Explosions were not the only danger: 75 men and boys died a lingering death by starvation when part of Heaton was cut off by flooding in May 1815.

24. **Pitts effigy**. William Pitt the Younger, then Prime Minister.

25. **Walter Trevillyan Junr**. Plumptre's companion on the journey described in the 1800 Cam Journal.

26. **C. Plumptre**. Charles, a clerical cousin whom Plumptre had just visited at Longnewton, County Durham.

27. **Dibdin**. Charles Dibdin (1745–1814), a versatile composer and performer known for entertainments like the one he has brought to Morpeth. Plumptre's parlour repertoire included many of Dibdin's songs.

28. **her devotees**. Plumptre may well have glimpsed them through his sister Anne, who moved in the same circles as the feminist Mary Wollstonecraft.

29. *Ned Cake*. Knead (or kneaded) cake.

30. **scarcity in 1795**. A year of bad harvest and bread shortage. See also the Cheap Repository Tract mentioned in the 1800 Cam Journal (18 December).

31. **Cheviot beyond**. Thomson's *The Seasons* (*Summer*, line 1167): 'Far seen, the heights of heathy Cheviot blaze'.

32. **Grose's Antiquities**. Francis Grose's four-volume *The Antiquities of England* (1773–76) was well respected in its time, though Grose was better remembered for his slang dictionary.

33. **E.O. table**. For a gambling game like roulette, in which the players threw balls into niches marked E and O.

34. **fitted up**. By Robert Adam in the 1760s.

35. **fees of admittance**. Quoted from Mavor's abridgement of Pennant's 1769 tour (*British Tourists*, 1: 15).

36. **his gates**. Adapted or misremembered from Exodus 20:10 and Deuteronomy 5:14.

37. **Prov**. Proverbs 22:2.

38. **Rogero**. 'Doomed to starve on water gru-el', according to his song in *The Rovers*, a lively spoof of German drama reprinted in *The Poetry of the Anti-Jacobin* (1799) from the short-lived Tory journal.

39. **Fraser Tytler**. Later Lord Woodhouselee (1747-1813), Judge Advocate of Scotland and a Professor at the University of Edinburgh. The friend who had advised Plumptre about guides before he set out, he entertained him in Edinburgh.

40. *Apron Play*. A puzzling reference. What Plumptre saw could have

been a procession of burgesses and craft guilds, whose members would have worn aprons (like Freemasons).

41. **and thunders.** Part of the passage from Thomson's *The Seasons* (*Winter*, line 105) already quoted in the 1792 Journal.

42. **Cowper's Hope.** The lines (353–6) describe the effect of a gun being fired in the silence of an abbey ruin.

43. **We crossed.** Plumptre's companion is Mr Palliser, the Duke of Atholl's factor.

44. **Ossian's Hall.** A hermitage built for the third Duke of Atholl in 1758 and redecorated in 1783, when it was named after the Gaelic poet whose reputation had been revived by James Macpherson's spurious translations in the 1760s. The National Trust for Scotland now owns it.

45. **Gow.** Both performer and composer of fiddle music, Niel Gow (1727–1807) published several collections of Strathspey Reels, met Burns and sat for Raeburn. Nathaniel (1766–1831) was the most successful of the sons who followed in his footsteps.

46. **a servant.** Plumptre had changed his original plan and put off hiring a guide at Edinburgh, Perth or Dunkeld because he did not like the looks (or the fees) of the candidates he interviewed.

47. **Poet Struan.** Alexander Robertson of Struan (1670?–1749), Jacobite chief and author of vigorous, sometimes obscene poetry. Plumptre gives colourful, inaccurate details of him when he gets to Carie, Struan's estate on Loch Rannoch.

48. **Poetry.** Presumably Macpherson's 'Ossian'.

49. **finding its attraction.** A famous experiment in which the Astronomer Royal, Nevil Maskelyne (1732–1811), and his companions measured the deviations of a plumbline. The mathematician Charles Hutton deduced the mean density of the earth from the result.

50. **the gravel.** Sand-like concretions in the kidneys or bladder.

51. **Camel Driver.** The finished poem is given on 6 July.

52. **know her not.** An adaptation of Malcolm's remark about Ross (*Macbeth*, IV.iii.160).

53. **i' th' north.** An adaptation of the king's exchange with the Earl of Derby in *Richard III* (IV.iv.483–4).

54. **We were next conducted.** Plumptre has joined a party from his inn at Kenmore.

55. **Parnel.** Slightly altered from the opening of Thomas Parnell's *The Hermit*, a narrative poem published after his death by Pope in 1721.

56. **People's eyes.** Adapted from Gray's *Elegy Written in a Country Churchyard* to compliment the Earl of Breadalbane and his 'model' village.

57. **turns to thee.** From Goldsmith's *The Traveller* (1764).

58. **Caledonian's regions.** Johnson's description of Iona in *A Journey to the Western Islands of Scotland* (1775).

59. **Journies in Scotland**. Pennant's 1769 tour briefly mentions the McNabs as smiths established here since 1440 (*British Tourists*, 1: 81). The geologist Barthélemy Faujas de Saint-Fond, whose book appeared in English as *Travels in England, Scotland and the Hebrides* (1799), falls upon them as if they were a lost tribe in the Andes (1: 264–302).

60. **see Ossian**. Luno was the smith who made the hero Fingal's sword in Macpherson's *Temora*.

61. **reliques of Ossian**. 'A precious manuscript', according to Saint-Fond, who had not been allowed to see it (1: 290).

62. **Elizabeth Woodcock**. In February 1799 she survived a week buried in a snowdrift. Her death in July resulted 'more from having had spirits given her, and from the fatigue of visitors, than from the effects of the cold', insisted Plumptre in a note to *Winter* (*Original Dramas*, 77n), a play much concerned with snowdrifts. See also the 1792 Journal (Llandrillo to Oswestry).

63. **about you**. Slightly misremembered from the Duke of Buckingham's theatrical satire *The Rehearsal* (1671). The playwright Bayes has fallen down and hurt his nose (II.v).

64. **Here I rested thankfully**. On his previous visit, recorded in the Memorandums of his 1796 tour (3 August), Plumptre had left a piece of paper with the following lines: 'He who up this mountain climbs,/Will grateful rest his weary limbs;/But greater thanks that place shall meet,/Which gives me both to drink & eat'.

65. **Ode to the Sun**. 'O thou that rollest above, round as the shield of my fathers! Whence are thy beams, O sun! thy everlasting light?' and so forth, from the ending of Macpherson's 'Carthon'.

66. **she was such**. Adapted from Banquo's greeting to the Witches (*Macbeth*, I.iii.46-7).

67. **Adelphi window**. A vivid image, but inaccurate if it refers to the Adam brothers' development by the Thames, which had plain façades.

68. **Sycorax**. The witch displaced by Prospero in *The Tempest*.

69. **thick and slab**. Like the contents of the Witches' cauldron (*Macbeth*, IV.i.32).

70. **throng**. Crowded or busy.

71. **map of Scotland**. John Ainslie's *Scotland, Drawn and Engrav'd from a Series of Angles and Astronomical Observations* (1789), at four miles to the inch. The sheets measure about two feet by two feet, so no wonder the tube in which he carried them attracted attention.

72. **tricksey spirit**. Prospero's description of Ariel (*The Tempest*, V.i.226).

73. **chumb**. A slang term fashionable in the universities, derived (as Plumptre's spelling suggests) from 'chamber-fellow'.

74. ***Highland Eclogue***. Begun 'half in earnest and half in jest' to relieve the miseries of 20 June, finished and copied out in the entry for 6 July. It parodies 'Hassan; or, The Camel Driver', the second of William Col-

lins's *Persian Eclogues* (1742): 'In silent horror o'er the desert waste/The driver Hassan with his camels passed'. Collins's flimsy combination of pastoral and Orientalism was still popular enough to invite the treatment Plumptre gives it.

75. **sewins**. Welsh, not Scottish, dialect for 'salmon'.

76. **Cadell**. Probably William Archibald Cadell (1775–1855), a gentleman of means who interested himself in science, antiquities and travel.

77. **Mrs Siddons**. Sarah Siddons (1755–1831), then at the peak of her career as a tragic actress, in Edinburgh with several of her most famous non-Shakespearean roles, familiar to Drury Lane audiences since the 1780s. In John Home's Scottish tragedy *Douglas*, first performed at Edinburgh in 1756, Lady Randolph is the mother briefly reunited with her long-lost son. Plumptre adapted it for his *English Drama Purified*.

78. **Henry Siddons**. An undistinguished actor, who had joined the Edinburgh company in 1793 and later became manager of the New Theatre Royal. He died in 1815.

79. **Woods**. A long-standing member of the company, then approaching the end of his career. He died in 1802.

80. **Otway and Rowe**. Thomas Otway, whose *Venice Preserv'd* (1682) gave Sarah Siddons one of her most famous parts, and Nicholas Rowe, whose tragedies of *Jane Shore* (1714) and *Lady Jane Grey* (1715) Plumptre included in *English Drama Purified*.

81. **the Gamester**. Edward Moore's domestic tragedy (1753), in which Beverley is destroyed by gambling and the villain Stukeley. Plumptre included a version of it in his *English Drama Purified*.

82. **only tears**. Prompted by Spranger Barry's rivalry with Garrick in 1756, usually given as: 'The town has found out different ways/To praise its different Lears;/To Barry it gives loud huzzas/To Garrick only tears'.

83. **the Grecian Daughter**. An exotic melodrama (1772) by Arthur Murphy, in which Euphrasia suckles her starving father Evander and kills the tyrant Dionysius.

84. **the Stranger**. Benjamin Thompson's English adaptation of a play by August von Kotzebue, first performed in 1798, gave Sarah Siddons the part of an erring but finally penitent wife. Plumptre greatly disliked Kotzebue and the new German school of Romantic drama: see also Birmingham, 11 September.

85. **Sir John**. Formally Sir John Dalrymple Hamilton Magill (1726-1810) of Oxenfoord Castle, lawyer, historian and, as Plumptre discovers, a man of versatile interests.

86. **Jameson**. George Jamesone (1589/90–1644), the 'Scottish Vandyke', known for his portraits of the nobility.

87. **Preston Hall**. A show house in the Robert Adam style, begun by Robert Mitchell for Alexander Callander in 1782.

88. *hattered ket*. Usually called 'hatted kit', made from buttermilk, mild

and sugar or spices.

89. **soap from fish**. Patented the previous year on behalf of John Crooks. A report for the Board of Trustees in Edinburgh, published in 1800, judged it unsatisfactory, expensive and very smelly.

90. **black soap**. Taking its colour from charcoal or ashes.

91. **the brown**. Presumably either mottled or yellow, both hard soaps made with tallow. Soft soap used whale or fish oil and potash.

92. **not to the means**. Plumptre's original Memorandums are more forthright in calling Sir John and his family 'oddities': 'S^r. J. is full of projects. S^d. he would make my fortune by letting me make his soap at Camb.—I make a fortune by setting up as a soap boiler!!!—L^y. D. is civil and goodhumoured, tells droll stories and bursts out laughing at them.—The Miss Ds. make y^r. own cloaths, L^y. D. breaks the sugar herself.—S^r. J. calls L^y D. "Bessy"—and "Madam Bess"'.

93. **Dilly**. The Diligence, or public stage coach.

94. **taking of the Cape**. The Battle of the First of June (1794), when Admiral Howe had captured seven French ships off Ushant, and General Craig's capture of the Cape of Good Hope from the Dutch (September 1795).

95. **travelling on a Sunday**. The Memorandums book adds: 'Ye Great, ye will answer this!!'

96. **virtues and the vices of every condition**. The Memorandums book spoils the effect by adding: 'Robert, the coachman came in to tea. With this I could have dispensed, but he was very well behaved'.

97. **useful hints**. In the 'Essay on Artificial Water' added to the 1796–98 edition of Uvedale Price's *Essay on the Picturesque*. For Price and his essay, see 'The Picturesque' (3 September).

98. **Char**. A small fish of the salmon family, prized as a delicacy.

99. **my former memorandums**. Iron Crag has not changed its name; Boater Crag is now Boathow Crag, Ravlig is Revelin Crag, and Angling crag (or Angling stone) is Angler's Crag.

100. **the troubles**. The rebellion by the United Irishmen, defeated at Wexford in June 1798.

101. **Lingmel beck … Row beck**. Either Plumptre was muddled or the names have changed: the stream to the south-east is now called Lingmell Gill, while to the north Lingmell Beck joins Mosedale Beck.

102. **rock rising up**. Presumably Castle Howe.

103. **whole process**. Near the end of 'Spring', the first of *Walks in a Forest* (1794), a sequence of Picturesque poems by Thomas Gisborne, a leading Evangelical clergyman. In the Lake District charcoal was used in the gunpowder industry.

104. *reedy* **lake**. Grasmere, to the north.

105. **engaged and re-engaged**. The Memorandums book notes that those booked to lodge with the Misses Newton included Sir George Beau-

mont, art connoisseur and, later, Wordsworth's benefactor. Plumptre himself made the Salutation Inn his base until 2 August.

106. **delicious Grasmere**. 'Delicious Grasmere's calm retreat', from Richard Cumberland's *Ode to the Sun* (1776), a briefly popular poem reprinted in later editions of West's *Guide to the Lakes*. Cumberland was best known to contemporaries for his sentimental comedies.

107. **becoming attire**. A famous passage from Thomas Gray's letter to Thomas Warton describing his tour of the Lakes in 1769, first published in the posthumous edition of his *Works* (1775) by his friend William Mason (as Section 5, Letter 4).

108. **Wests first station**. Thomas West's *Guide to the Lakes* (1778), the first such book and for many years the most influential, reached its seventh edition in 1799. Adopting the Picturesque approach, West organised the landscape into 'stations', or viewpoints; his taste in choosing and describing them was widely admired. The first Windermere station (seventh edition, 55–60) was among the most famous.

109. **Pennants remark**. In fact, Pennant compared Derwentwater, not Windermere, with Loch Lomond (and Lough Leane in Ireland), while politely refusing to choose between them (*Tour in Scotland*, fourth edition, 2: 40). The passage was omitted from Mavor's abridgement.

110. **our whole party**. John Dudley, his companion on the 1792 and 1793 tours, had arrived on 31 July with—to Plumptre's surprise and annoyance—his wife and brother-in-law, a Mr Kirkby.

111. **Helvellyn ... Wyburn**. From Cumberland's *Ode to the Sun*.

112. **Finkle street hause**. Perhaps Newlands Hause. Plate 6 in James Clarke's *Survey of the Lakes* (1787), which Plumptre knew, marks the road from Portinscale to Newlands as Finkle Street.

113. **Queen's Head**. Which Plumptre had made the setting for much of his comic opera, *The Lakers* (1798).

114. **Crosthwaites Museum**. Peter Crosthwaite (1735–1805), 'Admiral at Keswick Regatta, ... Guide, Pilot, Geographer & Hydrographer to the Nobility and Gentry' as well as museum keeper, outshone rivals like Hutton in exploiting the Keswick tourist trade.

115. **11 different names**. Spelled out in Plumptre's note: 'Brook, Burn, Beck, Gutter, Gill, Gole, Race, Rill, Runner, Sike, Sow'.

116. **Pocklington**. Joseph Pocklington, originally a Newark banker, owned Barrow Hall, the Bowder Stone and, most notoriously, Derwent Isle, where his sham castle and other follies attracted almost universal derision as examples of false taste. In her *Companion and Useful Guide* to Scotland and the Lakes (1799) the Hon. Mrs Murray complained that 'Mr. Pocklington's slime may be traced in every part of Keswick Vale' (21–2), while Plumptre had a character in *The Lakers* mistake the island for a tea-garden (I.iii).

117. **Wests 3d. station**. Between Stable Hills and Walla Crag on the eastern

shore: 'Here all that is great and pleasing on the lake, all that is grand and sublime in the environs, lie before you in a beautiful order, and natural disposition' (seventh edition, 88).

118. **kiddyish**. In contemporary slang a 'kiddy' was a flashily dressed thief, but Plumptre may be thinking specifically of his own creation Bob Kiddy in *The Lakers*, an empty-headed tourist interested only in food and drink.

119. **his Ramble**. The second edition of *A Fortnight's Ramble to the Lakes* (1795) by Captain Joseph Budworth (afterwards Palmer), another pedestrian. It mentions watch towers and beacons on pages 120 and 167.

120. **our glasses**. See note 5.

121. **dotrell**. A species of plover, 'fat and sweet flavoured', according to Captain Budworth (223).

122. **Ormathwait and the Vicarage**. Discovered by Gray, who thought the view from the vicarage a picture 'that would fairly sell for a thousand pounds' (*Works*, Section 5, Letter 4), and discussed by West as his eighth Keswick station (seventh edition, 104–6).

123. **the cannon**. The most popular of many stationed around the Lakes so that tourists could artificially recreate the sublime effects of thunderstorm and chaos.

124. **black wad mines**. Black lead mines, supplying the Keswick pencil industry.

125. **Masters of the ceremonies at Bath**. A tradition established by Richard 'Beau' Nash (1674–1761), who put visitors to the spa under the rule of etiquette.

126. **Will Hearty**. 'A plain honest soul', sings Sir Charles Portinscale (*Lakers*, II.iv).

127. **Wests IVth. station**. 'A most astonishing view of the lake and vale of Keswick, spread out to the north in the most picturesque manner' (seventh edition, 93).

128. **Wests Vth. station**. Specifically recommended for evening viewing, 'when the last beams of the sun rest on the purple summit of Skiddaw, and the deep shade of Wythop's wooded brows is stretched over the lake' (seventh edition, 103).

129. **Druid's Temple**. Castlerigg Stone Circle.

130. **Mell fell on our right**. A slip of the pen: Great Mell and Little Mell must have been on their left.

131. **the *Palace***. Patterdale Hall, home of the Mounsey family, so-called Kings and Queens of the dale.

132. **hurt it**. The Memorandums book adds: 'She asked me if I w^d. chuse *clean* sheets. She shewed me some, which had only been slept in once by a woman and her daughter "and they were quite wholesome people, they had very clean shifts on!!!"– I however expressed my custom of sleeping in coarse sheets, and was indulged in them'.

133. **take me in**. Plumptre quoted the relevant statute in a footnote, adding: 'This was the first time during my long tour that I had met with any reluctance at receiving me'.

134. **the mail**. The mail coach from Lancaster to Preston.

135. **Quick**. John Quick (1748–1831), a popular comedian at Covent Garden, said to be George III's favourite actor.

136. **iron trade**. Memorandums book continues: 'Visited Rover. Had tea ½ p. 7. Another Bagman and his customer, in volunteer uniform came in and called for bottle of wine. They seemed to have some difference about the weight of the goods—I believe copper—and about the casting up of their accounts. The volunteer swore very shockingly. After tea again bathed Rover's shoulder with brandy. When I came in again the volunteer was gone, and the Bagman asked me "if I came from Liverpool? He thought I was a *Grocer* there"'.

137. **third conveyance**. The Memorandums book adds: 'Dined with the Waggoners. If not so elegant they were full as orderly in their behaviour as their betters'.

138. **wake**. A local festival.

139. **Gresford**. Home of Rev. Henry Newcome and his family, connections of Plumptre's mother. He (and Rover) had visited them on his 1797 tour.

140. **I think otherwise**. Plumptre is adapting the lament for the dead ass at Nampont in Sterne's *Sentimental Journey*.

141. **care of my church**. William Wilson, Fellow of St John's College, whom Plumptre looked up to as a spiritual mentor. He died the following March at the age of thirty-eight, after the offer of the fashionable rectory of Keston, unwelcome to one of his retiring habits, had 'materially affected his mind' (obituary in *Gentleman's Magazine*, June 1800).

142. **another friend**. John Haggitt, Fellow of Clare College and Vicar of Madingley, who arranged for the services at Hinxton to be taken by John Palmer, Arabist and traveller, of St John's.

143. **head of my village**. Edward Green (1770–1804) of Hinxton Hall, a close friend and ally in efforts to improve the parish. His first son, Edward, had been born on 2 August.

144. **Task Book 3**. Lines 349–51, the last originally reading: 'I knew at least one hare that had a friend'. Like Sterne's lament for the dead ass, Cowper's account of his pet hare typified the new tenderness for animals which marked the sensibility of Plumptre's generation.

145. **Camus**. Milton's personification of Cambridge in *Lycidas* (line 103).

146. **stream**. 'Deva spreads her wizard stream': *Lycidas* (line 55). Deva, of course, is the Dee.

147. *a bed*. *Cymbeline* (III.iii.33).

148. **fellow Collegian**. John Gibbons, Fellow of Clare and later Rector of Harley near Shrewsbury.

149. **brazed to it.** Adapted from Gloucester's words about his bastard son Edmund in *King Lear* (I.i.10).

150. **Ladies at the Cottage.** For Plumptre's earlier visits see his 1792 Journal and 1797 Journal ('The Ladies of Llangollen', 7–8 August).

151. **Lady Stanley.** Margaret, Lady Stanley of Alderley Park, or her daughter-in-law Maria Josepha (1771–1863), friend of Edward Gibbon.

152. **Chapellow.** Rev. Leonard Chappelow, amateur botanist and poet, and admirer of the Ladies.

153. **Eggington of Birmingham.** Plumptre had visited the studio where Francis Eginton (1737–1805) made his painted glass in 1797.

154. **Fairy Palace of the Vale.** From the poem *Llangollen Vale* (1796) by Anna Seward.

155. **Mr Arnauld and Mr Varley.** The landscape painter John Varley (1778–1842), on his first Welsh tour, and George Arnald (1763–1841). Both exhibited Welsh views at the Royal Academy in 1800, and Wales remained Varley's favourite subject. When he next met Varley, Plumptre judged him 'a Genius without Education' (1800 Memorandums, 8 June).

156. **my companion.** Leonard Chappelow.

157. **Watt.** Gregory Watt (1779–1804), son of the engineer James Watt and a partner in the Soho works.

158. **Avon Vour.** Afon fawr.

159. **Barkers painting.** Thomas Barker (1769–1847), the most famous of the 'Barkers of Bath', had exhibited canvases of Rhaeadr Dhu and the Swallow Falls at the Royal Academy the previous year. Plumptre had seen the painting of Pistyll Cain when he dined at Acton Park, home of the Cunliffe family at Wrexham, on 21 August.

160. **Snowdonia p.100.** That is, Thomas Pennant's *The Journey to Snowdon*, the first part of Volume 2 of his *Tour in Wales* (1778–81), which Plumptre had consulted for his first Welsh tour of 1792.

161. **Morver Rudland.** 'Morfa Rhuddlan', a plaintive tune which takes its title from Caradoc's defeat by King Offa of Mercia in 795.

162. **as well as others.** The Memorandums book for the previous day noted: 'The Guide a great Lyar, cannot depend upon him. He is 74 years of age—some allowance is to be made for that: but he is not fit to act as guide any longer. He has a son 19 years of age: he should make over the business to him'.

163. **accommodations . . . indifferent.** The Memorandums book is specific: 'Mrs Williams asked me if I had any objection to those two gentlemen sleeping in my room (there being 3 beds.) I said no. They went to bed in another room and when I went to bed Mrs W. said the Maltster of Machynleth was to sleep in one of the beds that he was a very good man. At 12 o'clock he came to bed and was sick. Perhaps he had been drinking his own beer.—Got into bed & fell asleep—when I made the ch-maid take away the pot. He then only disturbed me by his snoring'.

164. **Wales p.94.** Richard Warner's *Walk through Wales* (1798) described Jones as 'a Welshman whose natural *ingenuity* had been sharpened into *cunning* by a long residence in England'.

165. **teaboards.** Tea trays.

166. **men's blood.** *Julius Caesar* (III.ii.25).

167. **Price.** Uvedale Price (1747–1829) of Foxley, Herefordshire. His *Essay on the Picturesque* (1794), combining aesthetic theory with advice to fellow landowners on improving their estates, rejected the smooth effects of 'Capability' Brown and Humphry Repton for a Picturesque characterised by roughness, sudden variation and irregularity.

168. **not greatly discouraged.** Plumptre here quoted a lengthy passage, from the expanded 1796–98 edition, arguing that landowners do not make improvements just for their own pleasure.

169. **Engl. Garden.** William Mason's *The English Garden* (1771–1781), still popular with enthusiasts of the Picturesque despite its praise of 'Capability' Brown.

170. **seat of Sʳ. G. Cornwallis.** Monnington and Moccas Court, on opposite banks of the Wye, both belonged to Sir George Cornwall.

171. **thicket.** The dash indicates that Plumptre has left out a line and a half which do not fit the present scene.

172. **old Par.** Thomas Parr, a Shropshire man who died in 1635 and was said to have been born in 1483.

173. *neat picturesque.* Disagreeing with 'Capability' Brown, who brought his lawns up to the house, Price advocated formal gardens and walks (*Essay*, 1796–98 edition, 1: 37). William Gilpin used the phrase 'Picturesque Beauty' in the titles of his tours.

174. **Knight.** Richard Payne Knight (1750–1824) had rebuilt his house with a boldly Gothic exterior and neo-classical interior. He joined the Picturesque debate with *The Landscape* (1794), a didactic poem which agrees with Price, to whom it is addressed, in attacking Brown and Repton.

175. **Poem of the Landscape B.1. l.315.** Plumptre is citing the second edition (1795).

176. **Mʳ P.** Plumptre had been staying at Stone with John and Diana Plumptre since 5 September.

177. **Hagley ... the House.** Hagley Hall, notable for the grounds laid out by George Lyttelton, first Lord Lyttelton (1709–73) with the help of the poet William Shenstone (1714–63) and praised by Thomson in *The Seasons*. Shenstone's own estate, The Leasowes, was a famous showpiece of Picturesque taste.

178. *Informer.* Traditionally despised, informers were widely used by Evangelical groups like the Society for the Suppression of Vice and approvingly portrayed by writers like Hannah More.

179. **Pizarro.** Sheridan's highly successful adaptation of *Die Spanier in Peru* by August von Kotzebue, a playwright Plumptre particularly dis-

liked (see 'At the Theatre Royal in Edinburgh', 15 July). The remark that Sheridan had altered the original for the worse is a propitiatory nod in the direction of his sister Anne, who published a rival version of *Pizarro* among her translations of Kotzebue.

180. **Elliston**. Robert William Elliston (1774–1831), a versatile actor who went on to play Rolla at Drury Lane, where he became manager.

181. **shew and noise**. The phrases are borrowed from Hamlet's advice to the players (III.ii.1–35), except for the pun '*higher*lings'.

182. **Powel**. John Powell (1755–1836) had joined the Norwich Company in 1786 and by 1799 was beginning a thirty-year association with Drury Lane, where he usually played supporting roles.

183. **Harley ... Johnson ... Biggs**. George Davies Harley, Elizabeth Johnson and Anne Biggs, all briefly successful at Covent Garden but better known on the provincial circuits.

184. **Spike Hall**. Presumably the home of a successful bayonet manufacturer, of whom there were several in Birmingham at this time.

185. **Humberston**. Humberstone, John Dudley's parish.

186. **Skeffington Hall**. Where he visited Lumley Skeffington in the 1790 Journal.

187. **Stamford ... my brother**. Joseph, who had moved from Wisbech since Plumptre visited him in the 1790 Journal.

188. **Stukeley**. Mrs Bayley and her family ('From Cambridge to Little Stukeley', 30 April).

1800 Memorandums

1. **Richard Scott**. His parish clerk.

2. **grounds formal**. Audley End park was laid out in the 1760s by 'Capability' Brown, whose belts and clumps of trees particularly offended the next generation of Picturesque theorists.

3. **Hockerhill**. Hockerill, the coaching stop at Bishop's Stortford.

4. **Johnians**. Members, in this case Fellows, of St John's College: Robert Boon (the Bursar), John Romney (son of the painter) and Joshua Smith.

5. **bodkin**. That is, wedged in without proper room.

6. **Irish Giant**. Patrick Cotter, who used the stage-name O'Brien customary with Irish giants, was then nearing the end of his long career as a public show. He died in 1806. Estimates of his height varied from 7 feet 10 inches to 8 feet 7½ inches.

7. **N°. 14 Caroline Street, Bedford square**. Apparently the home of Plumptre's mother and sisters Anne and Bell, though they had chosen Hampstead when they first moved from Norwich to London in 1797.

8. **Assassinate the King**. James Hadfield, a deranged ex-soldier, fired at George III as he entered his box at Drury Lane on 15 May. The king was not injured.

9. **Russian officer**. Russia had been Britain's ally in the Second Coalition against France since the previous December.

10. **powder tax**. To raise money for the war against France, William Pitt's budget in 1795 had introduced a one-guinea licence for the wearing of powder (usually flour) on hair and wigs.

11. **Robert, Jemima and Miss Taylor ... M**rs **P.** Plumptre's lawyer brother Robert, then aged forty, with his wife Elizabeth, and his unmarried sister Jemima, then aged thirty-one. Miss Taylor may well be a member of the Norwich Dissenting family then represented by the hymn writer John Taylor (1750–1826) and his wife Susannah.

12. *Gilpin*. William Gilpin (1724-1804), author of travel books which made him the leading authority on the Picturesque, as well as a clergyman of Evangelical leanings. Since 1777 he had been Vicar of Boldre in the New Forest, where he had established his school and workhouse in the early 1790s.

13. **Holden**. John Holden, Fellow of Sidney Sussex and a distinguished preacher.

14. **Amusements of Clergymen**. *Three Dialogues on the Amusements of Clergymen*, which Gilpin published under the pseudonym of 'Joseph Frampton' in 1796, warned against blood sports, gambling and (in most circumstances) plays and dancing.

15. **Baker ... sermon**. A pamphlet originally published in 1791 and later (1795?) included in Hannah More's influential series of Cheap Repository Tracts. A parishioner at Boldre, Baker was a rogue whom Gilpin mistook for an example of honest and cheerful poverty.

16. **Mr G's printed account**. A pamphlet published in 1796.

17. **his drawings**. Plumptre was presumably interested in the aquatinting process Gilpin used, and to some extent pioneered, for the illustrations to his tours. Contemporaries often remarked Gilpin's habit of reorganising the details of a scene to increase its Picturesque effect.

18. **Francis Henry Newcome**. Plumptre's exact contemporary Frank, youngest son of the Hackney schoolmaster Henry Newcome. He had graduated from Trinity Hall and entered the Middle Temple in 1792.

19. **Math ... Mark**. Presumably the episode of the Gadarene swine, in Matthew 8:28–34 and Mark 5:1–19.

20. **Green**. Edward Green of Hinxton Hall, for whom see also the 1799 Narrative ('Rover's Last Journey', 14 August).

21. **Speare**. James Speare, elected Fellow of Clare the previous year.

22. **offsets**. Offshoots.

23. **Auctioneer**. By Charles Dibdin, for whom see the 1799 Narrative ('Morpeth', 24 May).

24. **Honeycomb**. Adapted from Psalms 19:10.

25. **his mode of life**. Plumptre defended Frank's behaviour to his relatives in London later in this tour, and gave a tantalisingly brief glimpse of his

eventual fate in a diary entry for 11 November 1805: 'By Fly to Hockerill whence I took a chaise to Mr Jacobs at Much Hadham, to see my cousin F. Newcome, in confinement. His intellect evidently weakened, but seeming more *happy* & contented than I ever saw him before. F.N. and his Keeper (Joseph Baldrey) walked with me to Hockerill, and staid and eat cold meat till the Fly came'.

26. **Chiswell**. A merchant with antiquarian interests, Richard Muilman assumed the name Trench Chiswell on inheriting Debden Hall, near Newport. He committed suicide in 1797 after losing money on West Indian speculations.

27. **Beauchamp**. Henry Pratt Beauchamp, who entered King's College from Eton in 1798 and became a Fellow in 1801. He was removed from the curacy of Kirton and Lindsey in 1809 for neglect of duty.

28. **George Moore**. Farmer, shopkeeper and churchwarden: 'honest, sober and remarkably industrious' but 'too indulgent a father' (according to Plumptre's 'Account of Hinxton 1802'). His son Richard had been committed to Chelmsford Jail on 10 May, charged with stealing a saddle and a whip. The charge may well have been dropped, for there is no record of his being brought to trial.

29. **Dennis**. Not mentioned in Plumptre's 'Account of Hinxton 1802'.

30. **Luke 16**. In fact Luke 15:18–19.

31. **Anne Bates**. She had already given birth to two children, presumably by Richard Moore. He finally married her in September 1801.

32. **Duties of Religion**. A catechism which the pupils at Boldre were required to learn by heart, published in 1798.

33. **Lydia**. Plumptre's unmarried sister, then aged 38. She apparently stayed as housekeeper at Hinxton Vicarage until November 1801, when a Mrs Mary Sutton arrived.

34. **Haggitt**. John Haggitt, for whom see the 1799 Narrative ('Rover's Last Journey', 14 August).

35. **Sumpter**. Thomas Sumpter, a native of Histon and Fellow of King's College until his early death in 1803.

1800 Cam Journal

1. **Hartshorn**. A solution of ammonia in water, originally made from shavings of hart's horn. Whatever its efficacy against gnats, it makes an odd remedy for an upset stomach, though this is how Trevelyan uses it at Ashwell.

2. **sleep's disturbers**. Richard III's description of the Princes in the Tower (IV.ii.73).

3. **Wilkin's new-built house**. Newnham Cottage (still standing) on Queens' Road, built for himself by William Wilkins (1747–1815), licensee of the Theatre Royal in Norwich and the Barnwell theatre on the out-

skirts of Cambridge. His son, another William Wilkins, was the architect of Downing College and the National Gallery.

4. **Pemberton**. Lord of the Manor of Trumpington. He had died in March.

5. **Ways and Means**. The two heroes of George Colman the Younger's comedy (1788) blunder into the wrong bedrooms when trying to elope with the heroines, a chaste echo of the clerks' misadventures in 'The Reeve's Tale'.

6. **stewponds**. Fish ponds.

7. **Overseer**. The parish official responsible for poor relief.

8. **called in the map**. A mistake apparently started by John Speed (or his engraver) in the seventeenth century and copied by mapmakers until R.G. Baker's county map of 1821.

9. **triumphal arch**. Added by Sir John Soane c.1794.

10. **Pavilion**. Built in 1774–77 by James 'Athenian' Stuart, altered by Humphry Repton soon after Plumptre described its decay, and demolished later in the nineteenth century. The engraving which Plumptre mentions appeared in the *Westminster Magazine* for February 1777.

11. **Gothic tower**. A sham ruin, built by Sanderson Miller in 1750. It still stands.

12. **Gilpin**. Plumptre noted Gilpin's practice of taking liberties in his drawings to create the desired Picturesque effect in his 1800 Memorandums ('William Gilpin', 27 May).

13. **moralist to die**. From Gray's *Elegy Written in a Country Churchyard*.

14. **spear**. 'The unsteadfast footing of a spear': *Henry IV, Part One* (I.iii.191).

15. **den of thieves**. 'My house shall be called the house of prayer; but ye have made it a den of thieves': Christ's denunciation of the moneychangers in the temple (Matthew 21:13).

16. **Stat. 1. M. C. 3 . . . 1 W. & M**. An Act Against Offenders of Preachers and Other Ministers in the Church (1553) and The Toleration Act (1689), which, among other provisions, fixed the penalty for interrupting a clergyman during a service at, respectively, three months' imprisonment and a fine of £20.

17. **Fuzellis source of the Nile**. 'The Fertilization of the Nile', drawn by Fuseli and engraved by Blake for Erasmus Darwin's *The Botanic Garden* (1791). To justify his impudent comparison, Plumptre added a note citing the explorer James Bruce, who recorded that the Blue Nile was not strong enough to turn a mill until it was two miles from its source.

18. **Turno**. Isaiah Turnough, Vicar of Gamlingay from 1765 until his death in 1802.

19. **that branch**. Bourn Brook.

20. **Rev^d. Mr Say**. Francis Say, incumbent of Robert Plumptre's old parish of Whaddon and a clutch of nearby livings. He had died in 1796.

21. **Downing College**. Sir George Downing died in 1749, but legal disputes

about his will prevented the charter for his college being granted until September 1800. Building began in 1807.

22. **joice.** To juice, or gise: to put cattle out to grass for a fee.

23. **Great Gransden.** Plumptre's own living from 1812 until his death.

24. **Barnabas Oley.** A Royalist divine (1602–86), who also built the vicarage and almshouses at Great Gransden and started the new buildings of Clare College in the 1630s. He published George Herbert's prose portrait of the model country parson in the poet's *Remains* (1652).

25. **William Caxton.** In fact he came from Kent.

26. **formerly was my Fathers.** Robert Plumptre had left his property in Great and Little Eversden to his wife. George Hewitt, elected to his fellowship while Dr Robert was President and appointed Rector of St Botolph's in 1799, was 'a scandalous old reprobate' at odds with the evangelical tone Isaac Milner established at Queens'.

27. **Coleseed.** The source of rape-oil.

28. **(mentioned p.23).** Page 198 in this edition.

29. **Green.** Edward Green of Hinxton Hall, for whom see also the 1799 Narrative ('Rover's last journey', 14 August) and the 1800 Memorandums ('Visiting a cousin', 2 June).

30. **Thackeray.** Probably Dr Frederic Thackeray (1774–1854), though Plumptre was friendly with several members of the family, powerful at King's College, that produced the novelist. Joseph Thackeray vaccinated the Hinxton parishioners a few years later.

31. **York.** Lady Anne Yorke, the Earl of Hardwicke's eldest daughter. She married the third Earl of Mexborough in 1807 and died in 1870.

32. **Rumford's plan.** Benjamin Thompson, Count Rumford (1753–1814), pioneered new designs for stoves, kitchen ranges, chimney flues and utensils. The first part of *On the Construction of Kitchen Fire-Places and Kitchen Utensils*, later collected as the tenth of his *Essays*, appeared in 1799.

33. **New Monuments.** Thomas Banks' monument to Philip, second Earl of Hardwicke (1720–90), and John Bacon's monument to Joseph Yorke, Lord Dover (1724–92), stand near three much grander ones: by Peter Scheemakers and James 'Athenian' Stuart to Catherine, mother of the third Earl (died 1759), and Philip, the first Earl (died 1764), and by Scheemakers alone to the Right Hon. Charles Yorke (died 1770), father of the third Earl. A small wall tablet jointly remembers Rev. Charles Isaac Yorke (1762–91) and his sister Mary (1767–95), children of the Bishop who ordained Plumptre.

34. **16 poles.** A pole is 30¼ square yards.

35. **Information for Cottagers.** A pamphlet published by the Society for Bettering the Condition and Increasing the Comforts of the Poor in 1800, offering a ragbag of practical and moral advice: a recipe for stew, information about Friendly Societies and Sunday Schools, and the

'Twelve True Old Golden Rules' (for example, 'INDUSTRY will make a man a purse, and FRUGALITY will find him strings for it').

36. **Macfell's construction**. James McPhail's *Treatise on the Culture of the Cucumber* (1794) advocated frames with brick sides and flues.

37. **in illis**. 'The times are changed, and we (and you) are changed with them'.

38. **The Cottage Cook**. One of Hannah More's own contributions (1797) to her Cheap Repository Tracts, it offers only a few simple recipes, and concentrates instead on the story of how Mrs Jones discovers 'the Way To Do Much Good with Little Money': prosecuting the baker for giving short measure, getting one of the village pubs closed, and so forth.

39. **Digesters**. Papin's Digesters: pressure cookers, approved by Count Rumford, for boiling meat quickly or softening bones.

40. **Thoughts on the Scarcity in 95 and Tom White**. The shortages and high prices of 1800 have made Plumptre turn back to *Hints to All Ranks of People on the Occasion of the Present Scarcity*, an anonymous Cheap Repository Tract intended as Sunday reading for August 1795, which viewed the bad harvest of that year as 'a call to repentance, a punishment of our manifold sins' and 'a trial of our faith'. Hannah More's *Tom White* (1795) tells how a virtuous postilion became a prosperous farmer.

41. **£50 curacy**. Roughly the value of Plumptre's own appointment at Hinxton, though his annual income was swelled to more than four times this figure by his college fellowship and his father's legacy.